The
Darkest Jungle

Commit yourself to the Virgin Mary

for in her hands is the way into the Darién—

and in God's is the way out.

A SIXTEENTH-CENTURY SPANISH EPIGRAPH CARVED IN
STONE SOMEWHERE IN THE GULF OF SAN MIGUEL AND
SAID TO BE OBSERVABLE ONLY WHEN THE EARTH, SUN,
AND MOON ALIGN TO PRODUCE THE YEAR'S LOWEST
SPRING TIDE.

R.
Rano
Rancho 6
Rancho 5
Rancho 4
Rancho 3
Rancho 2
Virago Tree
La Villa
Rancho 1
Site of F.te de Princip.
R. Lara
R. Savana
Periaki
Fairfax & Eliza I.s
R.
Indi
R. Tuvra
Cr. Gual Gu.
Boca Gde
S.Miguel Harb.r
Boca
Chica
Rock
Darien
Harbour
Bank
PACIFIC
OCEAN
R. Buenaventura
Gorda Pt.
Farallon Ingles
P.ta Gorda
P.ta Brava
Buey Bank
Buena Vista
Iguana
Chapi
P.ta Colorado
P.ta Patina
GULF OF SAN MIGUEL
N
W   E
S
Garachiné Bay

I.Pinos

Sasardi.Pt

ATLANTIC

OCEAN

Prevost's farthest 12
Rancho 12
R.Prevost

Rancho 11

Rancho 10
Rancho 9

Cordillera

Sasardi

Sasardi Is.

Sasardi I.

Ustucarguna R.

Indian Rancho

R.Morti

Morti

I.d'Oro

R.Aglasenica

CALEDONIA BAY

Caledonia R.

Devil's Own

Asnati R.

Asnati

+Port & Pt.Escoces

Pas

Lioma Descada

Recovery
Camp

R.Lara

Sucubdi

St.John Pk.

Cordilleras

Sucubdi R.

Camp Beautiful

Parting Camp

Careto B.

Careto Pt.

Hospital Camp

R.Chuqunaque

ISTHMUS of DARIÉN

BETWEEN SAN MIGUEL AND CALEDONIA BAY
AS SURVEYED IN 1854

Adapted from a map appearing in the
Journal of the Royal Geographical Society in 1857

R.Inglesias

Commander Prevost's Route.............

Maury-Truxtun Route — — — — —

*Strain's Route

Gisborne's Route

(*Strain went 2x's up & down)

R. Tuyra

R.Tiuati

15 Miles

Yavisa

Santa Maria el Real

ALSO BY TODD BALF

The Last River

The Darkest Jungle

The True Story of the Darién Expedition and

America's Ill-Fated Race to Connect the Seas

TODD BALF

CROWN PUBLISHERS
NEW YORK

Published by Crown Publishers, New York, New York.
Member of the Crown Publishing Group, a division of Random House, Inc.
www.crownpublishing.com

CROWN is a trademark and the Crown colophon is a registered trademark of Random House, Inc.

Printed in the United States of America

Design by Lauren Dong

Library of Congress Cataloging-in-Publication Data
Balf, Todd.
     The darkest jungle : the true story of the Darién expedition and America's ill-fated race to connect the seas / Todd Balf.
     Includes bibliographical references.
          1. Panama Canal (Panama)—History—19th century.   2. Darién Ship Canal Expedition (1853–1854).   3. Darién (Panama and Colombia)—History—19th century.   4. Strain, Isaac G., 1821–1857.   5. *Cyane* (Sloop-of-war).   I. Title.
     HE537.1.B35 2003
     917.287'78043—dc22
     2003012509

ISBN 0-609-60989-0

10 9 8 7 6 5 4 3 2 1

First Edition

To Patty, Celia, and Henry

Contents

Maps appear on pages iv–v and 78–79.

Dramatis Personae

Darién, 1853–54

Principal Expedition Members*

AMERICAN "ADVANCE PARTY"

LIEUTENANT ISAAC STRAIN, thirty-three, of Springfield, Ohio.
   Commander U.S. Darién Exploring Expedition
FREDERICK AVERY, thirty-four, of New York City. "Pioneer"
   volunteer hired in Cartagena
JAMES GOLDMAN, twenty-two, of New York City. Seaman, crew of
   Cyane
HENRY WILSON, age unknown, of New York City. Landsman, crew
   of *Cyane*

AMERICAN "MAIN PARTY"

PASSED MIDSHIPMAN WILLIAM TALBOT TRUXTUN, twenty-nine, of
   Philadelphia. Acting master and executive
JOHN "JACK" MAURY, twenty-eight, of Virginia. Principal engineer,
   appointed assistant astronomer and secretary
SAMUEL KETTLEWELL, thirty-one, of Baltimore. Draftsman and
   journal keeper
ANDREW F. BOGGS, thirty-five, of Springfield, Ohio. Special
   assistant engineer

* *ages at time of expedition*

EDWARD LOMBARD, thirty-eight, of Norfolk, Virginia. Seaman and expedition boatswain's mate

ADDITIONAL U.S. OFFICERS

GEORGE N. HOLLINS, fifty-four, of Maryland. Commander of sloop-of-war *Cyane*

THEODORE WINTHROP, twenty-five, of New Haven, Connecticut. Volunteer "pioneer"

BRITISH EXPEDITION

LIONEL GISBORNE, thirty-one, of London. Chief engineer of the Atlantic and Pacific Junction Company

DR. EDWARD CULLEN, of Dublin. Volunteer and self-proclaimed ship canal route "discoverer"

JAMES C. PREVOST. Commander of Her Majesty's steamship, *Virago*. Leader of unofficial exploration across Darién

DR. WILLIAM ROSS. Assistant surgeon of the *Virago* and supervising physician of joint British-American rescue

Capitalists

WILLIAM H. ASPINWALL, of New York City. Railroad magnate

SIR CHARLES FOX, of Britain. Director of the Atlantic and Pacific Junction Company, the London-based firm backing the Darién route

Men of Science

BARON ALEXANDER VON HUMBOLDT, eighty-four. World-renowned nineteenth-century scientist and traveler

AGUSTÍN CODAZZI, sixty-one. Italian-born geographer in charge of the national survey of New Granada (Colombia) from 1850 to 1859

ADMIRAL ROBERT FITZROY of the Royal Geographical Society. Darwin's famous companion aboard the *Beagle*

MATTHEW FONTAINE MAURY, forty-eight, of Washington, D.C. Director of the U.S. Naval Observatory

The
Darkest Jungle

PROLOGUE

March 9, 1854

Isthmus of Panama

IN THE STEAMY, LATE-AFTERNOON heat, the long dugout canoes ascended the tapering jungle river. For hours the native boatmen paddled a zigzagging course, idling near the steeply undercut, green-walled banks to listen and look. As they prepared to turn back, they glimpsed something—a strangely shaped piece of river debris, some knot of dark logs worked free by the tenacious outgoing tide. Their paddles stilled.

It was a raft, two skeletal, corpse-white figures aboard, one crouching. His wild blue eyes were sunk deep into cavernous sockets, a beard piling down. He wore a wide-brimmed hat, a torn blue flannel shirt, and a single leather moccasin—the ragged remains of a uniform. His skin, tight on bone in some places and flapping emptily in others, was a hieroglyph of rashes, boils, and insect bites. The man's companion, a young seaman, was stretched out and listless, as though he had already let go. On the sodden deck between the two lay a handful of gnawed-over palm nuts.

As the boatmen pulled closer, the blue-eyed man jerked himself up and stared hard at them, as if he couldn't comprehend what was taking place. His voice low and cracking, he sternly hailed them to stand off. Then it became clear . . . his rescuers. For a moment he was oddly conscious of everything, he later remembered. He raised his hand and with difficulty lay two fingers on his opposite wrist like a doctor to that of a sickly patient. He thought he might feel a fatal spike in his pulse and know, at least for a comforting instant, that it was the shock of being found that killed him, not the hardships of being lost. He was the commander of the United States Darién Exploring Expedition, he told them; his name was Lieutenant Isaac Strain.

During the journey downstream he took his offered place in one of the canoes; his alertness fell for a time and then rose again as he busily scanned the near banks, anxiously glaring at the high, cloud-draped mountains from where he had come. The same lands were terra incognita to the boatmen. They had never explored the greater territory next to their own, never traded nor fished in the tightest folds of the upstream forests. The land had a fearfully savage and bloody past. The question they wished to ask the officer wasn't what the world wanted to know—had he found the ship canal route—but rather something a good deal simpler. *What had he seen?*

But shortly after the lieutenant reached their village, he stumbled and collapsed. He had been lost 49 days and weighed, perhaps, 75 pounds. Yet at dusk on March 9, 1854, Isaac Strain's suffering had only really just begun. His ship lay an ocean away. *"Donde están mis hombres?"* he managed when the boatmen pulled him to his feet. "Where are my men?"

1 / GALES of DECEMBER

And we Americans are the peculiar, chosen people.... God has predestinated, mankind expects, great things from our race; and great things we feel in our souls. The rest of the nations must soon be in our rear. We are the pioneers of the world; the advance-guard, sent on through the wilderness of untried things, to break a new path in the New World that is ours. In our youth is our strength; in our inexperience our wisdom ... And let us always remember, that with ourselves—almost for the first time in the history of the Earth—national selfishness is unbounded philanthropy; for we cannot do a good to America but we give alms to the world.

HERMAN MELVILLE,
WHITE-JACKET (1850)

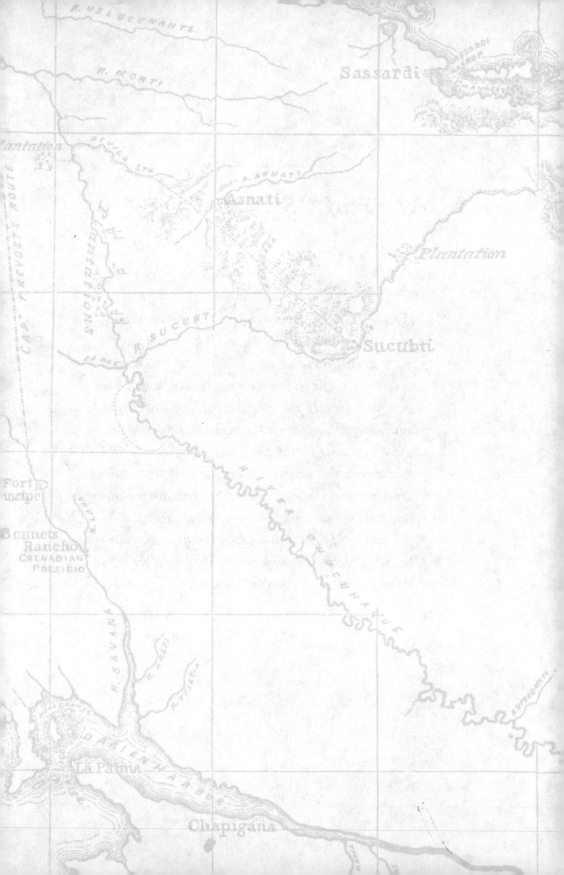

December 19, 1853

39° 56′ N, 75° 8′ W
Philadelphia

THE SHIPS ROUNDING CAPE HENLOPEN at the mouth of the Delaware River were rushing home to port. A blockade of frost had fastened upon Delaware Bay and was spreading up the river's winding, 100-mile course to Philadelphia. Already two merchant ships, the bark *Louisa* and the brig *Loretto,* were bound up near the breakwater. Another few days of single-digit cold and even the port's steam tugs might not make it out. The river would be corked until March. Along the bitterly cold Southwark waterfront, where the long wood-planked wharves and the brick-walled Navy yard thronged with officers and merchantmen safely back, the talk wasn't of Christmas or the New Year but the coming ice. Few could recall it fixing so early.

At dockside the sloop-of-war *Cyane*'s preparations drew curious onlookers. She wasn't one of the American Navy's powerful new steamships, but an old square-rigged man-of-war whose heyday was the Mexican War, almost a decade before. There wasn't a graceful line in her 132 feet of running length, critics said, and the secretary of the Navy seemed to agree; her active duty in recent years had been confined to quiet coastal cruises. Of late the vessel had gone nowhere. A year earlier, at port in Hampton Roads, Virginia, a near mutiny had erupted, and the subsequent trial had kept the ship in limbo for months. Only in recent weeks had the *Cyane* received the okay to return to duty and with the order a different, more restorative kind of attention. Her hull was newly coppered and her decks and hold meticulously disinfected with a purging vinegar wash.

She was crammed with personnel. In addition to the standard two-hundred-man complement for a vessel her size, she carried an unusual number of supernumeraries—a party that included three additional naval officers, a trio of engineers, and two civilian volunteers, one of those a surgeon. The extra outfit was evidently getting a lift somewhere. The *Cyane* was said to be headed south on Home Squadron business, but where exactly, nobody knew. The hustle and bustle suggested she had little time to lose.

In fact, throughout the frigid winter day the activity intensified. The ship's carpenters banged together chicken coops and pigpens, and the boatswain's mate's silver whistle pealed insistently. A "high die" or "heave hard" command boomed from the deck officer's speaking trumpet with enough venom to awaken the dear departed souls on Chestnut Street. Man-hauled sail bundles rose up the fore, main, and mizzen masts, and late-arriving stores, livestock, and sea trunks coursed across the gangway. By the locals' rough estimate there were well over 15,000 pounds of sea biscuit and salted meat bound for the hold—sufficient provisions for a three-month cruise, maybe more. Barrels of fresh water and spirits went down the hatchways with a number of less recognizable containers. Theodolites, sextants, spyglasses, mountain barometers, and leather cases of mathematical instruments—the exotica of a precise land survey—were being salted away too.

On the morning of December 20 the *Cyane* made final preparations to get under way. The long-awaited steam tug, *Thunderbolt*, had arrived during the night to tow them out. At 10 A.M. the topmen went aloft and the crew hauled up anchor. They would be making sail and tracking south along the Gulf Stream in less than forty-eight hours. The ice shattering over *Cyane*'s bow notwithstanding, a young, adventure-driven lieutenant named Isaac Strain could not remember a time when he had felt more fortunate.

THE NAVY DEPARTMENT, in response to the wishes of President Franklin Pierce, had assigned *Cyane* to "special service," specifically a reconnaissance of a prospective Atlantic-Pacific ship canal route through the Isthmus of Darién in present-day Panama. After a series of autumn meetings with the secretary of the Navy and Pierce, Strain unexpectedly won the command, his first. His crossing party, officially known as the U.S. Darién Exploring Expedition, was to locate what until recently had not been thought to exist: a break in the mountains across the narrowest portion of the isthmus, the so-called Darién Gap.

The tropics location had the whiff of freshness in an otherwise old and costly battle to link the seas. After centuries of being battered on the endless ice of the Canadian Arctic and never finding the storied Northwest Passage, the first nations saw something a good deal brighter in the warm crease of a slender forest. Great Britain and France were simultaneously mounting a joint survey expedition of the same Darién route, with Her Majesty's Admiralty said to be sending three English vessels, including a man-of-war and an advanced survey ship, the steam-powered *Scorpion*. Naturally the governments pledged cooperation. Privately, it was a different matter. Like their successful race to summit Everest a hundred years later, England saw an undertaking that would define her people's greatness. President Pierce, an aggressive expansionist who viewed the country's borders expanding to Cuba and beyond, was no less determined. Isaac Strain was his Hillary.

THERE ARE NO SURVIVING PHOTOGRAPHS of the *Cyane*'s crew. The exploring party didn't bring a camera, a bulky contraption still in its infancy at midcentury and rarely used outside the popular city portrait studios. Instead the journey was expected to be recorded with a draftsman's faithful and exuberantly detailed line drawings.

The first of the images, a wardroom tableau, is telling. The thirty-three-year-old Strain was a small man, but he dominates the frame. He is the lone figure standing at a large table of his fellow officers. The ship's stout captain, George Hollins, appears almost a spoof of the old Navy: rotund, sedentary, dispassionate. The ship belonged to Hollins, of course; he was the permanent commander. But the coming expedition command was Strain's, and he is Hollins's dashing opposite: lean and all storm-trim—more the sinewy bow-sprit than the dense mainmast. His shoulders are right-angle square. He has an aquiline nose and a full but slender brown beard that seems to wrap his jaw like planking on a well-formed bow. His head, with its boyish thatch of brown hair, is luminous, bathed in light where the others are not. His physical posture, left arm bracing the top of a chair and right tucked inside a full-length, high-collared naval coat, is intensely attentive. The portrait seems to describe a new kind of leader, one defined by movement and stirred by the remarkable ambition of the age.

An "interoceanic" ship canal was not just a gigantic task, said one statesman, "but the greatest the world has ever known." The canal's creation would defy nature in the most fundamental way imaginable—dividing the Americas in two. The rising tide of the Pacific would flow right through a man-made, 150-foot-wide channel (bringing Atlantic-bound ship traffic along with the flood; on the receding ebb tide the vessels would cross in the opposite direction, Atlantic to Pacific).

It was an audacious plan but it was a confident time—genius was everywhere. Steamships and mail packets cruised the waters of the world, and where they stopped, the newly lain railroads started. Where a river stopped, an American engineer saw another beginning. By 1850 hundreds of artificial waterways webbed the East. It was the Canal Era.

Darién, the grandest canal of them all, would change the world all over again. No railway crossed the North American continent in 1853, and none would for another fifteen years. If a "gap," or low pass existed in Darién's Atlantic mountains, as it was hotly rumored to, then the tunneling work would be minimal and the seas would be joined with relative ease. Suddenly goods, from mail to gold, might be shipped to distant places like California, or even Australia, in a fraction of the usual time. The traditional sailing route around Cape Horn, one of the most storm-ravaged passages in seafaring, might be avoided, sparing lives and millions of dollars in wrecked shipping. The four-month voyage from New York to California would take half as long.

Darién was a project whose commercial advantages were hardly possible to overrate, Strain wrote the Navy Department on November 3, when he formally accepted his command. "As an American officer [there is nothing] I should feel more pride in connecting my name," he added. If commerce was king, then tiny Darién was potentially the most gilded terrain on the vast planetary map.

And yet Darién wasn't a new idea—it was the oldest. In 1503 Christopher Columbus, on his fourth and final voyage, futilely combed the Panama coast, believing the isthmus was merely a peninsula and that in the vicinity of Darién he would find its termination and thus a passage through. *El estrecho secreto*, the secret strait, never revealed itself, of course, and after failing to establish a settlement, Columbus dejectedly turned away from the palm-fringed shores of Panama for the dreary homeward voyage to Spain.

The search was famously resumed by Vasco Núñez de Balboa. In 1513, from a peak in Darién, Balboa became the first European to see the vast Pacific. The Spaniard's Darién settlements at Santa María del Antigua and Acla, the first mainland New World colonies, thrived on the promise of a transit route across. When none materialized, the settlements succumbed, the ruins overrun by emerald jungle. By the time the Spanish left they had come to equate Darién with the fictional hell of Dante's *Inferno*. In 1698 the quest was revived again, this time by a charismatic Scot named William Paterson. In a grand colonizing scheme, he proclaimed the geographically charmed Darién as "the door of the seas and key to the universe." The Scots died in diseased droves and lasted less than a year. Sickness was inevitable in the tropics, a colonist lamented, but death swept Darién. The land was cursed.

From his first research Strain—one of the few Navy men who had traversed and studied jungle habitats—saw himself drawn into Darién's orbit, its history and tragic protagonists. It was the most written-about and trod-upon bit of blank geography on the globe, only the writing seemed to tangle like spidery jungle vines, each account twisting into another until it was impossible to tell right from wrong, real from imagined. Not a single fact was reliable. The information, maps included, was either dated or distorted to advance someone's scheme—or to savage another's. For the first half of the century not a single expedition had even dared to cross. Between the two oceans seemed concentrated the obstacles of a continent, one account read: a maze of precipitous mountains, whitewater torrents, and impenetrable swamp.

But the geographic rumor persisted. There was a way through, a gap neither the pioneer Spaniards nor the native Indians wished to make known. The rumor gave rise to a belief that took hold in Europe and quickly spread to a watchful America. Darién, the vengeful and defiant wilderness at the crossroads of the world, was a myth. Strain was certain his party, with its "well imagined plans," would be the first to offer a correct view.

ACCORDING TO THE SECRETARY of the Navy's orders, the *Cyane* was to sail first for Cartagena, at the northern tip of South America in present-day Colombia, then on to Caledonia Bay, where Lieutenant Strain would lead a "speedy" overland crossing of the isthmus in an attempt to map and survey the route. He was to do so without disrupting or antagonizing the native Indians, and he was to report his instrumented findings directly to the department.

Getting the *Cyane* ready in time seemed a long shot. Strain's $1,500 budget, the best the department could do, was barely enough for slop clothing. In the few weeks he had, the lieutenant flew into motion. "I have asked as little as compatible with the execution of the work, and will with pleasure devote my own limited means to cover any margin which may be left," he explained with the presentation of his extraordinary budget.

The technical survey instruments, he pointed out, required no outlay; they came on loan from the National Observatory in Washington. The arms, which would be returned, were from a friendly quartermaster. They included the best guns then available: twenty percussion muskets, ten Jenks carbines, and eight Colt pistols. Firearms, given the many hazards, were a first priority.

But his attention to detail was evident everywhere. Food came from the *Cyane*'s stores, but Strain requested and received permission to significantly rework the standard ration. The jungle could be a hostile environment: hard to hunt in and difficult to provision for. Beef, the lieutenant wrote the department, "would be ill adapted to land transportation, and contains in the same bulk and weight much less nutrients [than pork]."

Strain also dispatched friends to chase down more background journal articles and books from the best private libraries in New York, Boston, and Washington. From the Philadelphia Academy of Natural Sciences came tin collecting boxes and reams of coarse paper for botanizing, one of Strain's many hobbies. A well-known businessman who saw Strain in ceaseless action prior to December 20 marveled at his "great enthusiasm" and ingenuity. He had no personal liabilities— he was not married and had scrupulously avoided owning a home. Every time he left for sea he brought his treasured books and personal journals with him, as if one day he might not be coming back. Few could imagine a man better suited to exploration—or more desirous to follow in the footsteps of the famous pioneers who came to Darién before him.

STRAIN WAS ENCOURAGED by their transit of the Delaware. The ice had slowed but not stopped them. Sixty miles along he and much of the crew regarded the progress of Fort Delaware, a massive granite fortress somehow rising out of the compressible river mud. As the three-masted *Cyane* eased past the long, low southeast bastion, Strain gave the order for a formal salute. The island construction site, with wharf builders and stonecutters astride thudding pile drivers, was a vision of American willpower and industrial ingenuity. The cannon blast crashed through the overcast sky to massive cheers, aboard and ashore. Curiously, their 77 degrees west longitude was a magic number of sorts, the same looping meridian shared by the tiny Pennsylvania burg where Strain was born and, after a considerable expanse of ocean, the Isthmus of Darién.

On the afternoon of the 22nd they unhooked from the steam tug, made sail to royals, and rounded the Cape May and Henlopen lights on a southeast course. "Passed several sails standing on different courses," the log recorded. Their 8 knots felt like 80 to the ship's sailing master, William Wilcox, after the cautious crawl downriver. Seemingly by the minute the temperature rose. At midnight it had climbed to 50 degrees Fahrenheit, a 15-degree spike over twelve hours earlier. By noon of the 23rd it was 60.

At 72 degrees west longitude, 37 degrees north latitude, their position was the western edge of the Gulf Stream, a few miles northeast of Cape Hatteras. The Atlantic's hue, once the deep dark blue of their upturned naval collars, was translucent. Silver flying fish broke the surface and glided from crest to crest with their winglike fins. Their raucous emergence from the ocean depths seemed to mimic the seamen themselves, who joined the morning watch on the sun-drenched weather deck. Of course, the Gulf Stream came from where they were going. The birds shadowing it were tropical exotics. The warm seawater drawn for baths brought with it bits of waxy leaves and shavings of dark tropical woods. Mindful of the chock-ablock chill they came from, most saw the "river in the sea" as a promise-filled tiding.

Hours later, however, the sea began to increase, lightning flashed in the northwest, and the barometer fell rapidly. Their arrival was spectacularly ill-timed. The cold upper-atmosphere air, which had followed them out to sea, was about to collide with the unnaturally warm air and seawater around them. Modern meteorologists have a term for the uniquely unstable winter conditions that can congregate off Hatteras—bombagenesis. The phrase is perversely apt. To the unfortunate bystander the storm erupts with such sudden malice, the only true comparison is to an enormous bomb exploding.

Almost on theatrical cue, the darkness fell and the sea rose. At 6 P.M., only hours after their arrival in the Gulf Stream, a hurricane-force wind tore through the rigging. "A terrific squall struck her from the N.W. forcing her lee rail nearly under water," wrote Wilcox in his personal log of the storm, describing a thunderous gust that laid the

800-ton fighting ship almost on its beam-ends. The sky was black with clouds, the rain poured in horizontal sheets, and in all directions vision was limited by roaring billows, white with froth and foam.

Sudden as the storm was it wasn't without warning. *Cyane*'s officers (presumably Strain included) had seen *something* coming but Captain Hollins "insisted on making sail despite appearances," complained Wilcox in his personal account. Perhaps the sultry Gulf had lulled Hollins into complacency, but more likely he wished to make a resounding statement to crew and officers alike. Laying on canvas with a storm coming on was a defiant old-school gesture—to the sea and to the men. Perhaps the order was directed to Strain, to test his loyalties and define the limits of his command. Strain was known to be a favorite of the junior officers and a bit feisty at times with his superiors. It *was* Hollins's ship. Or maybe he simply saw an irresistible chance to shorten their passage—perhaps even to break a record. The following northwesterlies weren't just favorable to their southeast course, they were perfect.

Whatever the rationale, Hollins's order to set sail only hours prior to the storm's full onset was a disaster. Standard heavy weather precautions—striking sail and yards, battening hatches, and stowing the ship's deck ordnance below—were put off. It wasn't until 4 P.M., about three hours after the weather abruptly worsened, that Hollins finally relented and reversed his command, sending the crew aloft, screaming "jump men, jump." But by then the gale was upon them.

With all of seventy-two hours to acclimate himself, Strain found himself at the helm with a green, questionably loyal crew, an old second-rate ship he had never sailed, and a hundred-year storm gathering behind him. Nothing challenged personal courage and conviction more than the darkness and a great sea coming on, Strain once wrote. Here it was.

CHASED BY STRAIN'S TRUMPET-amplified voice, all hands raced to the main deck. The topmen, lashed by flapping lines and struggling in the dark, flung themselves into the shrouds; others raced below to ready the bilge pumps. Already seawater was pouring down the hatches. The seasick civilians were herded into the wardroom, where they were instructed to lie prone on the sloshy wet floor. Throughout the night, they clung to whatever they could, only to be repeatedly tossed against the oak bulkheads as wave after wave struck tremendous blows, seemingly hell-bent to bury them all.

Hard up the helm or hard down were the navigational choices in a hurricane-strength storm. But circumstances beyond their control— "a furious gale & the wildest kind of sea," in Master Wilcox's words—forced their hand, making the ship near impossible to bring to, and driving them south. Near midnight on the 23rd, the sea reached its terrible peak. It was a perfect hurricane. "The old crosses [the perpendicular spars] making frightful lunges—taking in water over both bows & each gangway," reported Wilcox. He thought their fate spoken for. The topmen couldn't get out to the end of the violently flailing, gale-scoured yards. Loose sails, bursting with the foam-filled air, needed to be flattened down, fisted-up, and "gasketed" to the yards with stout lines. If they weren't, the masts, already bending grotesquely under the strain, would almost certainly snap. As if to cruelly destroy any chance for rescue, a 40-foot wall of wind-driven sea had collapsed the aft davit (the bracing that secures the auxiliary boats) and was threatening to pitch the 20-foot-plus dory-like vessels overboard. Near midnight their lone sail gave way, the steel fastening hanks popping off like shirt buttons. The sheet anchor men got to the staysail and secured it, but actual repairs were impossible. The ship's bowsprit was consistently underwater, plunging in the sea's deepening troughs. A temporary sail a bit further aft would have to do.

In the tumult the commands from the quarterdeck couldn't or

wouldn't be heard aloft. The seamen, some new, were exhausted after hours of punishing struggle. Their will was faltering. Seeing everything slip away, desperate, Strain drove the ship's second lieutenant up the rigging to spur the men. He was to provide their will, even if it meant threatening court-martial or, in the worst possible case, exacting the order behind a raised pistol. There was no choice; the ship's survival was at stake.

Amazingly, the extraordinary errand succeeded. In the early morning hours the topmen bulled their way to the outermost end of the yards and secured the sails. No one was blown off or sucked into the sea. The moment they were able to safely scramble down, the off-watch turned in, and the hatches were battened down behind them.

As the ship ran ably before the storm, almost bounding from sea to sea, a drowned-out but distinct chorus of huzzahs rose up. Sure enough, the *Cyane* was racing before the wind. Her 11 knots felt like 50 as every timber groaned to the breaking point. The old ship held.

Others weren't so lucky. The "gales of December," as the two-week-long storm came to be known, would exact a massive toll in life and property. Dozens of ships from several nations were severely damaged or lost. The most notable disaster was the luxury passenger ship *San Francisco,* a fully loaded steamship on its celebrated New York–to–California inaugural run. In the last hours of the tempest a single enormous predawn sea rose—"more like a mountain than anything else," recalled a survivor—crushing the deck cabins and sweeping hundreds into the sea. It would be weeks before help got to her, and in that time dozens more would die as overcrowding and unsanitary conditions bred a lethal outbreak of cholera.

Off Jamaica, a sister storm slammed into the *Espiégle,* the isthmus-bound British ship carrying Lionel Gisborne and Edward Cullen, the two men whose recent books and maps had revitalized the Darién route and brought it to popular attention. The chaotic seas pouring across the deck ripped away the lee quarterboat, sending both it and the boatswain's mate overboard. Only after numerous abortive attempts "owing to the height of the sea" was the crew able to rope in and snatch the half-drowned man out of the water.

The *Cyane* was one of the fortunate few. Her repairs were minor. The same 50-foot seas that dismasted the gargantuan *San Francisco* merely stove in *Cyane*'s quarterboat. The night-long Force 12 winds shredded the foretopmast staysail and mizzen top gallant sail but nothing else. A courageous effort by several seamen had secured the launch boats—the same ones that would be used to land the exploration party at Darién—lashing them with tackle at the height of the storm. Not a single life was lost, nor were there any serious injuries.

The *Cyane*'s unlikely deliverance uplifted all, but perhaps none so much as Theodore Winthrop, one of the late-joining civilian volunteers. During the darkest hours of the storm he had given up, figuring the holocaust above him was his punishment for glory seeking. Now, as the *Cyane* threaded the Mona Passage between the Dominican Republic and Puerto Rico and stood down the sunny isthmian coast, he took to the deck, opened his pocket diary, and recorded a new world: "Ten knots an hour down the N.E. trades; sheltered under a sail from the sun of the tropics; a fresh cool breeze following fast; a brilliant sea with sparkling foam crests; a clean ship with black contrast of battery; plenty of sailor life strewed over the decks in Sunday rig; a dim outline of Hayti on the starboard quarter, hopes of Carthagena & oranges in four days—these are the pleasures of our New Year's day."

Isaac Strain's plague of black luck, a rather unfortunate legacy to his seventeen-year naval career, seemed mercifully over. He had not only been spared but sped toward his destiny. The waters were getting warmer.

2 / The SEA and the JUNGLE

The beauty of the surrounding fertile and highly cul-
tivated plain reminded me of the more cultivated
portions of my own country, and recalled to my mind
a period, before my wanderings over the ocean had
commenced, when I lived quietly, and in seclusion,
upon a farm, far from the stir and bustle of the world.

ISAAC STRAIN, *CORDILLERA AND PAMPA,*
MOUNTAIN AND PLAIN (1853)

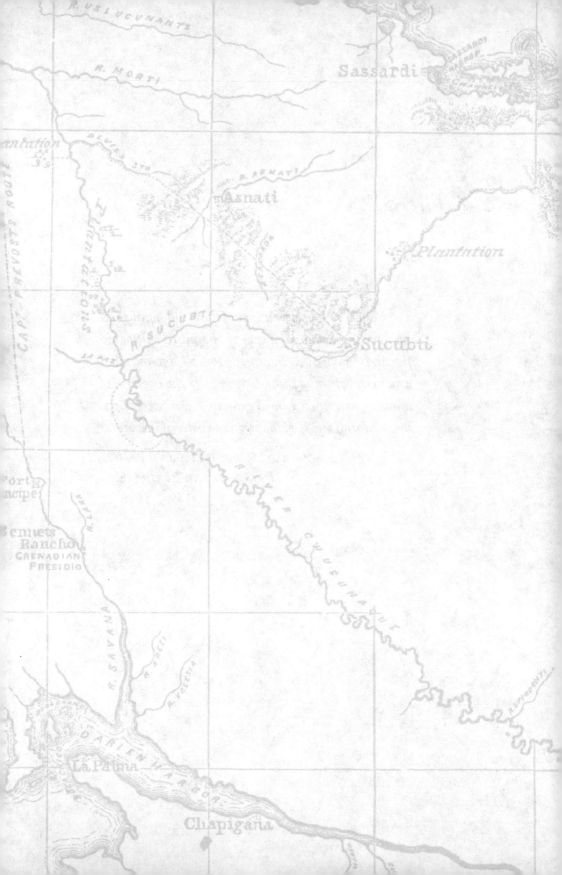

January 2, 1854

15° 12′ N, 70° 21′ W
West Indies

A SHIP IN THE TORRID ZONE took a while to heat up, but
when it did the sticky warmth drew around everyone. The
coppered bottom of the ship began turning algae green,
and the ordinary smells of human living became extraordinary.
They were enriched with those of freighted livestock, of course,
with vermin, tar, linseed oil, wet wood, stale water, and the first
stores turning in the hold. In compressed, low-overhead places like
the berthing deck the fumes thickened as they cooked. In as little as
a couple of days the overwhelming stench caused green newcomers
to retch practically each time they went below. When the battened-
down ship was vented after a prolonged tropical storm like the one
Cyane had been through, it wasn't uncommon for a noxious column
of air to rise through the hatchway like smoke, prompting more than
one captain to send someone down below to see whether the ship
was on fire.

Undoubtedly the *Cyane*'s crew was logy from the building tropical heat, but most were badly hung over too. Predictably, the New
Year's allowance of grog had resulted in trouble, and in the captain's
oak-paneled aft cabin a four-man court of inquiry was in session to

hear the ugly particulars, make judgment, and advise a course of discipline.

The ship had left the Atlantic and was, in the view of the young midshipman keeping the day's log, "running through a large space of light green water." They were in the heart of the Caribbean Sea, almost equidistant between the Tropic of Cancer and the Equator and only a day or two from their first stop, at Cartagena.

Isaac Strain and his Darién shore party were comfortably encamped on the wide-open weather deck. Extra sail, strung up like a quilted awning, sheltered them from the broiling overhead sun and a sudden afternoon shower. A 10- to 12-knot trade kept the sails full. The earliest Spanish navigators dubbed the Caribbean the "Ladies Gulf" because, they said, a girl could safely take the helm within its lovely borders. The New Year, at least for the expeditionary portion of the *Cyane*'s crew, had dawned perfectly. An engine seemed to be behind them—due to the following seas, the old *Cyane* was threatening the speed record for the Philadelphia-to-Cartagena passage. The conversation, about the expedition and themselves, came easily.

Their land party was small, only eight at present, but expected to near thirty by the time they got on the ground and added seamen volunteers and local guides. The leaders were Strain, two passed midshipmen, William Talbot Truxtun and John Minor Maury, and the civilian Winthrop. Truxtun, of Philadelphia, and Maury, from Virginia, were each in their late twenties and early in their much-anticipated careers; they were from two of the most decorated families in the U.S. Navy. Of the two, only the quieter one, the handsome Truxtun, had yet seen any "special service," as the Navy called its prestigious scientific cruises. Winthrop, a recent Yale graduate, was a descendant of Massachusetts Bay Colony governor John Winthrop. He had just returned to the East Coast from six months of rambling in the Northwest wilds when he impetuously signed up with the exploring party, telling his startled family that the "object is one which would start the most stationary of mortals; the stoniest statu-quoite would move his petrified pins when a trip was proposed to him the object of which is to make South America an island and the Atlantic and Pacific one ocean at the Straits of Darién."

The dockside arrangement happened so fast that Winthrop didn't have time to collect his things but instead dispatched his mother to send by express "all my shirts & flannels, socks Hakfs, shoes 2 pr, my white blanket, a pr of worn moccasins with red cloth front (on the floor in the nursery)—a blue hickory shirt, my butcher's knife & sheaf, my saddle bags—my belt (leather), old pantaloons & coat hanging in closet—any thin clothes of mine—all the light reading there is including E. Warburtons Darién—Davies Surveying—if there is a Spanish Oblendorf or Dictionary and on the whole anything you can think off [*sic*] that will be useful omitting none of the above."

Like Truxtun, Maury, and Strain, he had agreed to volunteer for the duty. In Winthrop's arrangement, he was accorded the stature of officer but received no pay and had for the time being no specific duties. The junior officers took a deep pay cut, forgiving the government their standard salary in order to accommodate the lean expedition budget. The privilege of participating in such an adventure was also a consideration. Part of his compensation, a genial Maury assured his southern sweetheart, was escaping the glacial Northeast winter. Their pay was $12 per month, or $36 for the entire three-month special service in Darién.

An obvious added benefit was the fare. They would likely eat well. They were all experienced woodsmen, particularly Strain, who had a marksman's eye. Above the improved daily ration—roughly a pound of salted pork, a half pound of rice, and 14 ounces of hardtack—the party anticipated adding tropical fruits, fish, and fresh game meat. Winthrop, the only one of the gentlemen to have visited the Isthmus of Panama, could attest to its richness. On a brief sojourn in the Pacific forests he saw all manner of wild animals, he told the others, including a plump alligator he easily dropped with his five-shooter. Tumbling mountain brooks were everywhere, meaning an unequaled supply of fresh drinking water. None of them would be surprised to leave the isthmus a little thicker on the bone than when they started.

Flung open on the quarterdeck's low signal locker, a spate of impressive, newly authored maps of Darién drew their almost constant review and comment. Less than one-ninth of the land surface of the globe had been surveyed at midcentury, with only the Dutch East Indies, India, and Venezuela mapped in tropical latitudes. The planet's interior, inhabited by almost one billion people, was unknown. In the meridian grids and section grades, they saw both order and immense opportunity. That night, the sky was brilliant, a gauzy firmament set against slowly flickering stars and a lovely quarter moon. The confidence the maps inspired was unmistakable: The dash across was unlikely to present any serious difficulty.

Strain had earlier drawn up a command structure along ship's lines. On a ship there was a captain, a first officer, second officer, and so on. Truxtun was the equivalent of the first officer, Maury the second. Each had his prescribed duties. Truxtun was to look after the main body, supervising the particulars of the march, the provisions, and the native mule drivers they planned to hire in Cartagena. Maury, a first-rated engineer, would oversee the levels and command the chain bearers, the thick-shouldered laborers who would spool out 100-foot lines of steel links to get an accurate measure of distance traveled. Strain was the chief pioneer, entrusted with route finding, discipline, and the overall welfare of the party.

None of them, Strain included, had ever set foot on Darién terrain before. They would rely heavily on Winthrop's Panama expertise, and he and Strain had talked nearly nonstop since coming out of the storm. (Panama and Darién were then neighboring provinces belonging to New Granada, or present-day Colombia.) "Our party will be the first to cross from sea to sea—if we do cross and we do not intend to be stopped," a stirred Winthrop wrote home at the time.

Strain, he enthused, was a special man who had traveled to the most amazing places. He wasn't a northerner like Truxtun, or a southerner like Maury, or a Yankee like himself. He was a westerner with all the hope, hardship, and enterprise that implied at mid-century.

ISAAC G. STRAIN WAS BORN in 1821 in Roxbury, Pennsylvania, a burg set fast in the oak and maple forests of the Appalachian mountains. At the peak of the **A**-shaped Franklin County, Roxbury claimed the western end of a picturesque valley that was merely the trace portion of a much grander valley, one following the great Appalachian Divide and extending from Vermont to Alabama. Neither winters nor summers were extreme, and because of the vigorous brooks and mountain streams crosshatching the valley the climate was a temperate ideal. The fertile, well-drained soil produced not only prodigious harvests of wheat and corn (and flush orchards in its higher reaches) but the best type of manhood, locals believed, one steeped in the magic of the dull soil beneath their feet.

Isaac's family were of Scotch-Irish stock, descendants of Ulster Protestants who fled the bloody sectarian violence of northern Ireland at the outset of the eighteenth century. The Scotch-Irish settled the central Pennsylvanian wilderness rapidly, expanding ever deeper into the Six Nations hunting territories until the long, tense standoff erupted with the outbreak of the French and Indian War in 1753. Savage raids and counterraids razed the countryside for the next decade. For the vast majority of Scotch-Irish the diaspora resumed. They fled in terrified numbers. But Isaac's ancestors were part of

those who stayed, barricading themselves behind a string of rudimentary forts raised on the county's exposed western flank at Cove
Gap, Path Valley, and Parnell's Knob.

At the time of Strain's birth the valley held some three hundred
people, mostly miners, loggers, and farmers with several shopkeep-
ers and millers, a few of them German Lutherans but most God-
fearing Scotch-Irish Presbyterians who came from miles out every
Sabbath, traversing mountain roads and cold creeks to attend the
daylong services in the redbrick Middle Spring church, whose white
bell tower soared over the countryside. Strain made the journey from
as early as he could remember. He, however, seemed to have had his
spirit awakened in a more unlikely place: a tidy, hand-hewn cabin
neighboring the church, presided over by the ministerial presence of
John Cooper.

Hopewell Academy was one of the state's last log cabin schools.
There was a single entrance, sliding windows, and a gable projecting
over the end where the busy public road to Newburg ran past the
"academy building." Day-tripping students could be seen continu-
ously traveling the valley road, often exhorting their horses to a
gallop as they approached the steep hilltop on which the little
oblong-shaped school stood.

Isaac's classroom contained a woodstove, table, professor's chair,
and benches. John Cooper, the son of an influential local pastor and
a graduate of nearby Dickinson College, required his pupils to learn
and apply "with much exactness" the rules of grammar and analyze
and parse sentences and words, taken at random from different parts
of the lesson. He was a kinsman of Strain's on his mother's side, part
of a long line of robust churchmen and scholars. His gentlemanly
disposition and scholarly range left its mark on Isaac, instilling him
with generous doses of Latin and literature, but also a sense of their,
and their country's, keen future. Hopewell Academy, wrote an ad-

miring local physician, "sent forth many from its unpretending portals to act well their part."

John Cooper wasn't a proselytizer, but he shared a common trait with his minister father: charged patriotism. Father Cooper, a moderator of the synods of New York and Philadelphia, in May 1776 preached the cause of American independence as a divine one. Not only the rights of men, but the sacred interests of Christ's Kingdom were involved in the struggle. His words didn't go unheeded. It was said that no church in the Cumberland Valley (which then included Strain's neighboring Franklin County), or possibly any valley in America, sent as many men into the war of independence as the Rev. Mr. Cooper's Middle Spring church. At the Battle of Trenton, the minister himself shouldered a musket.

Hopewell's Latin scholars had no war to fight. Not a conventional one, at least. The idea was to brandish their distinctive frontier intelligence in a way and with a humility that would be the envy of any county, any state, any nation. In a one-room schoolhouse, on the edge of a farm in the middle of nowhere, and in church every Sunday, Isaac trusted in "a destiny that shapes our ends, Rough hew them as we will."

Often in the evening, recalled one of Cooper's pupils, "some of the boys would be pitching iron rings by the roadside, near the gate, whilst others on the porch were playing checkers, and others still, with violin and flute, were making sweet strains of music. . . . Now and then a fishing in the creek was resorted to as an expedient for enjoyment. With well prepared torch lights, nets and poles, all the students would march about dark to the Condoguinet, and spend five or six hours wading in that beautiful stream, often returning with success, at midnight, to their homes, sometimes with no success, but always with glad hearts, making the surrounding woods echo with their songs."

Isaac's home in Roxbury, where the sinuous Condoguinet origi-nated, was literally an extension of the sylvan setting. His grandfa-ther Captain William Strain, a Revolutionary War hero, had grown up here and for years ran a large gristmill. The fields waved with golden grain, and the deep pools of the plunging Condoguinet pos-sessed the best fishing in the county. In the smoky postdawn morn-ings, with the valley wrapped in a heavy fog, a boy might trace the forests for deer, or after the harvest, the innumerable wild turkeys.

Isaac, all of ten, understood he was lucky. He was a farmer's son in a time when sons followed their fathers into the fields. Many of the boys he knew couldn't read or write. His family was different. He wasn't being prepared to turn earth and tend crops. As a young boy freely moving over countryside where his name was known, Isaac could not have felt anything other than blessed by his birthright. People could scarcely imagine what he might do one day.

BUT THE TOWN WAS FADING. A few years earlier the valley had been a prosperous trading center and a popular layover for wagoners on their way across the Alleghenies, west to Pittsburgh. But the new mountain roads, wider and smoother to accommodate horse-drawn wagons, were built in the southern part of the county, bypassing Roxbury. The new era of "smooth ways" and wagon trains made the pack horses obsolete, and with their obsolescence the town receded back into the boreal wilderness.

The town's demise was mirrored in the hardships of its families. Many of the houses were identical to those of their settler descen-dants: one-story log homes with floors of split and hewed hardwood and benches for chairs. The burials came in chilling waves. A devas-tating fire at the Middle Spring church was considered a fateful blow. A treasured record of the territory's births, marriages, and deaths— including those of Isaac's pioneer ancestors—went up in flames.

In the early 1830s the twelve-year-old Isaac and his father, Robert, moved on. His birth mother did not. There's no record of what happened to Martha Grier Strain, the eldest daughter of a prominent church family in Franklin County. Robert's marriage to Martha on December 7, 1820, at Middle Spring Presbyterian Church is all that survives in print, that and the occasion of Isaac's baptism on April 13, 1824. His mother's story is a mystery. She was not at his baptism, or at least she wasn't credited with being there, and she didn't become a member of the Middle Spring church when her husband did. After the May 15, 1827, meeting in which Robert was voted in, Martha's name appears next to his for the last time. "Martha dis+," the log entry reads, the *dis* shorthand for *discharged* and the cross a common symbol for *deceased*. But she didn't die. In 1836, in another county in Pennsylvania, she remarried and had two more children. The puzzle is what happened in the years between, the years with Isaac. Perhaps the "+" meant an illness, not the physical kind but the more incapacitating, less easily talked about mental sort. Depression and madness were all too common. In the 1830s in Roxbury everyone was just holding on. A beautiful young sister of Isaac's mother had just died. Perhaps she broke down.

The middle initial in Isaac's name, G., likely stood for Grier. The name Isaac descended to him from his maternal grandfather, a college-educated minister with a roaming spirit. The Rev. Isaac Grier's earnest diary of his three-year-long wilderness mission up the west branch of the Susquehanna is as good as a DNA match to his namesake. Yet the Grier name was never acknowledged by Isaac. Clearly there was a terrible upheaval in Roxbury. When Isaac and his thirty-five-year-old father left, they left everything and everyone they knew forever.

It's possible Isaac had been on his own from a very young age, looked after by his extended family but mostly dependent on his wits and resiliency. The makeup of an explorer is impossible to divine.

But in Isaac's case, you could almost hear the refrain from those he left behind: *We knew it all along.*

ISAAC AND HIS FATHER joined the great westward migration looking for a fresh start. They stopped in Springfield, Ohio, and stayed. The newly built National Road, all 350 potholed miles of it, ended in Springfield. Beyond lay the frontier. For a young boy already engaged by thoughts of what lay elsewhere, the daily sight of family wagon trains stopping, storing up, and rolling west was impressive. The regularly scheduled stagecoaches, egg-shaped and brightly painted on the outside, deposited presidential candidates in black claw-hammer coats, celebrity actors, and adventure seekers. Military regiments stormed through en route to remote garrisons, and boys Strain's age delivered the mail for the Pony Express, swapping mounts every six miles and galloping into town in showy breakneck final sprints. Springfield, in its pre-railroad days, was the end of the road but the beginning of a thousand voyages. By one estimate twelve hundred wagons a day were coming into town in 1836. For those that went on, future prospects never looked so good and optimism never ran so high as the day they left Springfield.

Even at the edge of the inland frontier, the teenage Strain was aware that the Navy was on the brink of a new seafaring era. For the last ten years, but particularly in the several leading up to Isaac's enlistment, public and prominent forces were at work to fund a national scientific expedition to the ends of the world—the Antarctic region and the South Pacific.

In 1838, after years of battling in Congress, an agreement was struck authorizing the first large-scale U.S. Navy exploring expedition. The Wilkes United States Exploring Expedition, named for its fiery commander, Lieutenant Charles Wilkes, was a massive enterprise comprising six ships and a dozen "scientifics." In January 1840, he would famously claim discovery of the Antarctic continent, beating his British exploratory counterpart, Sir James Clark Ross, to the 66th parallel by mere weeks. The trip was the envy of every midshipman in the fleet, a veritable broadside to the perception that Americans were Europe's exploratory inferiors. No one had ever navigated further south, and few had advanced the scientific cause the way Wilkes had. They were gone four years, in which time they sailed some 85,000 miles while surveying hundreds of islands and collecting hundreds of new species. The expedition would usher in a dozen more "voyages of discovery" over the next two decades, one of them the Darién Exploring Expedition. Not coincidentally, the week the secretary of the Navy's proposal for a national scientific expedition reached Congress in 1837—an item well reported in the Ohio newspapers—was the week Strain decided he wanted to be a sailor.

On February 6, 1838, a wide-eyed, sixteen-year-old Isaac reported to the sloop-of-war USS *Erie* at the Boston Navy Yard. By all accounts Strain was a quick and eager understudy on his yearlong training cruise, receiving high marks from his commanding officer and a warrant as a midshipman after the minimum six months of sea duty. His next four years were spent almost exclusively at sea, marked by his regular requests for transfers to ships exploring deeper, less charted waters than that of the North Atlantic and Caribbean. His only hindrance was his health, which sometimes seemed less resolute than Strain wished. He was hospitalized at Pensacola and later in Brazil, where he was abruptly sent home by a board of medical officers and was issued an eight-month furlough to regain his health. The generous leave was likely a nod to circumstances at home. His forty-year-old father, only recently remarried for the third time, had succumbed to pulmonary consumption over the winter, dying December 20 at the Springfield home of George Brain, his father-in-law. That same winter Isaac's infant half brother, Montgomery, was also buried.

His father had left Isaac a small plot of land in Springfield and $20. After just a month of his allotted eight months, Isaac wrote the department of his recaptured health and his intention to attend naval school in Philadelphia to prepare for his midshipman's examination. He sold the inherited land for cash and shortly thereafter wrote a friend that he had severed his ties to his Ohio home. He was striking out for the East, its culture, its energy, its change.

Isaac was only twenty-one. His stepmother, father, and half brother had all died in the last five years. He was old enough to have already served five years in the U.S. Navy, but he was young and impressionable enough to wonder if he, like Charles Darwin ten years earlier aboard the *Beagle,* might be on the brink of changing his life and everyone else's forever. Darwin too had been in his early twenties when he embarked on his famous voyage. Darwin's book, with the *Beagle*'s British naval commander Robert Fitzroy, had been published to thunderous accolade in 1839. Like many of his generation— but also for personal reasons all his own—Strain was in a terrible hurry.

Increasingly he began to plan his own journey. In Philadelphia, the fever for exploration burned as hot as anywhere. The leading philosophers, naturalists, and statesmen marched through on a regular basis, flinging themselves against one another in a parade of popular lectures. In the few months Strain was stationed in Philadelphia to prepare for his naval exam, the touring lecturers included the Prussian naturalist Alexander von Humboldt and anthropologist John L. Stephens (whose thrilling *Incidents of Travel in Central America* would introduce Mayan civilization to Americans for the first time). Midcentury Philadelphia itself was a frenzied hub of natural history, anchored by the redbrick edifices of the American Philosophical Society and the Academy of Natural Sciences. Within each was unfolding an astonishing diversity of work, from Audubon's ornithological portraits of the American West to Samuel Haldeman's ethnological investigations of Indian languages. Artifacts came in a voluminous flow as ships from all points of the compass entered the yawning mouth of the Delaware and rode the incoming tide to Philadelphia with strange boxed bounties of bones and bugs.

But the bones and bird skins, delightful as they were, didn't compare with the personalities roaming the salons and lecture halls. Swarms of voices made themselves heard, their travels explained, and access was often available to all, even to those without significant means.

Improbable alliances were possible, and Strain was the beneficiary of one. In those months in Philadelphia he managed to introduce himself to one of the acclaimed giants of science. His name was Samuel George Morton, and his newly published best seller, *Crania Americana,* purported to scientifically prove what the country already had a good deal of faith in: the uncommon and unequaled breadth of Caucasian intelligence. Morton made his case with a vast collection of skulls, a bounty he hoped the enthusiastic midshipman might add to in his future naval travels.

Strain's future direction was never more certain than on February 28, 1843. That was the day observers in the Northern Hemisphere saw the brightest comet observed in seven centuries. Each evening that March, Strain and thousands of Philadelphians stood in rapt wonder, eyes turned heavenward for the nightly displays. The comet came so close to colliding with the sun (a mere 89,000 miles) that it was "fragmented like buckshot, its gas and particles blown back by the powerful solar wind to form a broom tail that stretched for more than 50 degrees of arc in the southwestern sky." The event was interpreted in widely different ways, but for Strain and a rising class of scientific-minded young men the great comet of 1843, the finest of the entire nineteenth century, was seen as the purest symbol of their extraordinary future path.

Isaac, on the verge of twenty-three, was certain he would lead America into a new seafaring era. He had a new life, influential friends, and a hell of an idea. Acquaintances saw him as incredibly self-assured and a bit hungry for notoriety. He said he was going to the deepest, darkest jungle on the planet, and he worried somebody might beat him to it. He needn't have worried. In 1843 almost nobody wanted to go to the jungle.

By late summer he had outfitted, staffed, and arranged partial sponsorship for an extensive reconnaissance of Paraguay, Colombia, and unexplored portions of Brazil. It was a phenomenally ambitious undertaking, one echoing that of Darwin in scientific scope but also those of the voyageurs in physical audacity. He would be gone two years, travel the courses of the major South American river systems, and map the uncharted interior. The department provided an outgoing passage for him and his team and arranged for the loan of a dip circle, diurnal variation apparatus, and circle of reflection, a trio of instruments to make magnetic observations. Specifically, the department instructed Midshipman Strain to determine geographic localities and glean "other important scientific information." Morton and others from the Academy of Natural Sciences anticipated a windfall for science: bird skins, bugs in spirits, and Morton's peculiar obsession, crania, but also perhaps a sampling of the "early man" remains then being mined in the bone caves of Minas Gerais. Isaac's team expanded to become a mini corps of discovery, with three naturalists, a civil engineer, and a legal expert to analyze the Brazilian judiciary.

None had come before him. He was twenty-three when he and the others boarded the naval ship USS *Levant* for the passage to Rio. Strain's confidence and energy were limitless. Unfortunately, the trip was a disaster. Men deserted, equipment failed, and flooded rivers rose like walls around them. Fear of killing fevers and age-old tribal conflicts made native volunteers impossible to hire, and thousands of carefully gathered specimens rotted in the rains. The Navy Department either ignored or never received his repeated pleas for more men and supplies, and after six backbreaking months in the jungle, a heartsick Isaac was forced to retreat to Rio and accept a berth aboard the USS *Constitution*.

The ensuing journey was itself newsworthy, taking him around the world to Madagascar, Borneo, and other exotic equatorial ports that spawned more ideas for more expeditions. Physically the 80,000-mile, three-year cruise put oceans between him and the men in Philadelphia and Washington Strain felt he had let down. But the aborted South American expedition gnawed at him. He seemingly thought of little else. When the *Constitution* stopped at Rio in 1846 he did not take the ship on her homeward leg to New York. Instead he requested to stay in Rio, where he began to plan anew. "He has a plan for exploring South America," gushed Samuel Greene Arnold, a New Englander traveling through Rio at the time. "He will build a schooner to draw 6 feet of water . . . make her so she can be turned into a steamer drawing 2½ feet. He has been three years making up a party for the trip, actually educating some of the men for their parts. This is all done on his own account, but the U.S. govt will probably aid him eventually."

But his redemptive, steam-powered return to Brazil's emerald-green interior was not to be. Instead Strain received orders to the Pacific aboard the battleship-of-the-line *Ohio*. The United States was in the final stages of its war with Mexico. By the time he reached Callao Bay, Peru, Strain learned the trip had been for naught—the war was over—and he quickly petitioned for his release from the Pacific squadron, hopeful of returning to Rio and re-forming his expedition. In June of 1848 the department detached him from the squadron but left the timing of his release to the discretion of his commander. The *Ohio*'s captain kept him an extra six months and tabled Strain's request to visit South America "at his own expense."

The tense atmosphere aboard the *Ohio* was unlike anything Strain had encountered. Each of the ship's stops, at La Paz, Monterey, and finally San Francisco, was worse than the one before. In the last port the outbreak of gold mania caused virtual anarchy. Seamen were denied shore leaves, and naval vessels were kept circling at sea to forestall wholesale desertions. In October Strain watched in horror as two Navy seamen, John and Peter Black, swung from the fore yardarm of the USS *Savannah,* executed as mutineers for their role in attacking a midshipman and commandeering his launch.

Around the same time, Strain was court-martialed. Like several other young officers, he had earned the enmity of the famously volatile Pacific Fleet Commander Thomas ap Catesby Jones. When a ship's surgeon preferred dubious charges against Strain for a verbal insult, Jones took the opportunity to show the uppity young explorer his place. The court found Strain guilty of insolence and recommended a minor reprimand, but the commodore, unsatisfied, asked the court to reconsider its finding in favor of a harsher penalty. The judges complied, revoking Strain's appointment as "acting master" and dismissing him from the squadron. Officially, Strain's career was in ruins.

One can imagine Strain's precarious emotional state upon leaving California on November 15, 1848, aboard the store ship *Lexington.* His dream of either a command or building "a boat in which I can transport myself from place to place to explore rivers . . . and publish popular works" was drifting further away. At some point on the homeward voyage from San Francisco Strain scrambled together a new plan, receiving permission from the *Lexington*'s captain to take leave of the ship at Valparaíso and return to her three months later at Rio de Janeiro. In order to do so Strain would need to cross the southern portion of South America, traversing over the snowcapped

Andes, and across the wildly desolate pampas of Chile and Argentina, a distance of some 800 miles. Strain's desperation to get off the ship was understandable, but his proposed course made no sense. If he had chosen to risk his life and suffer hardship to get to California, as so many did, he would have been understood. Instead he was relinquishing a perfectly comfortable berth and crossing in the wrong direction, west to east, and doing so not to chase a fortune but to . . . well, nobody knew what.

He set out for Santiago in a *birocha,* a rude horse-drawn carriage, on February 18, 1849. Ascending a steep range of hills, he looked out over Valparaíso and her deep, wide-mouthed bay. "As I turned to take my last look of the Pacific, upon whose bosom, owing to the caprices of fortune, and those in authority, I had passed some of the most disagreeable months of my naval career, I could still discern the massive black hull of the old 'Lexington,' between which and myself was commencing a race to Rio de Janeiro."

After a furious, high-speed descent of the cordillera—like "being in the tow of a locomotive"—he exchanged the *birocha* for a post horse, pairing himself with a mail courier named Don Antonio and galloping "whip and spur, whip and spur" across the pampas on a daily exchange of mounts, each morning whipped forward by his *compañero*'s charged "*Pega fuego al campo*—Set fire to the plain!"

In May Strain arrived in Buenos Aires with a wealth of geographical and political facts—but he was also barely ambulatory. He had suffered immensely, almost unmindfully, and especially in the latter stages of the crossing. A raging bilious fever turned his skin a pale yellow and prevented him from walking without assistance. He managed to gain passage on a Rio-bound vessel, but the ship sprang a leak and nearly sank. He missed the New York–bound *Lexington* by four days.

In spite of the near catastrophe and his "loss" of the race, Strain felt victorious. Completing the crossing erased the stigma of Brazil and the bitterness of his Pacific tour. His health returned quickly, and four years later he produced a narrative of the trip, his first published book, *Cordillera and Pampa, Mountain and Plain: Sketches of a Journey in Chili, and the Argentine Provinces, in 1849*. What he had attempted and why seemed to astonish even him. What kind of traveler, he openly wondered in the book's first few pages, seeks such an unconventional journey? He professed not to have the answer and left the decision to his readers. Friends put Strain in an elite adventuring category all his own. He had the stamina, and the restlessness, to walk anywhere on the earth's surface . . . up the highest, newly discovered Himalayan peaks, across the frozen and desolate tundra of the poles, through the hottest jungles of Africa, Asia, and America. What's more, as the South American crossing proved, he could do it, and might even prefer to do it, all alone.

In late 1849, Strain appeared poised for a major breakthrough. He had visited the most remote corners of the globe, traveled nonstop for almost six years, and still was only twenty-nine. The Navy reinstated him after a few months, undoubtedly aware that the court-martial charges were probably frivolous (in the interim Commodore Jones had been brought up on charges himself—embezzling the *Ohio*'s funds to speculate in the San Francisco gold market). Significantly, Isaac had succeeded in achieving one of his earliest goals: He'd fully occupied, and been occupied by, the "stimulating world of action."

In 1850, those like Strain who were trying to accomplish things saw a world spinning so much faster. In the proverbial blink of an eye, men ricocheted from poverty to wealth, from rogue to royalty. Around the same time a morose Ulysses S. Grant was drinking his career away at California's Fort Humboldt, seemingly bound for nowhere. But fortunes changed, sometimes with very little warning. Strain was one of the blessed. In the common vernacular Strain was a perfect gentleman—worldly, facile in conversation, and relentlessly enterprising. Naturally he had relocated to New York City, the self-proclaimed center of the American universe.

In the spring he was rewarded with a principal position on the Mexican Boundary Commission, the expeditionary outfit charged with surveying lands newly won from Mexico. The commissioner was John Bartlett, a New York bookseller whom Strain had come to know in his increasingly frequent visits to the Ethnological Society.

The soldier Strain and the scholar Bartlett were a fine team who dreamed up an inspired scientific agenda: They would conduct a complete topographical survey of the 2,000-mile line, a task that involved endless astronomical observations and chains laid end to end over "thorny and angular" land. Touchy instruments such as chronometers and mountain barometers would need to survive thousands of jostly, desert-hot miles. The job before them ranked as "the most extensive geodetic work ever projected by any nation, either in ancient or modern times," one surveyor extolled.

The technical matter was difficult enough, but en route Strain and Bartlett planned to study everything that moved, or didn't. A scientific corps was to take the full botanical, zoological, and anthropological measure of the present-day Texas, Arizona, and New Mexico landscape. The scientific party included a geologist and mineralogist, botanist, naturalist, taxidermist, entomologist, and historiographer. An artist was even hired to document the journey.

Strain outfitted the 105-man expedition (including overseeing a custom-made fleet of mule-drawn wagons) and arranged the sea transport to Texas. It was an overwhelming and thankless duty for such a staggeringly large, logistically challenged party, and one the commissioner was happy to delegate. Strain's dispatches to Bartlett estimate everything from the amount and weight of mule shoes and hard bread rations to the number of flannel shirts and blankets to issue out. In May he also advised Bartlett on personnel decisions, in one case dissuading him from hiring an acquaintance as an engineer,

but noting that "after a hard day's march with his cheerful songs
he has no superior and would be worth a liberal salary for that purpose above having the best tenor voice I have ever heard." On the
downside, Strain's humor still intact, "a Mexican fandango [native
dance] would lead him off from any pursuit in which he might be
engaged."

Strain's field assignment was the command of a reconnoitering
party. The plum for Strain lay literally and figuratively down the
road—an exploratory of the lower Colorado River below its junction with the Gila, a territory newly acquired, and less known than
"any other part of this continent."

Strain's hands were in everything, which is exactly how he
wanted it. One the eve of the expedition, a breathless Bartlett was
convinced this "will be a great affair" and that a finer set of "intelligent, good-looking young men was never collected together for a
similar object." The newspapers were captivated by the possibilities,
christening the expedition "the most important to set foot in the
United States since Lewis & Clarke's [sic] expedition under Mr. Jefferson's administration." At Indianola, Texas, on the eve of the cavalry's departure, a fellow officer toasted Strain as the person "to
whom we owe more now than any man."

But for Strain the trip ended almost before it started, echoing his
Brazil trip. His elaborate preparations were left for others to make
use of. The iron-hulled boats he'd had made for his run of the Colorado never saw the water. Intramilitary feuding—the command included both Army and Navy officers—undercut Bartlett and Strain's
"great affair." Outranked and unable to manage the men the way he
wished, Strain abruptly quit his post shortly after arriving in Texas.
The humiliating public imbroglio to follow seemed to chase him to
sea. In January 1851, only weeks after returning from Texas, he exiled himself to a new post on the *John Adams* and began a long cruise
off the sweltering West African coast, the least popular station in the

Navy service. In his lengthy absence even his supporters back in the States supposed his spirit shaken, perhaps irrevocably.

And yet when the lieutenant returned to New York City in the late summer of 1853 he was visibly renewed, stronger and more determined than ever. His book *Cordillera and Pampa* was newly published and had brought him back into public notice. Evidently he gave no thought to settling, a state of being that many officers his age found themselves preoccupied with. "I begin to think that I shall not have a chance of even trying to get married until I am entirely too old for that species of amusement," wrote a friend of Strain's, hurried off on another assignment. Strain at some level had to feel the longing too, but what he talked about, again, was *going*.

He applied for an exploratory of the East Indies, willfully vowing to supplement the enterprise, as he had in Brazil, with his own money if need be. He informed the department, as well as old acquaintances, that *that* was what he had been doing during his three years at sea— planning, preparing, and teaching himself the Malay tongue (only a handful in the States were proficient in the obscure language). Isaac had somehow mined a deeper and richer vein of Calvinist faith. He had two letters of recommendation written on his behalf by commanding officers, one of whom talked of his unsurpassed professional abilities and spirit and energy for travel; another complimented his leadership.

Isaac might have pointed out his intriguing obsession with those parts of the map that were emerald green: The sorties up uncharted Borneo rivers when he served aboard the *Constitution*. The time he'd been told about the sickest, most fever-ridden island in the entire Indonesian chain, a place Singapore natives refused to visit, and how he'd paid a visit, hopeful he might glean something scientific about the causes of tropical disease. In Brazil he'd once walked 28 miles in a single day, "though the nails of my toes nearly all came off." In other instances he had averted starving by living off palm nuts.

Yes, he had traveled across mountains and plains and deserts, but he felt he belonged in the jungle. In 1853 there were no jungle explorers like him, and he knew it. None who wanted to do everything, from cataloguing insects to opening trade routes. None who saw and was prepared to use the full magnificent potential of modern technology. The jungle need no longer be the surveyor's nightmare, Strain said.

Compasses and chronometers could be placed in a man's pocket, the long, brass-encased telescopic levels and transits (and even the tall glass columns of a mountain barometer) slung over shoulders in leather or India-rubber carrying cases. Isaac could readily imagine a tropics notebook brimming with more calculations and precise geographic observations than any American explorer before him.

Isaac was, it seemed, the realization of a strange and perfectly new kind of species. Others had faltered, stumbling in the heat and fever and the wilderness of the unknown. But he saw himself as adapted, perhaps even deserving.

Others had noticed. He wasn't selected for the East Indies expedition, but in October, the lieutenant got the order to come posthaste to Washington. The government had another proposal in hand.

NEARING LANDFALL, THE *Cyane* was forced to lay to on January 3 or risk overrunning the port. A gale was bullying them along. La Popa, a landmark peak announcing the still-unseen city of Cartagena, came into view at dawn the following morning, looming grandly above the low coast. They were at the well-fortified crown of South America, a few hundred miles north of Caledonia Bay. In the foreground lay the harbor's guardian headlands, each with its own battery, gapped by a narrow channel of treacherous water. The massive seventeenth-century Castillo San Felipe de Barajas, built from the natural coral rock, rose above them mythically, half mountain and half structure. The natural topography and man's sculpting hand were rarely put to better or more potent use, Strain thought.

Two hours later they were through Boca Chica and beating up the magnificent bay, the squally ocean gusts calmed by the shielding hills rising all around them. "The bay is not merely quiet but as solitary as a lake," wrote Winthrop, stunned by the contrast with the tossing ocean.

At sunset on January 4, 1854, they came abreast of the fabled old walled city. Part of the coral-block seawall was whitewashed and dipping into the blue water, overhung by a canopy of wild cocoa-nut trees and stained by a creeping mildew. The Moorish towers of the old city, their rooftops red-tiled and patchy gray, fanned the skyline. Cartagena was an empire's stronghold erected for the ages but crumbling far sooner. Still, from the quarterdeck rail where Strain stood, the allure was little diminished. The lonely outline of a neglected city, the landlocked mountain setting, and the wavy trails disappearing high up on the ridge sparked an unanticipated bond: the continuation of an adventure he had begun long ago.

The next morning, just before the exploration party boarded a launch for the city to commence a rapid round of final preparations, the *Cyane* boomed a salute of seven guns. They made the passage from Philadelphia in a near-record thirteen days. From the mainland batteries came an auspicious and thunderous reply, a full twenty-one.

3 / TORRID ZONE

The increase of human knowledge ... have given us powers which only call for application. Everything depends upon energy and perseverance.

BARON ALEXANDER VON HUMBOLDT, WRITING ABOUT THE PROPOSED DARIÉN SHIP CANAL IN 1853

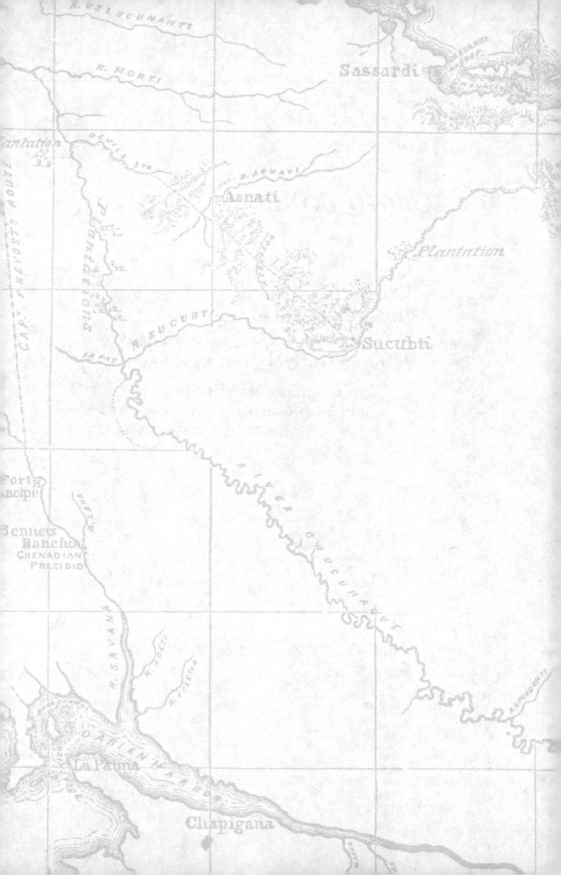

January 4, 1854

10° 44′ N, 75° 38′ W
Cartagena

A BOARD THE *CYANE*'S LONGBOAT, the exploring party made the lengthy pull to shore in late afternoon. The Cartagena boat wharf, slack and disappointingly small in the estimation of most New Granada travelers, was stirring with uncharacteristic vigor. At the grand stone arch entrance into the city Strain, Hollins, and the other officers were met by National Guardsmen and the fife and drum of a modest marine band. A few hundred infantry stood in formation in the plaza. To Strain's great interest, they wore northern-style military attire except at the feet, where the trials of the climate and the requirements of marching had driven them to something new and a bit drastic: the sandal-like *alpargata*. Beyond the soldiers, on the ground and the limestone ramparts above, the city's citizens were assembled for a long look at their handsome visitors. It had been years since an American man-of-war had called at the port.

Strain was impeccably dressed for his official debut: He wore a long, double-breasted blue cloth coat, cocked hat, and laced pantaloons, his full dress uniform. Two rows of nine large brass buttons fronted his breast, and a long gold-handled sword dangled off his left

hip in a black leather scabbard. The regulation uniform was altered
slightly for tropics duty, with white pantaloons instead of dark blue
and a coat of lighter "summer cloth." It was a pleasant 75 degrees,
and the martial airs that filled the old square reminded him of Rio.
Out of the corner of his eye, he saw some white in the sea of dark;
several straw-hatted English gentlemen were watching too.

"Delighted with terra firma!" wrote Winthrop of the spirited re-
ception to greet them. Each American carried his dark blue, gold-
embroidered cap in his right hand, and a small marine escort carried
the thirty-one-star flag, which waved softly in the light offshore
breezes. The governor of the city, having invited the officers to a formal interview, looked on approvingly. The distinguished American
entourage and its "great enterprise" at Darién were symbolic of a
new and better day. Better still, the Americans weren't the only
courtiers soon expected.

A faded and not unappealing elegance flourished in Cartagena,
with its whitewashed palace walls, wild courtyard gardens, and lively
balcony scenes. Though lacking the seaside promenaders of busier,
more fortunate ports, there was a simplicity and civility inside the
ancient, weather-beaten walls, where the men found "doors nor windows never need be shut." When some of the party rode up to La
Popa's 500-foot summit the next morning and looked down on the
red-tiled roofs, small plazas, and numerous church domes, they
would remember the equatorial sun parting the morning mists over
the bay and washing the city in a flood tide of tropical light.

One could easily imagine the comings and goings of centuries: of
homeward-bound Spanish caravels groaning with the bloody spoils
of Peru, of Balboa's triumphant march to the sea with his weary *ex-
peditionares,* of the race to shelter as the buccaneering fleet of Francis Drake blew through the Boca Grande gap to take a turn at the city
ramparts.

Founded in 1533, Cartagena was once one of the great centers of

Spanish commerce, second only to Mexico City in importance. The revolutionary Simón Bolívar liberated the "Pearl of the Indies" in 1821, but some three decades later the state of things in Cartagena, as in many of its sister South American cities, was less than robust. Civil war and high tariffs had taken their toll. The British mail steamers made regular monthly stops, but the bulk of coastal traffic now called at Santa Martha, a neighboring port. Only a rough old bridle path connected Cartagena with the interior, and an effort to construct a modern canal connecting the city with the Magdalena, the immense river system at its doorstep, had recently failed—surging floodwaters had descended from the jungle highlands and collapsed the works in a single swipe, leaving the city as isolated and "romantically ruinous" as ever.

The official interview with the governor and the American consul, Ramón Sánchez, took place in a large high-ceilinged room, the participants seated across from one another in two rows of rocking chairs. An eager Strain carried letters of introduction from New Granada's representative in Washington, encouraging full cooperation, and the friendly, English-speaking governor gave every indication he intended to comply.

In spite of the auspicious beginning, Strain was quickly sobered by the practical reality. Cartagena was only 150 miles and a couple of days' sail from Caledonia Bay—and technically Darién was a province of New Granada—but in the course of the afternoon it became evident that their hosts knew little more than they about the interior. There were no Darién guides in the city. Neither their own revolutionary republic, formed some three decades earlier, nor the Spanish rule to precede it had had a presence in Darién for almost a hundred years. Native load carriers and muleteers would be scarce, the governor predicted, since those who were willing to risk isthmus living had likely been recruited already. They were working further up the isthmus, the peaceful part, where a New York company was paying premium $1-a-day wages in a desperate attempt to finish a trans-isthmus railroad track. "Nobody here has been there [Darién] & they are all afraid of the Indians," scribbled Winthrop.

Adjacent to him, William Talbot Truxtun rolled his rocking chair to curb the rising heat. Clean-shaven, with a ridge of lustrous dark hair and an earnest gaze, he looked far younger than the men around him. It was possible the governor's reports of savage Indians were gross exaggerations and that help might be forthcoming once they socialized with the city's denizens, but it was also likely they might soon be under way with little more assistance than wood, water, and stores. His responsibilities and that of his fellow junior officers, such as Maury and Winthrop, were certain to expand, yet Truxtun's would increase the most as second in command. Truxtun had met Lieutenant Strain long ago, almost a decade earlier at Rio, but had never served with him. He also had never been on a tropical land expedition; he was from a family of seafarers, and fighting men at that.

Born in Chester, Pennsylvania, in 1824, just off the Queen's Road from Philadelphia, William Talbot (W.T.) Truxtun was the grandson of Thomas Truxtun and Silas Talbot, the first commanders of the U.S. Navy. Thomas Truxtun was the most storied privateer in the country's history, capturing numerous vessels in the earliest days of the Revolutionary War. Known to relish odds-against engagements, Truxtun's career sparkled with improbable victories, including a shellacking of the massive French frigate *L'Insurgente* off Hen's Island in the West Indies. In a battle that lasted little more than an hour, his *Constellation* suffered only a single casualty in routing the opposition. Talbot's record was nearly as glorious. Though wounded a total of thirteen times (five of the musket balls he would carry with him to the grave after his death at sixty-two), Talbot captured some ten vessels during the war before the British managed to defeat him. William Truxtun, W.T.'s father, was on his way to similar renown, but contracted yellow fever in the tropics and was cut down as a young lieutenant. His son was only six at the time and had known little of his father. Scarcely more than a decade later, however, W.T. would follow in the family path and attend the naval academy at Philadelphia—he was one of eight Truxtun grandchildren there at the same time.

Much of Midshipman Truxtun's early career was conventional, neither brilliant nor flawed, and altogether consistent with a peacetime Navy that offered few opportunities to make one's mark. The Navy's senior rank was top-heavy with old warriors, many of them veterans of the War of 1812 and most disinclined to retire their commission. Battle victories were the standard determiner of a soldier's upward rise, but with few battles to fight, the younger officers languished sometimes decades without a promotion.

In his mid-twenties Truxtun seemed more enlivened by his Philadelphia social life than anything the Navy promised. "Trux," as his friends called him, had a winning aristocratic air about him. Well-groomed, bright, and socially deft, he circulated among the fine young socialites of the city and began courting one of its belles, Annie Elizabeth Scott, when he was assigned to the *Dolphin* in the summer of 1853.

The "special service" cruise was a turning point. For several months he repeatedly crisscrossed the Atlantic Ocean in the first successful effort at mapping the sea floor for a submarine telegraph cable. The sounding work in the stormy Atlantic was one of the most difficult and dangerous tasks imaginable, and the crew's ability to skirt disaster was a virtual miracle. Their closest call was Columbus Day, when a predawn hurricane rolled the *Dolphin* onto her beamends—a "knockdown," in sea parlance—forcing Truxtun and the rest of the crew to man the bilge pumps and heave overboard everything from the sounding leads to barrels of beef to save the ship. Truxtun's stalwart service had not only saved his life and many others but earned him the Darién opportunity. The invitation, arriving only weeks after he returned from sea, was eagerly accepted. Of course, it was not an opportunity for an almost-thirty-year-old midshipman to pass up, but there was a part of him that wondered about his readiness, his future marriage state, and the details of a long ago cruise to similar waters, the one that had cost his father his life.

In the chair next to Truxtun, Jack Maury was reminded of an Englishman's warning about full dress in the tropics: It is a bath you won't wish to repeat. Junior to Truxtun, Maury wasn't one to second-guess himself. He was known to be one of the most fearless and technically gifted officers in the service. Before being reassigned to the Darién party on November 1, he had been successfully applying himself to the mechanical woes of the Navy showpiece USS *Alleghany,* an iron-hulled gunboat. Few would seem better suited to assess and advise the engineering aspects of a proposed canal. He had come to the meeting prepared, if the governor wished, to ride out to inspect the wreckage of the ill-fated Cartagena canal works.

Like Truxtun, he came from a strong family. He was two when his pious thirty-two-year-old mother, Lucy, died. In the words of her obituarist, she fell "a victim to a malady which blighted her in the morning of life" and before "breathing her last, bade a mild adieu to all around her, and like a broken lilly, bent her head and died." He and his sister were orphaned with the death of their father, Richard, in 1836. The ten-year-old Jack was immediately incorporated into the larger Fredericksburg, Virginia, clan under the stewardship of his father's first cousin, Matthew Fontaine (M.F.) Maury.

M. F. Maury was the superintendent of the National Observatory and a whirlwind of a man said to control the makeup and design of almost every exploring expedition that left the shores of the United States. He had wrung out the mysteries of the sea in a groundbreaking, world-acclaimed book, depicting how and why the ocean behaved the way it did.

In 1853, M.F. was at full stride. His "voyages of discovery," as they were dubbed, wrapped the globe, from Japan to the Amazon.

Commodores Matthew Perry and Cadwallader Ringgold were in the Far East, the former poised to open relations with Japan and the latter commanding a Bering Strait– and North Pacific–bound expedition that Maury touted as "the largest surveying squadron now afloat under any flag." Elsewhere, Lieutenant William Herndon, M.F.'s son-in-law, was concluding a pioneering, source-to-sea exploration of the Amazon valley, and Lieutenant Thomas Page was in the Brazilian south, probing the tributaries of the Río de la Plata, which were "long sealed" and represented a "vast territory of boundless resource." Also under way were river exploratories in West Africa and an Arctic expedition led by an assistant surgeon, Elisha Kane, that would sail up the Greenland coast to 80 degrees 35 minutes north— the farthest north anyone had ever gone.

It was the greatest, most audacious year in the history of American seafaring exploration, one that drew notice around the world. Wrote a British correspondent to the Royal Geographical Society: "Never before did they [the United States], or any other government, set in motion so many exploring expeditions at once." The American capacity for "going ahead," its will to gain an exploratory foothold outside its borders, all had its origins at the Maury house, a small clapboard structure in Washington that in the years Jack and his sister stayed there had sheltered a small army of hard-luck kinsmen and relatives.

Jack had earned a cherished place in family lore when as a ten-year-old he climbed the lightning rod of old St. George's steeple in Fredericksburg so that he could touch the supposedly untouchable cross above it. On account of that and many other antics the local ladies publicly prophesied that the boy would never come to any good, and they were said to pray extra hard for him. He had a fire to him, but also a sweet naiveté. The summer of 1853 had been one of the best he had ever had, full of romance and crazy bareback romps in the rolling Virginia countryside—the highlight, he wrote a friend, of any young man's life. It had been his first summer in his native Fredericksburg for four years (on account of a long cruise to the Pacific), and it had been so good he doubted he would find anything either in Darién or anywhere else in the world to match it. His guardian, Matthew, a strong and vocal proponent of an isthmus ship canal, had gently prodded his twenty-eight-year-old ward not to let the opportunity slip. Thanks to Strain's colorful tutelage aboard the *Cyane* he was warming to the challenge at Darién, but he had also begun to rethink his naval career.

Jack's guardian, the so-called pathfinder of the seas, was a remarkable man and his home a kinetic place, full of ideas and passion and a steady stream of engaging visitors, from leathery sea captains to European savants. Yet the shadow he cast was sometimes impossibly large. As if his brilliance needed more confirmation, it was Maury who was asked by the owners of the ill-fated passenger ship *San Francisco* to provide a location in the vast Atlantic Ocean where rescuers might find their swept-away vessel. The last word of it had been off Cape Hatteras. Using his detailed knowledge of the Gulf Stream and its prevailing wind patterns in the North Atlantic, Maury came up with coordinates for a series of days in early January. On January 5, 1854, the shattered hulk was found exactly where he said it would be. Hundreds of men, women, and children were saved.

AT THE INVITATION of New Granada's governor, the American officers stayed in the city. Graciously, he had concluded their meeting by pledging his full support to the American survey, his only stipulation being that Strain wait for the arrival of the government's own topographical expert and bring him along for the crossing. He was expected daily but was coming on horseback from the capital, a rough transit of several days.

Strain and his officers stayed at the Hotel of California, the

German-run head inn in the center of the city, from which Strain could conveniently complete the party's outfitting. He had a few priorities: mules, which would carry his instruments in the crossing, and medicine.

The locally sold "preventative pills," which were loaded with the herbal antimalarial quinine, were highly endorsed by bush travelers. Quinine was to become the first wonder drug, but its routine, government-sponsored use was still years off. A prophylactic regimen was almost unheard of, and the ship's surgeons Strain knew preferred to bleed their feverish patients rather than dose them with the bitter tasting by-product of tree bark. (Only a few years later U.S. naval doctors would follow the lead of France and England and begin stocking tropical expeditions with large enough supplies of quinine for preventative daily doses. Malaria cases declined sharply.)

The pills were a sore temptation but one he ultimately could not justify. He deferred to medical wisdom: They were an expensive extra. The expedition would stick with what the then-standard Navy medicine chest did provide: calomel for the fever and fluxes, sulfur-based "blue pills" for bilious symptoms, chamomile flowers for a "cooling tea," and opium for when the excruciating end was near.

Ultimately, the only significant extra expense he incurred was for four mules and a backup chronometer, a crucial piece of survey equipment, and for that he was apologetic, assuring the department he would repay the cost himself if need be. The budget, tight and getting tighter, defined his preparations as much as anything. He also passed on the rain-repelling capes, which private parties stocked. Strain was acutely aware that the bulk of his funds had to be preserved for Caledonia, where the cost of procuring guides was said to be exorbitant.

In the aftermath of Brazil, he had vowed "not to allow myself to be hurried off in such haste that half my intentions were unfulfilled" and never to travel without a "sufficient supply of money." That he found himself in near identical circumstances might have caused him great alarm, but it didn't. Dreams and denial were the gift of his generation. "Hitch your wagon to a star," exhorted the essayist Ralph Waldo Emerson in his widely read *Self Reliance*. Great leaders were undeterred, resourceful, and uncompromising in the face of even overwhelming odds. In a sense, Emerson's was the voice of all expedition starts: The past dims and the future brightens.

PART OF STRAIN'S INFORMATION about Darién came from an almost nightly roundtable at the hotel's California Café. The nightspot brought to it the melting pot that was Cartagena: lonesome foreign diplomats, young cigar-smoking fishermen, and a growing number of engineers and adventurers sent from afar to probe the neighboring wilderness.

They were French, English, and American—erudite men in white linen suits and straw hats with dated London or New York newspapers passing among them. Strain enjoyed their company. There were colorful evenings full of the bonhomie one would expect when men from similar social strata stumble upon one another in an exotic and vaguely threatening part of the world. The tales they told, or had heard told, were fantastic, something the adventurer in Strain would have appreciated. He heard of an Englishman emerging from the Darién wood blinded and emaciated, of rainfalls that turned streams into killing torrents, of a suffocating heat that "prostrates all energy."

Some believed he needed to petition his government for a larger force in order to overawe the savages. Others said no, he was American, and the Indians would receive him well as long as he was conciliatory and didn't, with his chain bearers and instrument takers, project an image of arrogance and conquest. A few said there were better routes for a ship canal, several of which they had seen.

He heard many voices. Some he was inclined to trust, some he was not. In certain cases the men were working on competing projects, sent to the jungle by a new fever of another sort: what the newspapers in London and New York were calling "canal mania."

A half dozen different ship canal routes, from Mexico to Darién, were now on the table, each backed by a distinguished capitalist and vying for a popular mandate. Five separate sets of surveys were in progress. New York's Cornelius Vanderbilt had invested in a line across Nicaragua, declaring it the "natural route." Others advocated a railway at the Gulf of Tehuantepec in Mexico—the so-called high road to California. Present-day Panama, however, was the true epicenter of the canal rush, its narrow neck and unknown terrain a canny speculator's dream. There were three possible routes, the westernmost being at Panama City and the easternmost at the Atrato River, one of the largest river systems in Central and South America. Darién was presently the golden line in between, but competitors had yet to concede anything.

Of all the rumors Strain heard, the Indian stories concerned him most. The other routes didn't have that hazard. For days he had tried to recruit muleteers in Cartagena, but nobody, no matter the terms, would accompany him on account of Darién's forest inhabitants, known variously as the Kuna, the Tule, the San Blas, and Kuna Bravo. Stories of their savagery persisted, including a supposed practice of slicing off and roasting the flesh of bound Spanish intruders. "They have cherished such a jealousy of their independence that, to the present day, no white man has been permitted to land upon their shore," read one reputable account. "Every attempt to explore their country has been uniformly resisted."

What Strain knew from the historical record was that that was only partially true. At the outset of the Spanish conquest, Vasco Núñez de Balboa had allied with the Kuna chiefs on the Atlantic coast, and their assistance had helped him sustain colonies first at

Santa María del Antigua and later at Acla, a settlement near Caledonia Bay. His famous first crossing to the Pacific was aided by a thousand Indians and a series of treaties arranged in advance. When he reached the vicinity of the Gulf of San Miguel some four weeks after he set out, he entered the Pacific surf, with sword and buckler, and took formal possession in the name of the king, his master, vowing to defend it against his enemies.

Of course, Balboa's worst enemies turned out to be his own cutthroat countrymen, and after a circus trial for phony treason charges, they beheaded him at Acla. Balboa's conciliatory policy toward the Indians was immediately reversed by his successor, Pedrarias Dávila, and the horrific genocide began. "The friendly chiefs who called Balboa Elder Brother and Father and Lord had been tormented and plundered, and some of the best had been killed. The days when sociable tribesmen wandered in and out Santa María were done forever," writes Balboa's biographer Kathleen Romoli. Much of the population went into hiding as vast Spanish columns with their war dogs marched on the isthmus. Thousands of Kuna were enslaved and killed.

Despite the persecution, the Kuna were never fully subdued. They had learned to expertly hide themselves in the terrain, recognizing the jungle as their best weapon. They also played traditional European rivalries to their advantage. In the seventeenth and eighteenth centuries they repeatedly led English buccaneer raiding parties across the isthmus to Spanish gold depots on the Pacific. The Spaniards' gold mines in eastern Darién at Cana, an operation that annually yielded some 5,000 pounds of gold and was among their most lucrative possessions, were attacked in 1684, 1702, 1712, 1724, and 1734. Eventually they were abandoned. When forced to, as the Kuna often were, they would sue for peace. But each treaty was followed by an even bigger and bloodier revolt than the last.

In 1751, the seemingly pacified Kuna attacked in a major uprising, driving all foreigners from Darién, including French pirates whom they had allowed in their midst. Following the revolt foreigners were forbidden to marry Kuna or permanently settle in the territory. In 1785, the Spanish responded. This time they built four small forts along the San Blas coast and three more in the southern Darién to cut the Kuna off from their British allies. Again, the Kuna suffered steep losses and were forced to settle for peace, but in 1792 all the forts were abandoned and the weary Spanish retreated for good.

By the last half of the eighteenth century, war and epidemics had cut the Kuna population in half, to an estimated five thousand people. Many of the settlements along the rivers of the interior had been abandoned for safer, better-protected enclaves on the San Blas coast, or on the mangrove-rimmed islands. Yet the fiercest fighters were said to still live in the interior, independent of everyone, their fellow Kuna included. During the last Spanish exploration in 1788 by Lieutenant Manuel de Milla Santa Ella, the mountain Kuna were no less of a threat. They allowed his temporary passage but said any future attempt to connect the Pacific and Atlantic by road or canal would be met with deadly opposition. Soon thereafter the Spanish vanished and an uncommonly prolonged period of peace and isolation visited their quarter of the isthmus. The Cartageneans told Strain the same thing: No white man had crossed the Darién isthmus since.

THE ONE WHO FIRST articulated the idea that *someone* should was the Prussian naturalist Alexander von Humboldt. In 1853 he was eighty-four years old, a bit on the frayed side but no less influential, celebrated, or involved. In fact, the British surveyors bound for the isthmus had recently published a letter of his in the *Times* of London, which appeared to endorse the proposed route between Caledonia and San Miguel.

Humboldt had first come to Cartagena a full half century earlier on a four-year surveying trip of Central and South America. He quickly established his scientific zealotry and nerve with an ascent of the Amazon, where he made numerous astronomical determinations and observations on meteorological, botanical, zoological, mineralogical, geological, and ethnological phenomena. That was followed with an ascent of the snowcapped Chimborazo, a 19,000-foot Ecuadorian volcano that was then believed to be the tallest peak on the planet. His observations were made somewhat more difficult, he said, by the "rarefaction of the atmosphere and the intensity of the cold."

Baron von Humboldt was a giant, the author of dozens of books and the last of a race of philosophical generalizers who were considered capable of turning the ultimate scientific trick: putting into grand context, from earth to sky, all the "natural features and contents of a vast region." He was the dean of tropical field exploration, a pioneer with scientific discipline who wasn't afraid to mix it up with the landscape when it was far more common to make observations from the deck of a ship. He had literally put New Granada on the map; his wanderings, painstakingly recorded with a half dozen different survey instruments, resulted in the country's first modern maps. Scientists and gentlemen travelers applauded his work equally. In no small part due to Humboldt, tropical America suddenly interested everyone.

In a sense Humboldt had sparked the modern age of ship canal speculation with his own speculation: He believed there already was a sea path from Atlantic to Pacific. Its name was Raspadura. According to his best sources in Cartagena, "not even a ridge of partition" existed at Raspadura, and the Indians were able to pass from one side of the isthmus to the other in canoes. A monk was believed to have been the force behind the eighteenth-century project, directing Indians in his parish to dig the channel in order to connect two major rivers in northwest New Granada, the Río San Juan and the Río

Atrato. For a brief prerevolutionary period, large quantities of cacao made their way from ocean to ocean, arriving in Cartagena each year with the onset of the rainy season and high water. Humboldt's own limited investigation was inconclusive—he hadn't seen it—but he believed Raspadura "might be easily enlarged" to accommodate vessels with a larger draft. Whether or not the ravine of Raspadura could be unearthed again in the nineteenth century—something several speculators in the States were unsuccessfully pursuing—Humboldt made no secret of his belief that the "isthmus of Darién was superior to any other portion of the neck for a canal." Among other things in its favor was what he had observed as a geologist: the interruption of the mountain chains, and the depression of the Andean range, in eastern Darién. Somewhere in that low ridge, a breach, or gap, could be found.

Humboldt's reach and influence were universal, and Strain was no exception. The shipboard library included a copy of Humboldt's work, and he undoubtedly was tempted to explore the adjacent countryside and see the land the great one described. In fact, he encouraged Winthrop, who was finding himself restless, to do exactly that. He set off from Cartagena on the 8th and returned on the 9th, having visited the famous "mud volcancitoes of Turbaco." The mud springs with their bubbling air and barren footing were a mystery and had naturally inspired a riveting description and lavish illustration in Humboldt's *Narrative*. He had guessed they were of igneous action, which was vague enough, but Winthrop told Strain the anticipated spectacle was curiously disappointing. The "cones of disturbance" were half the size Humboldt had described, and the surrounding vegetation vastly different. Asking around, Winthrop said nobody recalled an event that might have altered the terrain. It was as if Humboldt—like the myriad people who described Darién—had never been there. Or perhaps the old chronicler, whose books fairly bubbled with facts, figures, and formulas, wasn't entirely immune to a fit of exaggeration. Either way Strain had to wonder if any story, out of any mouth, was worth listening to.

CARTAGENA'S THICK PERIMETER boundary walls, at once the envy of every visitor who saw them, were still walls. They gave the city a compressed feel. The streets were narrow, the houses of two stories, and the plazas small. After a week of mostly protocol the Americans had a growing sense they were trapped.

They had seen the city, walked the ramparts at dusk and dawn, and searched out the leading gentlemen. The ship had been supplied with wood and water, and fresh vegetables and meat delivered. The restless officers, taking Winthrop's example, were wandering further and further afield. "We looked into the old palace of the Inquisition," recounted one of the officers, describing a moonlit stroll, "and instead of instruments of torture were flowers and a pretty girl. I heard one of the party say something about a pain in his heart."

Meanwhile, the men stuck to the ship were broiling at anchor. The ship's surgeon took precautions to prevent sickness but the Americans weren't nearly as thorough or experienced as the English. In the Torrid Zone a British ship had a step-by-step protocol. Windsails aired the berth deck, and watches on the weather deck were protected from the sun's influence by awnings. During rain showers the men were under orders to take shelter, and "never allowed to work in the wet." Comparing the *Cyane*'s log with a British vessel cruising similar waters, the *Cyane* was daily averaging twice as many sick.

To Strain's disbelief, their departure was still days away. They were waiting on the country's topographical expert, Agustín Codazzi, who the governor insisted was coming. Codazzi, a celebrated Italian-born geographer who fought alongside Bolívar and mapped Venezuela, was getting along in years. He was sixty-one and a military veteran of the Napoleonic Wars and revolutions in Colombia and Mexico. His otherwise sterling career had taken an inglorious turn, however, after he directed an ill-conceived colonization scheme. His South American utopia had cost poor German émigrés their lives and fortunes. He was exiled from Venezuela, but Codazzi received sanctuary in New Granada and in 1850 was awarded the command of a countrywide topographical survey that would follow up on Humboldt's work from a half century earlier. By late 1853, Codazzi and his party of engineers, laborers, and artists had tramped an astounding 50,000 kilometers. He had been held up in Bogotá, where he was attempting to source old Spanish maps of Darién. Strain wasn't aware what was keeping Codazzi, but he didn't want to wait indefinitely. Captain Hollins informed the governor they would remain until the 13th, at which time they had to depart.

On January 10, Strain wrote his only official dispatch, telling Secretary of the Navy Dobbin there were "many rumors of English and French expeditions now on their way to the Isthmus, but as I do not place reliance upon them I will not trouble you by recounting . . . [also] many rumors in regards to the hostility of the Darién Indians some of which have been promulgated by parties interested in retaining the monopoly of the trade of the Isthmus."

In the same letter Strain touched on (but didn't explain) his encounter with a British government engineer the day before. There is something confusing and sneaky in the omission. They hadn't merely "passed," as Strain wrote, but had a tense and lengthy meeting. H. C. Forde was an emissary of the British Darién Exploring Expedition, with explicit orders to intercept the *Cyane* and ask Hollins and Strain to hold off sailing for eleven days. The British and French surveying parties were making final preparations in Jamaica and wanted to coordinate their arrival at Caledonia with the Americans. Forde's orders came from the chief of the English surveying expedition, the London engineer Lionel Gisborne.

Forde had every reason to think the Americans would comply.

For weeks high government letters had been crisscrossing the Atlantic, finalizing arrangements. Back in the summer the English government had broken the ice by inviting the Americans to join their Darién survey. A joint effort would eliminate the possibility of a confrontation and give credence to a recent treaty between the United States and Great Britain pledging neutrality on the isthmus. A multinational expedition would put ship canal investors at ease and substantiate the findings. Washington accepted the invitation and in the coming weeks regularly updated a British representative on the ship, officers, and size of the American contingent.

At some point, likely in one of the many private Navy Department meetings preceding *Cyane*'s departure, everything changed. Strain's final instructions said nothing about Great Britain, nothing about Gisborne, nothing about multinational cooperation. Washington had chosen—presumably with Isaac's encouragement—to do the ship canal survey independently. On the day of the meeting with Forde the Americans shared verbatim their official orders. Strain's subsequent letter to Secretary Dobbin offered nothing about the dramatic turn of events because, of course, there was nothing dramatic about it. It was the bully age of Manifest Destiny. The Americans were crossing independently and they, and they alone, had known it from the start.

The "love knot" of nations, never snugged tight in the first place, was officially undone. The Americans were leaving. The English, suckered good, were livid.

ON THE 12TH, the eve of their departure, the American officers were feted with a gala. The half-masked ball took place under an awning in front of the Old Palace of Inquisition. With his best accent, Strain raised a goblet of the native *guarapo* to "the good ladies of Cartagena," engendering a round of late-night toast making that encompassed everything to come. Heat lightning flashed on the distant horizon, and "the square was filled with the common people gambling & dancing and the tent lighted and crowded with promenaders & some dancers looked quite lively," observed Winthrop.

The *Cyane* sailed from Cartagena in the early afternoon on the 13th with a light breeze behind and cobalt blue skies overhead. With the notable exception of four jackasses now penned up on the weather deck, she looked very much like the ship that had arrived nine days earlier. Decks had been repeatedly scrubbed and the bilge had been scoured, but Hollins had decided not to repaint the hull white, a precaution that some thought reduced the suffocating heat in the body of a tropics ship. They were freshly loaded with thousands of gallons of water, and barrels of pitch and lime.

The English surveying schooner *Scorpion*, part of the British exploration fleet bound for Darién, entered the harbor as *Cyane* departed. England was on the brink of declaring war on Russia, yet the Admiralty was sending an additional brig and steam sloop. France, England's current ally, added its own warship. Under either steam or sail, the most heavily armed fleet since Spanish rule was days away from the isthmus.

Cartagena's poor reputation notwithstanding, the crew's health had stabilized and the sick rolls were down. Perhaps Strain's inability to hire local, tropically seasoned men would not become the problem he feared.

Strain's call for seamen volunteers was answered enthusiastically. In addition to his fifteen newly made "landsmen," he had also picked up two American volunteers at Cartagena. Frederick Avery, formerly of Connecticut, had spent several months on the Atrato River working for a New York company. R. W. Holcomb, also of Connecticut, had been on a survey of the Magdalena River and had extensive engineering experience on the Panama isthmus. Neither was the true native guide he had in mind, but Strain was happy to have skilled men aboard. His roster now stretched to twenty-seven. With the addition of an Indian guide or two at Caledonia he would be perfectly fitted out and on budget.

They were without Agustín Codazzi, who was still en route—a day behind them, as it would turn out. A map he carried, one from the last Spanish exploration of the crossing route in 1788, would prove to be very different from the ones in Strain's hands. It showed a major river called the Chucunaque corkscrewing down the isthmus lengthwise. Other rivers were dozens of miles removed from where they were supposed to be. Mountains were everywhere. It showed a patchwork, indirect route across the isthmus that bore no relation, in character or course, to the recent crop of breakthrough maps. Codazzi had come to the conclusion, after his research in Bogotá, that a large tract of land in the center of the isthmus, including the "chief cordillera," was still unsurveyed and would be a grueling test.

Whatever Codazzi had come up with, Strain felt certain they would survive without it. A man of Codazzi's stature—a friend of the famous Humboldt even—would undoubtedly have complicated matters. Strain was prepared to cooperate with him but was not disappointed it didn't work out. Darién seemed a problem best approached with nothing preconceived, nothing old. His young officer corps appeared undaunted. "But we require very little information," wrote Winthrop, reflecting the sentiment of Truxtun and Maury, "for [our] party will probably be the first to cross."

As they sailed south by southwest out of Boca Chica, following the rugged Colombian coastline to its juncture with the isthmus, the *Cyane* traced the identical route Balboa had taken on his momentous visit in 1510. Given Strain's high regard for him, perhaps their course was no coincidence. Balboa's determined crossing, with men as committed to go ahead as he, wasn't a parable but something approaching a plan of action. Just before nightfall they anchored at the broad, seaward end at the Gulf of Uraba. It was almost precisely where Balboa had been when he turned his caravel away from its intended landfall and instead set his party's sights on the low, dim hills of Darién.

4 / DARIÉN GAP

Not satisfied with crossing the isthmus once only in 1849, I returned again from the Atlantic to the Pacific, having cut a picadura, or track, for myself through the bush, from Port Escoces to the river Savana, which I navigated always, except on one occasion, alone, paddling myself in a little canoe. In 1850 I again crossed and recrossed this part of the isthmus, and again in August and September, 1851, I several times, and in different lines, crossed from the Savana River to the seabeach on the Atlantic, notching the barks of the trees as I went along with a machete or cutlass.

EDWARD CULLEN, IN THE *TIMES* OF LONDON,
FEBRUARY 16, 1853

51° 30′ N, 0° W
London, England

WHEN A YOUNG AMERICAN naval officer looked at the world in 1854 he invariably looked, a bit grudgingly, across the ocean to Victorian England. He saw a nation with superiority and strength in almost every realm that mattered, from seafaring to science. Her naval fleet, some five times the size of America's, was everyone's envy. Her Admiralty was the model. From whisker regulations to the 2-inch-wide collar of his frock coat lying "like strips of blue sky upon [his] shoulders," an American officer was made in her royal likeness.

At midcentury it was believed that the world was dramatically shrinking—drawn nearer by the electric wire and the coal-fired steam fleets—but where the affairs of Englishmen and Americans were involved, the oceanic divide never seemed greater. America was ever the rude frontier with its go-ahead zealots, England the paternalistic stalwart. Yankee strivers couldn't help but look over their shoulders to their British peers: oftentimes for approval, sometimes to see how fast they were gaining.

Isaac Strain's perceptions about the "discoverers" of the Darién miracle route had their roots in such a tangled place. He hadn't met either the engineer Lionel Gisborne or the Irish traveler Edward Cullen, but he felt he had. In 1854 one could make assumptions about a British engineer endorsed by the highest military, government, and financial leaders. As Strain sailed to Caledonia Bay he never felt as though he was sailing blind. He could be content in knowing whom and what he was dealing with. The principal information, maps, and testimonies in his possession bore Lionel Gisborne's signature, but more irresistibly they bore the larger, more indelible imprint of a peaking empire.

The Irishman's account always seemed a less crucial and relevant matter. Edward Cullen, a struggling Dublin physician, was an utter unknown. But if there was a law to storms, as the most learned men on both sides of the Atlantic supposed, he was that mystical start, the part before the wind began to blow when some perfectly inserted atmospheric disturbance rearranged sea and sky, igniting otherwise benign forces until in a blink of the eye it was too late—lightning lit up the horizon and the heavens appeared one vast sheet of fire. He set it all in motion; he was the incandescent torch to the dark dire isthmus, the light to spark the expectations of governments and kings.

Originally he hadn't set out to address the great ship canal question at all. The isthmus, in fact, was barely an interest. He had spent much of his adult life traveling, and successfully applying his doctoring skills in far-flung locales. In the early 1840s he had traveled in Venezuela; in 1845 he had been in Canton, China; in '47 he was chief physician and surgeon alongside General Flores during his failed expedition to Ecuador. In 1848 he was in Constantinople. Out of those experiences, and still thinking his future lay in medicine, he formed a prospectus for a group he called the Grand United Association of Medical Practitioners. Nothing came of it.

But in 1849, Cullen found himself in California. It would change his prospects—and the prospects of others—like nothing else he had ever done. It would also, in the crossing from Atlantic to Pacific, take him for the first time to the isthmus. The Darién route had yet to emerge but Panama's had. In their rush to reach San Francisco the '49ers were increasingly trying the rugged but well-known overland shortcut linking present-day Colón and the ferry lines at Panama City.

In California Cullen found neither gold, which he expected he would, nor good prospects for another moneymaking enterprise of his, an emigration plan for Irishmen back home. San Francisco, he reported, was an "extensive hell," where gambling was the real business and legitimate commerce was secondary. " 'Keep up the excitement' was the motto of the corrupt speculators," Cullen added rather peevishly, noting that actual sums derived from recent strikes would routinely be inflated one hundredfold.

The fertile countryside he thought he would see was another ruse. "It is difficult to conceive how a country, so burnt up in the dry, & so inundated in the rainy season can become a great agricultural country, as the writers on California would lead us to believe." On the long journeys between mines the "gravely [*sic*] plains, intensely heated, blistered the feet." Nightfall brought disagreeable cold and prairie wolves; in the mountains grizzly bears preyed upon parties, who had to keep nonstop watches to prevent attacks.

In the late summer of '49, Cullen shuttled between several mining hot spots. Like thousands of others, he left the Tuolumne for the Mariposa (a branch of the San Joaquin), where reports spread that miners were digging out $50,000 per day. After making the arduous 60-mile journey, "I dug for four days and satisfied myself of its poverty. . . . I was only three days without food; others who had much farther to go than I suffered much longer fasts as the people going to the Mariposa had eaten up everything on their line of march."

But worse than the privations was what Cullen perceived as the generally depraved and hopeless state of the American character.

Miners who fell ill in the camps—chronic dysentery being a result of what Cullen theorized was the tough and indigestible California beef—were heartlessly booted from tents to expire in the wilderness, their sullen companions not even bothering to provide decent Christian burials. At Stockton, the gateway city to the mines, he found a lawless environment where lynching was indulged for even the most trifling offenses.

Briefly, in the days before he departed in November, he attempted employment as a land agent in San Francisco. While there he stumbled upon an impoverished enclave at a sand beach north of the city. Happy Valley, he called it. "On this beach were congregated some thousands of unfortunates, some of whom had been landed without any means, could get no employment & could not raise funds sufficient to pay their passages up the river—starvation was the consequent result." Sometimes the corpses, which kept relatively well preserved in the arid climate, were found with flesh gnawed off their arms. "Suffice it to say, that, out of Ireland, I never saw such misery."

Undoubtedly Cullen's distaste for his California experience was genuine, but his "truth-telling" exposé, as he liked to frame it, also served to enhance a competing scheme: broad-scale Irish emigration to New Granada. Upon returning to Dublin, Cullen spent inordinate energy attempting to convince the Irish public and everyone else that the fertile countryside of New Granada, capable of producing the fruits of all climes, offered "the most desirable place on earth to locate a colony anywhere." In one year, an immigrant could attain the wealth, position, and standing that would require "20 years of hard labour & drudgery" in the United States. In a hint of his deft ability to rapidly mobilize a scheme, Cullen completed a minutely detailed prospectus only two months after his return from the isthmus ("potatoes grow very well at the elevation of 550 yds mean temp 76 degrees—at 1200 yards, mean temp 70 they are excellent"). It was the height of Ireland's potato famine. A few months later he told the New Granadian authorities he was awaiting their word to "forward out 700 or 800 people."

Much of this isthmian prelude was hashed out in correspondence with Dr. Morton Shaw, the longtime corresponding secretary for the Royal Geographical Society. The London-based RGS was the premier exploration society in the world, with an illustrious history of expeditionary discovery extending from the frozen zones of the Canadian Arctic to the archipelago of Malay. Their luminous membership included the savant Humboldt, African explorer Dr. David Livingstone, and the Admiralty hydrographer Sir Francis Beaufort. Cullen hoped to curry favor with the RGS, whom he trusted would give his career a much-needed boost. In one of his first notes to Shaw after his California trip, he employed a kind of scattershot tactic, listing his diverse travels to the East Indies, China, British Guiana, Venezuela, Spain, Turkey, and many other countries. Almost as an afterthought he mentioned, "During three months that I remained on the Isthmus, on my return from California, I traversed the isthmus of Darién in every direction." Evidently unaware of the depth of such a statement, Cullen said his immediate designs were to return to Darién to reopen the [old Spanish gold] mines of Cana.

One can imagine Shaw's start. He encouraged Cullen to tell him more, suggesting the Darién experience might make for an entertaining presentation before the membership.

Cullen did produce a paper, though he seemed to misjudge where the RGS's keenest interest lay and wrote almost exclusively about the Spanish gold mines at Cana. About the isthmus route, in that initial treatment, he said precious little, but what he did say offered the grandest, most dramatic news of all: "From a tree on the top of a mountain on the Río Lara, a branch of the Savana, I enjoyed a view of both Atlantic and Pacific, so narrow is the isthmus here."

With those words, written in the summer of 1850, the chase was

on. Unwittingly, Cullen had stumbled onto his elusive gold mine after all: a ship canal scheme at the forgotten Isthmus of Darién.

ALMOST IMMEDIATELY Cullen was asked to come before the RGS's
Edinburgh chapter and present a more complete paper on his Darién
route discovery, which he did. A few months after that he delivered
a report to Lord Palmerston, no less than Her Majesty's foreign minister. Weeks later he was off again to the isthmus to collect more information. In 1852 he published the first edition of *Darién Ship
Canal,* a book that compellingly outlined his case for the proposed
route between the late Scotch colony at Escoces (or Caledonia Bay)
and the Gulf of San Miguel. On the heels of his publication a company was formed, with Cullen playing a primary role. In late '52, he
returned to Darién for a third visit, this time detouring to Bogotá,
where he lobbied the New Granadian government for exclusive de-
velopment rights. The speed with which things were up and running
was astonishing.

The spareness of detail about his initial journey, the one where he
climbed a tall tree and glimpsed both oceans, did trouble some. But
his map was irresistible. Maps were the currency of the age, expertly
used to sink or elevate a given project. Cullen wasn't a cartographer,
but then, he didn't need to be. Old maps were routinely borrowed,
copied, and spiced up with imaginary topographical detail. Ac-
knowledgment not being absolutely necessary, or common, the
copyist was assumed as author.

Cullen's earliest renderings, what he called "rough sketches,"
were rather constrained, but his imagination grew. In a map drawn
from his surveys in 1850 and '51, he illustrated a cluster of mountains
split by a wide valley in the vicinity of Caledonia Harbor. "Not
high," Cullen labeled the western range, and "level grounds" was
written in large print around the proposed canal route. In a personal

note in the margins of a privately circulated version, Cullen jotted, "Crossed from Savannah [*sic*] to Port Escoces in six hours, no high ground, no difficulties." In another iteration was an inset navigational chart for the spacious harbors and a similarly unobstructed view of the interior. The coup de grâce, however, would be his "bird's-eye views," which faced the title page in the second edition of *Darién Ship Canal* and purported to show the heretofore unknown terrain between the Atlantic and Pacific Oceans. There were calm waters, lovely palm-fringed crescent-shaped harbors, distant uninterrupted views, low hills, and even an arrow-straight canal, with a handful of sailing ships in midpassage. The scene was glorious. Absent a photograph, which wouldn't be collected from Darién for another fifteen years, it was the most breathtaking image anyone had ever produced.

But by the time that second edition appeared in 1853, the worries about his original visit were vastly more pronounced. Perhaps the doctor's greatest skeptic, ironically, was also his initial champion: Sir Robert Fitzroy. Fitzroy was the most famous sea captain in Her Majesty's fleet. He had commanded the *Beagle* on Darwin's famous voyage to South America and pioneered the use of meteorological instruments for long voyages, but his passion and preoccupation in later years was the fact-finding for an isthmian ship canal.

Fitzroy reflected the persistent interest of the Royal Geographical Society itself, which had been largely formed around the futile nineteenth-century search for a Northwest Passage, the mythical interoceanic route in the Canadian Arctic. By the 1850s, that era, which is known for astounding geographical advances and desperate human disasters, was mercifully over.

At midcentury, the membership's eyes, with Fitzroy's leading the way, turned south. In November 1850, before the society's distinguished membership, Fitzroy read his exhaustive, highly technical review of the potential routes, whittling down the dozens to a

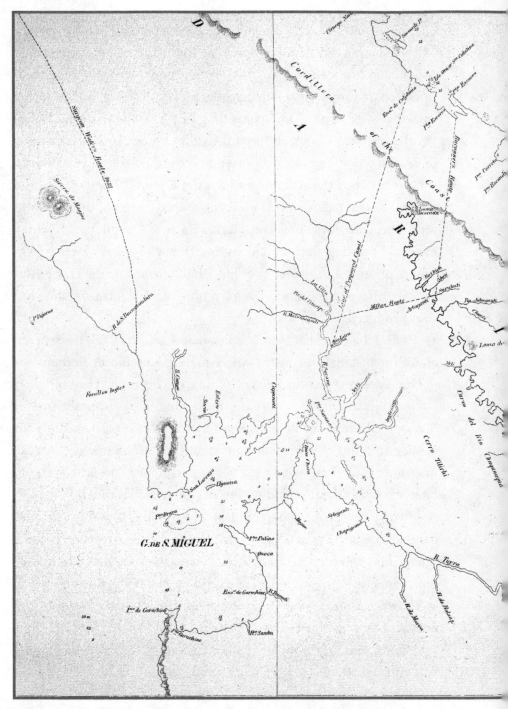

Edward Cullen's sketch of his "pioneering" route across the isthmus of Darién in 1850. The inset bird's-eye-view and the map both originally

MAP
OF
PART OF THE
ISTHMUS OF DARIEN
BY
Dr CULLEN.

N.B. The Soundings are in fathoms

Caledonia Bay

River Savana   Proposed Canal   River Lara   Cerro (Mount) Piriaki

Birds Eye View from the Junction of the proposed Canal with the Savana River to the Atlantic
by
Dr Cullen

appeared in The Isthmus of Darién Ship Canal, *written by Cullen and published in 1852.*

favored few. He left no stone unturned, assessing geology, topography, climate, and aboriginal hostility.

One candidacy inserted at the last moment, on the strength of Cullen's summertime correspondence with the RGS, was the Darién route between Escoces and San Miguel. Fitzroy knew that the buccaneers, in their sixteenth- and seventeenth-century accounts, reported a range of hills that was difficult to cross out of Caledonia, but he found a way to explain the conflict with Cullen's observations. It was plausible that the buccaneers' wary guides, the Kuna, hadn't showed the "best paths to their rather dangerous allies." Fitzroy went on encouragingly, explaining that any route that could be made available between the Gulf of San Miguel and Caledonia Bay, or the Gulf of Darién, would have the "advantage of excellent harbours at each end, and a great rise of tide in one of them [San Miguel]." Cullen's "discovery" was officially on the record, thanks to Fitzroy. Early on the two even collaborated with each other. When Fitzroy's papers were published in the influential annual RGS *Journal,* they came with a Darién Indian vocabulary credited to Cullen. Apparently he had collected the eclectic list of words during his extensive time in the bush.

The whole association with Cullen—and the brief suspension of his better instincts—was one Fitzroy almost immediately regretted. In January 1852, in a note to Shaw, Fitzroy sourly hailed Cullen's latest triumphant voyage to the isthmus: "In the *Times* I saw a notice of Dr. Cullen's return—I hope he has *really* been exploring *personally* . . . but perhaps I am too suspicious of him."

He was not. In February 1853, just days after Cullen had been inducted into the RGS and weeks after he had traveled to France as the project's envoy to Emperor Napoleon, a letter about him found its way to Lionel Gisborne. The informant was Andrew Hossack, a timber agent who had long lived on the Pacific side of the Darién near the Savana River. One of only a handful of white homesteaders in the territory, Hossack had been Cullen's host on his first visit to Darién.

The letter was an exposé, brimming with phrases like "monstrous falsehoods." It was impossible "for Dr. Cullen or any other in the state of health and circumstances in which he was at the time, to make any discoveries in a country like this when capital and a great deal of bodily exertion is required," Hossack ominously began.

Apparently Cullen had had a much worse time of it in California than he let on. Still intent on making a fortune, he had come looking for Hossack at his home with hopes of being guided to the abandoned gold mines at Cana. Hossack quickly sized up the doctor as one ill-suited to the rigors of gold mining in the jungle interior but brought to his attention "another speculation that he was better calculated to bring to the notice of the world, that is, the project of a ship canal from the Savana River to Port Escoces."

Cullen didn't do any exploring, but months later, Hossack received a letter from the now London-based doctor, asking for "all the information I possessed." Their speculation had found an audience in the Royal Geographical Society.

In September 1851 Cullen made his second appearance in Darién. Hossack wrote, "I advised him that instead of making stories of what he knew nothing, nor had ever seen to go up the Savana River to judge for himself, and then he could give a more correct account of it, and for that purpose furnished him with a boat, quadrant, compass and sounding lines, and also sent with him, at my own expense, a couple of Indians from my own house, to guide and pole the boat for him with instructions to get him . . . a considerable distance above Fuerte del Príncipe [the old Spanish fort on the Savana River] and directed the youngest of them to climb the highest tree and give Dr. C an account of what he saw."

Cullen never made it more than halfway across the isthmus, Hossack concluded, "although he pretends to have traveled the land from Sea to Sea and claims to be the sole discoverer of a route he never saw."

Lionel Gisborne promptly brought the bombshell letter to the attention of the Atlantic and Pacific Junction Company, the outfit inspired by Cullen's fieldwork. Gisborne and Cullen had never hit it off, starting with their own supposedly cooperative expedition in the summer of 1852. Cullen, who was to escort the engineer along the route he had personally crossed, never showed up at Cartagena, their prearranged meeting place, forcing the twenty-seven-year-old Gisborne to lead the survey himself. A government civil engineer, he had never conducted a jungle survey in his life, nor even been to the tropics.

The result was a much more limited investigation than had been anticipated. Gisborne suspected Cullen's absence had nothing to do with bureaucratic delays in Bogotá (Cullen's explanation) and everything to do with his fear of being exposed as completely ignorant of the country he supposedly "crossed back and forth many times." Actually, Cullen *was* delayed in Bogotá, but his efforts were focused on adding archive material to his thin first edition of *Darién Ship Canal*. The second would be greatly enlarged (204 pages versus the original 64), with new maps (including the striking bird's-eye depiction) and sections added on "ignorance respecting Darién," "discovery of the route," and "profits of a ship canal." When the reissue came out in 1853, it easily rivaled Gisborne's *Journal of the Expedition of Inquiry for the Junction of the Atlantic and Pacific Oceans* (which necessarily covered a lot of his waiting in Cartagena).

The irony is that Gisborne returned from his trip in 1852 not only corroborating Cullen's account but greatly enhancing it. His map was state-of-the-art. The rumored gap in the cordillera not only existed, he informed the company directors, but was quite a bit lower than expected. Gisborne hadn't accomplished an uninterrupted traverse (on the Atlantic side he was prevented from probing the interior by a band of Kuna after a few days of uneventful wandering), but he had reached the summit of the Continental Divide after restarting his examination from the Pacific side and the Savana River. The gap was near Caledonia Bay, just as Cullen said it was, and its height he estimated at 150 feet, not a serious obstacle to a sea-level canal. As Gisborne would point out to company directors, Hossack's letter didn't invalidate the route, only Cullen's discovery of it. "But not withstanding this [Cullen's false claim], the route is there, although none except myself or the Indians have traveled it since the time of the Spaniards," Hossack had written. He concluded with a final, almost gratuitous swipe at Cullen: "As for the vocabulary of Indian words Dr. C sent to the Geographical Society it was taken down from my table from the aforesaid two Indians."

Gisborne couldn't publicly expose Cullen without endangering the credibility of the coming expedition and causing panic among investors in the Atlantic and Pacific Junction Company. The prospectus issued on the news of Gisborne's report had raised $375,000 in capital on the initial stock offering. Several reputations were at stake, including that of company director Sir Charles Fox. He was the defiant genius who had drawn the plans for Crystal Palace at Hyde Park, the architectural wonder that housed the Great Exhibition of 1851 (the predecessor of the World's Fair). That vision had been repaid with knighthood. The Darién ship canal, even more jaw-dropping than a giant structure of cast iron and glass, was his daring follow-up. Fox knew the humiliating shock waves of scandal wouldn't stop at his door, but could extend all the way to *his* patron, Queen Victoria.

The Cullen/Gisborne contretemps was quietly taken care of behind closed doors. On the eve of sailing, at the last directors' meeting of the Atlantic and Pacific Junction Company, the matter was finalized. Cullen, who once had had his name on the letterhead with company headliners Messrs. Fox, Henderson, and Brassey, was removed from a leadership role and offered a vastly subordinate position, that of volunteer.

On the 17th of December, a trim, clean-shaven Gisborne left England aboard a private mail packet steamer. He wore a fashionable short-waisted monkey jacket and a look of annoyance. The stout Cullen, in his cocked Panama hat and long coat, with a telltale cigar waving about, was with him. Their feud was unresolved: Exasperatingly, Cullen refused to honorably capitulate, insisting he was the victim of a terrible misunderstanding that would be corrected only at Caledonia.

Without any impact beyond their own disgruntlement, the pair would have been comical. But their vendetta had warped everything, including the one thing nobody yet doubted: the professionalism of Lionel Gisborne's 1852 survey and the accuracy of his fine map. To English stockholders and those on the other side of the ocean awaiting the representatives of the Atlantic and Pacific Junction Company, nothing was amiss. Their entourage sailed at noon. Momentum, as always, was forward.

OF ALL THE UNLIKELY victims of the Darién fever, the most immediate was the *Virago*, a British naval steamship that arrived in the Gulf of San Miguel on December 17—the same day as Gisborne and Cullen's sailing from England.

The *Virago*'s unexpectedly early arrival at Darién came on orders from Her Majesty's Pacific commander, Rear Admiral Fairfax Moresby. The vessel's captain, James C. Prevost, was to attempt a traverse of the isthmus, from the Savana River to Escoces, gaining all possible information relating to the "portion of the Isthmus not actually trod on by Mr. Gisborne." Included with the order were copies of Gisborne's engineer's report to the Atlantic and Pacific Junction Company board, Cullen's book, and four maps, three of which were

Cullen's. "Much prudence will be required in the performance of this service," Moresby warned. "Should the time prove unfavourable or a prospect of delay beyond a week it must be abandoned."

Virago's mission was a renegade one. Neither Her Majesty's Admiralty in London nor the company directors relayed orders for an additional survey. It was certainly unknown to Gisborne, who had been extremely punctilious in his instructions to Forde and had pleaded for a coordinated action. The time constraint the rear admiral referred to was important, because if Prevost tarried, the *Virago* would be considered suspiciously overdue at Callao, its next scheduled port of call. It was a subterfuge that reeked of a go-ahead Yankee, not an august figure in the Admiralty's high command. Moresby's rationale was simple: A ship canal discovery was the stuff of immortality—and Prevost was his son-in-law.

Describing Darién Harbor at the mouth of the Savana River as a "magnificent sheet of water," Prevost proceeded up the river to a grass-hut village called Chapigana. There to greet him were assorted representatives, including Hossack, who gave Prevost a detailed description of the cross-isthmus route and made arrangements for native porters and guides. A few miles upriver, Prevost began the business of naming things, christening a pair of shapely midchannel islands the Fairfax and Eliza Islands in honor of his esteemed in-laws.

On Monday the 19th Captain Prevost formed the exploratory party, which included the ship's assistant surgeon, William Ross, and William Kennish, an Englishman now living at Chapigana who claimed to be acquainted with the route, the Indians dwelling in the interior, and the difficulties of the climate. To the latter point, his own broken constitution and faculties were rather sobering indicators. He was nearly blind from a parasite affliction. In all there were thirty-four, including a seaman who was chosen for his climbing talents (Prevost was hoping to certify the treetop where Cullen had said he spied both seas). Leaving the main ship at anchor with "three cheers," they advanced by small boats and canoe as far as possible (some 20 miles) before setting out on foot in a north-northeast direction, fully stocked with fourteen days' worth of provisions.

A recent cruise to the Pacific Northwest had brought Prevost significant overland and Indian experience, and from the beginning he was painstaking and surprisingly well prepared in his survey. A tape line was run to measure mileage, and track was cleared according to a compass reading, with the course set using the known latitude and longitude coordinates of Fuerte del Príncipe (the Pacific end of the route) and Port Escoces (the Atlantic end). Prevost's assistant, Acting Master Inkstip, blazed the trees with a small axe while double-checking the compass course. Each afternoon an advance party would strike out in search of an adequate, high-ground camp where the native assistants would construct a camp, or rancho, of enclosed huts roofed with palm leaves to protect against the unhealthful night dew. Prevost numbered them in ascending order, beginning with Rancho No. 1, which was on the east bank of the Savana. The fixed endpoint for measuring the trip's distance was "Virago Tree," a massive *cuipo* notched with the letters *V-I-R-A-G-O*.

Progressing steadily yet slowly—the four "pioneers" who used machetes to open the route could make no more than two or three miles a day in the dense forest—Prevost kept up a regular trans-isthmian communication using a system of runners with the ship, thus allowing him to request and receive resupplies of stores and men as needed. All seemed according to plan. As they reached deeper into the interior, cutting through impenetrable thickets of needly underbrush and crossing several major rivers, their anticipation of seeing the Atlantic was barely containable. Julier, their seaman climber, was instructed to hoist himself up trees at seemingly every hill crossed. More than ten days under way and certain they were nearing the summit ridge dividing the Atlantic and Pacific watersheds, Prevost wrote in his journal that the reward of a sea view was "more anxiously looked for by us than ever was the Pacific by Nunez Balboa." At various points Prevost alluded to possible sightings. "We fancied we saw the sea," he says at one point, making the occasion sound more like the mirage of overfatigued men (especially their poor tree climber Julier) or observer bias than absolute factual observation.

Thinking himself only hours away from the Atlantic, Prevost made a decision on January 2 to change tactics. Instead of pushing forward, as he had for the last thirteen days, with the entirety of his outfit, he decided to lighten their loads for one last rapid push. He was already overdue, but without the "heavy burdens on their backs" they would be able to speedily climb the steep and slippery hills of the cordillera. They carried only four days' worth of provisions—a biscuit and a half allowance of pork daily per man. The remainder of the provisions were left behind at Rancho No. 10 near a big unidentified river they had crossed, the food guarded by a detail of four armed soldiers. Since everyone wanted to go with the advance party, Prevost had the men draw lots to see who would be left behind. The unlucky ones were Thomas Hyde and James Perkins, both seamen, and Henry Windsor and Henry Robins, members of the ship's marine artillery. Prevost also said goodbye to the party's chief Indian guide, Pedro Punigani, whose health was failing.

Early on January 2, Prevost left with fifteen in number, including four native guides, hoping in the "providence of our God we should be allowed to see the Atlantic." Two days later, they were in the middle of the cordillera and "though within a very few miles of the object of our search," Prevost made the torturous decision to turn back. He was certain that given just a little more time—he mistakenly thought they had crested the dividing ridge—they would find a mountain stream leading them to the Atlantic. In fact, on their last day before turning back, Seaman Julier was sure he saw the route to follow. In a letter he sent to Rear Admiral Moresby shortly after his

return (and entitled "What I saw from the tops of trees while crossing the Isthmus of Darién"), the seaman described a "great gorge between overlapping mountains." It was the same gorge he had seen
from another tree days earlier and through which "I thought I saw
the sea."

Prevost's party had overcome fetid swamp, head-high thickets of
prickly palm, and the "full power of annoyance which the insignificant little sand fly is able to inflict." Yet on retracing their steps, they
were also struck by the Edenic qualities of the tropical forest. The
sight of a 150-foot waterfall and lush hillsides led Prevost to wax a
bit nostalgic about the "perfect solitude, perhaps never broken by
civilized man."

A day later, at noon on the 5th, they were back at their supply depot at Rancho No. 10. Mysteriously, it was abandoned. Believing his
men might have temporarily retreated to one of the earlier ranchos
(No. 9 was only a quarter mile away and No. 8 a mile beyond that),
Prevost pressed on. There were no signs anything was seriously
amiss.

On the approach to Rancho No. 8, at a bend in their newly cut
road near the western edge of a large swamp, he came upon the bodies of Hyde, Perkins, and Windsor. All three were lying on their
right sides. "My first impression was that they had fallen down exhausted with the weight they were carrying, as each had a load of
provisions, so unprepared was I [for an Indian attack]," Prevost
wrote. They had been shot at close range in an apparent ambush, a
pathside *cuipo* tree and its gargantuan buttresses providing the likely
cover. "The bodies of our poor fellows appeared in a sad putrid
state—seemingly they had been dead about forty eight hours. Nothing had been taken from them but their muskets, not even their ammunition or bayonets and a quantity of rum carried by Hyde was
untouched." Windsor had been shot through the pelvis and lower
part of the spine, Hyde through the left side of the head, and Perkins

through the head and throat. According to other accounts their throats had also been cut. With Robins missing, Prevost speculated he had either escaped, was somewhere wounded, or was being held prisoner.

Feeling they were in danger of an imminent attack themselves, and that those left behind at the other ranchos were also at risk, Prevost wasted no time in ordering an all-out march back to the ship. Wrote the surgeon, Ross: "Fearing we might now be surrounded by savages, and every moment expecting a volley from hidden enemies, we could not remain to afford Christian burial to our lamented comrades, however anxious to do so, and we continued our journey till dark, passing ranchos Nos. 8, 7, and 6, and sleeping at No. 5."

The night was impossibly long. "Without a fire or a light we lay down after marching sixteen measured miles, not to sleep but to listen for the slightest sound which might tell of the approach of the murderers." In the predawn, as soon as the bushes could be distinguished, continued Prevost, they were off again. By noon on the 6th they made the river boats; then, riding the high Pacific tidal flow, they reached the ship itself, still anchored at the mouth of the Savana River in Darién Harbor.

It was 2 A.M. on January 7 when they boarded. The men could barely walk, and one of them, an officer, never recovered from the effort, dying a few weeks later from expedition-related exhaustion. Prevost immediately dispatched a letter to his father-in-law, Rear Admiral Moresby, beginning with the precise results of the mission. They had advanced toward the Atlantic, he wrote, a distance of 26 miles and 14 chains. "Each day's halting place is marked by a rancho, numbered from 1 to 12, generally marked on some large tree, and the road between each a good bridle path clearly cut, and every conspicuous tree as clearly marked; thus leaving our route for the benefit of future explorers." Unable to ascend the Savana as far as the point indicated in Gisborne's map (the river in January being much lower than in July, the month Gisborne was there), Prevost estimated he had begun his overland portion only four miles downstream of Gisborne's. He was certain they had crossed Gisborne's track in the first few days, but had seen no evidence of it. However, due to the fact that Gisborne's published chart "differs so entirely, as regards distance and the principal features of the country, from that we travelled over, that I cannot positively say we reached 'that portion of the Isthmus not actually trodden on by him.' "

Only at the close of his report did he get around to the emotional business of his party's fatalities and what he called the determined opposition of the natives. "I cannot help thinking there must be some method in this cruelty," he wrote, alluding to the murders, ". . . a desire of striking terror upon the invaders of their soil." The otherwise peaceful tenor of their journey—they had seen evidence of local Indians and knew they were being observed—had maximized the terror. Up until the time of the strike, Prevost hadn't dreaded any opposition from the Indians, he said. In fact, he had actually gone looking for them in the waning days, with hopes of obtaining better route information. To overcome opposition, Prevost suggested a comprehensive treaty or a wider, well-fortified road.

He also dashed off a letter to the British consul general Donald MacDonald in Panama City. He informed MacDonald of the recent survey, including the murders of three and possibly four of his shipmates, and asked him to make "known this fact throughout your consulate and use every means in your power to obtain decisive information. . . . The missing man is 21 years of age, of middle stature, ruddy complexion, & reddish hair *and* whiskers. If alive I suppose him to be in the power of the Indians occupying the coast in the neighborhood of Port Escoces."

There was no mention of alerting the exploring parties on the Atlantic side, since Prevost was unaware of their existence (as they were of his). Since the British squadron was based in Jamaica, the ex-

pectation was that the warning would be forwarded across the isthmus to Admiralty headquarters. Which it was.

The dispatch was "expressed" across the isthmus by mule (the
trans-isthmus railway line was still 20 miles short of Panama), then
train, then sailing sloop for the penultimate leg from Aspinwall to the
docks at Kingston, Jamaica. More delays ensued when no private
vessel would make itself available for the last chartered leg to Caledonia. By the time Prevost's letter, warning of deadly Indian opposition, found its way to the vessels in Caledonia Bay the date was
January 27, 1854. The laggard piece of mail, its red wax seal em-
bossed with the arch profile of Her Royal Highness, was a stunning
symbol of the *true* distance, at least at Darién, from one coast to
the next.

Like the bloodiest chapters of the conquest, the Indians were now
on the move, folding deeply into the mountain forests, gathering
arms, and preparing for the deadly onslaught. The absent letter
wasn't merely an inconvenience. It was a death knell.

By January 27 everyone, including the Darién Exploring Expedition led by Strain, was long gone into the interior. In fact, the Americans were already well overdue.

5 / DOOR *of the* SEAS

Expecting to meet with our friends and countrymen, we found nothing but a vast howling wilderness, the Colony deserted and gone, their huts all burnt, their fort most part ruined, the ground which they had cleared adjoining to the fort all overgrown with weeds; and we looked for Peace but no good came, and for a time of health and comfort, but beheld Trouble.

THE REV. MR. FRANCIS BORLAND
ON HIS ARRIVAL AT CALEDONIA IN 1699 WITH
A SECOND WAVE OF SCOTTISH SETTLERS

R. USLUCUNANTZ

R. MORTI

Sassardi

DEVILA STN

CAP. PREVOSTS ROUTE

Plantations

R. ASNATI

Asnati

Plantation

R. SUCUBTI

Sucubti

RIVER CHUCUNAQUE

Fort Principe

R. MEMBRILLO

Bennets Rancho
GRENADIAN PRESIDIO

R. SAVANA

R. ARTI

R. FLECCIA

R. CUTIOGANTI

DARIEN HARBOR

La Palma

Chapigana

8° 51' N, 77° 38' W
Caledonia Bay, Darién

IN NOVEMBER 1698 the Scotsman William Paterson sailed into Caledonia Bay, bringing with him the first of several thousand colonists. His vision had been sweeping. He had come to settle the same bay Balboa had. On the remnants of the long-vanished Acla, Paterson saw a bigger and better colony. Something grander than a foothold on Tierra Firme, as the Spanish called the New World. He saw a place where the world united, her goods, her ships, her citizens. The harbor was sounded, her large guardian rocks charted, and houses built. The party comprised a large proportion of soldiers, but also merchants, tradesmen, and planters. Of the twelve hundred choice men, two hundred came from the best families in Scotland. Many brought wives and children.

The first of the projects, erecting a fortification at the harbor entrance, went swiftly. The star-shaped palisaded wall was framed with a double row of wooden stakes and sheathed with packed earth. Scores of jungle acres were quickly cleared and a treaty of perpetual peace and amity signed with the coastal San Blas Indians.

For his eager countrymen back home Paterson described a land of incomparable fruitfulness and a bay as still and serene as a loch. They had been delivered to their destiny. It was, he famously coined, the door of the seas. They called the bay Caledonia, the harbor Port Escoces, and their busy settlement on its sandy shore New Edinburgh. The company's investors were ecstatic at the first reports. The speculation at Darién was one of the most successful public ventures in history, drawing subscribers from every hamlet in Scotland, encompassing every class of citizen. National pride reached its zenith. Some £400,000, a full half of the country's circulating money, was devoted to the ships built, the provisions bought, and the tremendous stake made.

But the people kept dying, first on the harrowing ocean voyage and later in droves as unspeakable disease and famine took hold. Among the first to be buried was Paterson's own wife. The dead piled up faster than they could be properly buried. They were taken by the bloody flux, yellow fever, and malaria. The climate spoiled provisions, and the infernal rains drowned the few crops they got in the ground. But for the Indians, nobody helped them. The British, fearing their trade monopoly threatened, blocked ships from resupplying the starving Scotsmen. When a second fleet of ships arrived at Caledonia less than a year later, the company's thirteen hundred reinforcements gazed upon the "champion country" and saw nothing. Acres that had been cleared only months earlier were already overgrown. The huts had been burned and the fort dismantled. The newcomers tried to start over, but they were quickly set upon by Spanish warships; they abandoned Darién within months. Of the almost three thousand who came, it was said not more than twenty returned to Scotland. Paterson survived, but his spirit was crushed. "Grief has broken Mr. Paterson's heart and turned his brain, and now he's a child," a friend reported.

The Scots colony at Darién, however, was more than a national tragedy; it was another turning point in history. In large part due to the disastrous colonizing scheme, the Scottish economy failed. The

British bailout cost the Scots their political independence, forcing them into the Treaty of the Union, a pact making the two kingdoms one.

In time thousands of Scotch Presbyterians, following the trail of religious tolerance, once more took to boarding promise-filled ships, this time to America. Isaac Strain's forebears were among the émigrés, heading west, as it were. "Going from—toward," wrote Thoreau. "It's the history of every one of us." Strain's arrival at Caledonia, his ancestral countrymen would have said, was virtually predestined. Darién was in his blood.

AT DAWN ON JANUARY 17, the *Cyane* rounded the jutting cliffs at Punta Escoces and slipped into Caledonia Bay. The ship had been quietly shadowing the coast and cruising under light steering sails for hours. Well rested and bursting with anticipation, the men bent the starboard rail for their historic first look. No American naval ship had come before them. It was the noblest view, recalled an officer. Like a ship-of-the-line's gilded hull, the rich blue bay laid out long and deep.

Impressively framing the bay's eastern end was the narrow peninsula of Escoces, which bent like a cradling arm to semi-enclose the shoreline. At the westerly end, some 10 miles distant and hemmed by leggy mangroves, was Punta Sasardi. Clusters of coral islands, small native craft in the distance, and the melodic swells rolling beneath them felt almost divinely arranged. It wasn't unusual for an officer to see the work of providence in a wild stretch of coast so obviously meant to harbor his ship and a hundred like her. Veteran seamen recalled the thrilling experience of seeing the sloping green hills of San Francisco Bay for the first time. They knew otherwise, but there was nothing to visibly suggest that any white man, at any time, had been ashore before them.

Strain's first look probably ran to the mouths of several small rivers, each freshly graced by the new day's sun, each promising him a path to the other side. He saw a bay that was fit for a "place of great importance." There was spacious, deep anchorage, wooded shores, and the cooling trades. He would have lingered upon the tall cedars and exotic hardwoods forming the ridgeback of the thickly forested peninsula. A lyrical Scot had dubbed them "the Shades of Love." A green border of beach coconut trees, waving to a wind he could barely feel, probably bore enough fruit to fill the ship's hold. With a little imagination one could see the future: wharves and warehouses fingering the shore, flag-draped vessels spreading out behind him.

In attending to their anchoring—the harbor was not without its shoal grounds—Strain was prevented from continuing his observations. What he saw as he scanned the shore with a spyglass from *Cyane*'s maintop was as striking as his first view of the Darién a few hours before, only perversely so. Just beyond the bone-white shore and continuing far into the interior he saw mountains rising above mountains, a sea of high peaks clothed in dark forests, their tops trailing off into gray vaporous clouds. There wasn't the slightest suggestion of a gap. The news swept the ship.

"If one were asked to pick out a spot seemingly most utterly impracticable for anything like a canal . . . he could hardly select one more completely so, than this Isthmus as we look at it from on board," bemoaned Winthrop. "The eye hardly finds a resting spot of level ground."

In an almost welcome distraction, Strain's focus shifted to his dealings with the native Kuna Indians. They had, of course, tracked the American warship from the start, and a shore craft was already paddling furiously in the *Cyane*'s direction. Coming aboard, the men said they had been dispatched to ask the ship's commander to refrain from sending forth any landing parties until a conference could be held. Strain agreed, sending the men back with an invitation to their chiefs and those important men residing up and down the coast to gather on board the *Cyane* the following day for a "grand council."

Visitors arrived early the next morning and continued throughout the following day. Most arrived in good canoes, hollowed from coarse mahogany. *Cyane*'s officers found their state dress unexpectedly eclectic, with some of them wearing long European coats with no pants or shoes. They were small, remarked an officer, all under five feet, with large heads, copper skin, and black waist-length hair. They were all from the San Blas region of Darién, a territory that comprised Caledonia Bay in addition to dozens of miles of isthmian coastline. Thousands of Kuna Indians inhabited the Atlantic shore and islands. The general understanding was that they were an "insignificant race" but fiercely independent and so outsized in their forest environment that "one Indian-man is an army."

The grand council started poorly. As a quorum of sorts gathered in Hollins's cabin, the San Blas chiefs were unexpectedly stiff. Strangely, they "could not be prevailed upon to accept a present, however trifling, or valuable"; they also declined food and drink. Conspicuous in his absence was Calohgwa, the centenarian chief of the San Blas who lived down the coast at Carreto. Strain dispatched Winthrop and Truxtun in one of the ship's cutters to offer an escort to the "great old man," but he was evidently in no rush. Truxtun and Winthrop wouldn't return until the next morning, but when they did there was more bad news: they hadn't been allowed to land and had, as a consequence, been forced to spend the night on the water.

The chiefs of Putigandi, Sasardi, and Caledonia strenuously opposed the expedition's objective. They gravely shook their heads, an officer noted in his journal, and said they wanted no canal and would not sell the land which its Maker had given them. If a canal was meant to be, it would have been provided. But would they allow his party to cross the country? Strain repeatedly asked. The chiefs were evasive. The hills were everywhere, they replied. A canal made no sense.

In appealing to the men, Strain was at a personal loss. His adversaries knew more about him and other "outsiders" than he knew about them. Like the Japanese, they had kept themselves uniquely isolated from all intercourse with strangers. They traded with coastal vessels, exchanging their "much esteemed" cacao for shirts, utensils, arms, and ammunition, but they never allowed the foreign ships to land on their territory. Since the disappearance of the Spanish the routine had been unchanged: Each time a commercial vessel arrived at Caledonia it was met by Kuna boatmen and held offshore for the duration of the visit. They were expert with their guns, Strain had been informed, and more so with the bow and arrow. Surprisingly, the chiefs talked of their own far-ranging travels, and a few could converse in both English and Spanish. The message was clear: They were not ignorant of the world around them, nor were they unprepared to deal with it.

Strain was at a bigger disadvantage than he knew. Unlike Strain, the chiefs knew about the Prevost expedition. Whatever Strain's peaceful representations, they believed he would eventually turn his guns on the interior villages as he pursued a course of revenge. Their unwillingness to cooperate had nothing to do with "territorial exclusivity," as he suspected. A darkening fear of reprisal had been spreading across the isthmus for days.

As the mystifying standoff wore on, Strain found himself increasingly frustrated. He suspected they were hiding something, but he was inclined to believe it had to do with the gap. He saw that they were prepared to talk for days. They anticipated more chiefs coming, perhaps, even Calohgwa of Carreto, though nobody could say when. Endless delays were possible. And yet the British were expected shortly, an event that was certain to complicate matters and perhaps make the Indians more skittish.

Strain was left to his own considerable will. He took a harder line, impressing the men that he didn't intend to be the aggressor but that his party would be well armed and fully capable of defending themselves. The council represented villages extending 30 miles up and down the coast. Enough were present, he believed, to conclude a preliminary pact. After a hearty supper the chiefs seemed to soften. Just as likely they understood the futility of their filibuster. Strain seemed ready to proceed regardless of their opposition. An agreement was finally brokered around 9 P.M. Hollins ordered a feast and two volleys from the ship's carronade to punctuate the occasion.

As the shells exploded in the bay some saw in the chiefs' expressions "overawe." Others in the ship's company remembered nothing of the sort. "They were gratified by a display of fireworks," an officer wrote, "but manifested no great surprise." One can imagine a look of resolve. As the *Cyane* was celebrating peace, the Kuna were preparing for what they knew was war.

STRAIN'S SENSE OF RELIEF was profound. Using firmness and a bit of brinkmanship, he had conciliated the Kuna elders and overcome what he believed was the single greatest obstacle to his crossing. Notably, the treaty met the Navy Department's stipulation that he proceed only if he had assurances of no "unfriendly collision."

His confidence was high, so much so that he invited along Frederick Foster, a journalist. Foster was the editor of the *Aspinwall Courier*, one of two American newspapers based further up the isthmus, where U.S. enterprise was booming with the hordes of Yankees shuttling back and forth to California. If there was a hint of hubris, here it was: a chronicler to polish his trophy crossing. Strain knew an eyewitness account would reach every big-city newspaper. Foster's rival, the *Panama Daily Star*, had just published a teaser of sorts, an account of the Scots' disaster at Caledonia.

On January 19, Strain mustered the entire shore party on the weather deck and prepared them to land. It was midafternoon when Strain stood before his men to explain his accord with the San Blas chiefs. He and his officers wore Panama hats, not the blue caps of the men, but in all other respects the members of the party were indistinguishable from one another, with blue drill trousers and blue woolen shirts marked by a five-pointed white star on the collar.

The Indians who had come on board in recent days, he stated, were the principal men of the country. A treaty had been signed. The Americans would not be opposed, but neither would they be assisted. They were forbidden to eat from native plantations or stay in any of the villages. Though Strain had generously offered to pay up to $500 for a guide, he had been refused. Their undertaking, Strain continued, was simply theirs and theirs alone.

Strain's written instructions from Commander Hollins, which were nearly identical to the department's orders, were later read aloud. They directed the party to make a reconnaissance or survey "as speedy as possible of that portion of the Isthmus of Darién lying between this bay and the harbor of Darién on the Pacific." If the Indians opposed their progress, Strain was to resort to "every just and proper expedient to persuade them to abandon opposition and cause them to understand the peaceful object of the exploration." The arms at their disposal were to be used solely as a means of defense in case of attacks from Indians "who may at first seem friendly but afterwards prove treacherous."

Strain had selected his crossing party carefully, but there really was no such thing as a model jungle man. In the medical opinion, a pale skin and northern origin were innate disabilities. Strain had presumably watched how each man handled the heat, whether he sweated too much (something that might predispose him to illness), and whether he had undergone a fever yet (an advantage, since the ship's doctor thought a "seasoning" prevented a serious reoccurrence.) One of the men he chose was a black sailor, and—probably not coincidentally—several others hailed from southern parts of the U.S. where the climate was warmer.

If the men's adaptability was largely guesswork, their loyalty was not. Andrew Boggs, an assistant engineer on loan from the U.S. Coastal Survey, was a schoolboy friend from Springfield, Ohio. And draftsman Samuel Kettlewell, the tall, dark-haired son of a Royal Artillery general, had been with Strain in Texas during his difficult days on the Mexican Boundary Commission.

Even a few of the seamen had extra redeeming qualifications. James Golden, a young, sturdily built man-of-war man, had "studied" under Strain off Africa, preparing for what he hoped would be an adventurous turn. Edward Lombard was a revered sheet anchor man who had served with Strain on multiple cruises. He was to be the party's boatswain's mate, a role he won only after persuading Strain he would be as durable at Darién as he was in the "furious fifties." They constituted a body of men whose loyalty was almost open-ended. Regardless of his formal rank, they called Strain captain.

Everything seemed taken care of. The cutter and launch, loaded with arms and provisions, had been lowered to the water. The ship would remain in the harbor, ferrying out its boats to sound the harbor and conduct a complete hydrographic survey. Lines with lead sinkers would be fed out to determine depths and the composition of the sea floor. A gun was to go off each night so that the shore party might set their timepieces. The department had allowed the ship maximum flexibility, instructing Hollins that he was free to periodically leave the harbor if the climate proved sickly and his company was suffering.

Passed Midshipman Charles Latimer was the only roster change. His intermittent fever had spiked with the ship's arrival at Caledonia, and for several days he remained in the doctor's care. He "has suffered and continues to suffer from a chronic disease which though not at all dangerous, is painful," wrote Strain, reluctantly deciding to leave him behind.

It was a significant loss, but the party of twenty-seven boarding the ship's number three cutter and launch was still the largest, most experienced exploring corps to visit Darién in modern times. Those confided into his care, Strain predicted, would prove themselves "good men and true." His volunteers knew they would be acutely challenged, though not endlessly. They anticipated being back at the ship in ten days.

More than a century later the Army would solicit enlisted volunteers as scientific test subjects, offering them little pay or notoriety yet asking them to endure a battery of hellish trials. They were probed and prodded, run on threshold-testing treadmills, and exposed to extreme weather while carrying heavy loads for days on end. After it all, the supervising physician who designed the exams asked each man a simple question: Why had he volunteered to do it? The soldiers responded that they felt they were "signing on to something bigger than they were, something important." Another common answer was that they liked and trusted the supervising physician (the expedition leader). They often ran to the point of blackout.

The Darién volunteers, looking toward unknown forests and already slicked with clammy perspiration, were kindred spirits. Each surely wished to sum up his expedition experience the way another young seaman recently had: "I look upon my service as perhaps the most important that I ever rendered to the country."

INCREDIBLY, THE MOMENT THE party drew off the *Cyane* they found themselves in trouble. In truth, the breakers did not sneak up on them. The heavy surf had been running since their arrival. Having lost the entire morning awaiting the return of Truxtun and Winthrop, Strain was impatient. In the interest of time and the fact that the surf conditions weren't changing, he took a calculated gamble. The plan was to run in closer to the shore, scout a weakness in the surf, and crash through.

The closer they got, the more impossible their plan appeared. The long sweep of the Atlantic, backed by a freshening onshore breeze, was breaking against sandbars just below the surface. There was no chance of skirting the shoals, which were far more extensive than they first appeared and ran in a seemingly unbroken belt for miles. Instead Strain ordered a kedge anchor readied, anticipating that they would bottom out. They would use the kedge to haul themselves off or at least hold their stern into the surf until the sea eased. Strain hollered for his oarsmen to put their back into it, their only chance to time the break and pierce the white water with a burst. It was futile.

Only yards from shore the driving breakers lifted the 26-foot cutter, its several tons of contents, and dozens of men so that for an instant it felt like they were gliding in the air, absolutely without purchase. Moments later the thunderous surf overtook them, upending the cutter and launch and dumping the men and their belongings in the swirling blue-green sea. Hours were spent wading through the ocean salvaging the wreckage. By dusk Strain conceded that a significant number of their provisions, the launch's awning, and their 100-pound kedge had been either swept away or buried beneath the shifting sand.

Strain must have been deeply mortified by the episode. Military bearing was no small thing, and the way in which an American outfit carried itself and performed a deck drill, much less how it made a foreign arrival, was viewed with exaggerated importance. The eyewitnesses were few, but his own ship had had to look on, and that was bad enough.

That night they slept almost where they had emerged from the sea, in a string of deserted fishing huts near the mouth of the Caledonia River. Strain had wanted to start the march immediately, get into the cooler hills, and avoid a beach camp. He had practical reasons, yet he also knew Balboa and Paterson had buried scores of dead here. The former said the white-sand shore was formed on the bones of his men. Swatting at invisible sand flies, and so close to the crashing surf they could feel the beach heave beneath them, Strain spent a wakeful first night on Tierra Firme.

6 / DIVIDE

The hike had nothing to equal it during the War.

AN AMERICAN CIVIL WAR VETERAN, ON A LATER
DARIÉN EXPEDITION, DESCRIBING THE GRUELING ASCENT
OF THE ATLANTIC DIVIDE FROM CALEDONIA BAY

January 20, 1854

8° 52' N, 77° 41' W
Caledonia River

WHEN DAWN FINALLY CAME to Scotch Harbor, Strain was already up. As he waited for the final landing of replacement provisions, he ascended a steep hill to get a better view of their route. He panned the spyglass and saw nothing but an unbroken range of mountains. No gap. No depression. In his journal he recorded his first serious misgiving. The journey was hours old.

At noon the newly resupplied U.S. Darién exploring party headed single file up the Caledonia River, their gateway to the Pacific. It was not a major river, not like the Atrato, which they had anchored across from a few nights earlier. That was a large, delta-like river with an easy current and the deep, turbid water of the Mississippi. The heavy surf at the mouth of the Caledonia had, in combination with seasonal flood debris, formed a natural dike, a sand embankment that only ineffectually dammed the sea, or for that matter the river, but stood as if specifically placed to block a ship's passage.

They paddled and dragged a large cargo canoe up the "considerable stream" but soon found the going too rough and left the boat behind. The party intended to go as light and fast as possible. Strain had left his instruments and the mules to carry them back on the ship. A true survey featured endless measurements and trigonometric calculations. Bulky sextants, artificial horizons, chronometers, mountain barometers, and miles of topographical line had to be packed and repacked. Faulty equipment, a near certainty in the damp jungle environment, required time-consuming repairs. They didn't have the time.

One can imagine Strain's disappointment. He loved science, the certainty that a bright man with comprehensive training could bring to an unknown quarter of the world. Yet he would be able to perform only the most primitive topographical survey. Without a mountain barometer, which was used sometimes hourly to check atmospheric fluctuations in hilly regions, he couldn't precisely measure the height of land. Without astronomical tools he couldn't reliably determine latitude and longitude. Unable to fix the principal points, any intermediate points he picked up chronometrically were virtually useless. Without measuring chains to lay out as they went he could only guess at the true distance they traveled. Absent spirit levels, the foot-per-mile drop of the rivers would be an estimate. Of course, his sprint strategy—a run across the country to determine its general character, as he put it—meant something else too: He'd have to depend on somebody else's work, and more specifically, someone else's map.

Group supplies, parceled out among the seamen volunteers, were also kept to a bare minimum: only a single axe, not the six available, was taken. Individually, each man carried a large but reasonable 50-pound haversack containing a blanket, ten days' provisions, a single change of clothes, a carbine, a cartridge box, and 40 rounds of ammunition. Their most important items, as a weight scale would have confirmed, were their weapons and ammunition. A musket alone weighed almost 10 pounds.

In rearranging the expedition he transformed a plodding scientific party, the kind he'd take back into the wilderness *after* he had reconnoitered the crossing, into a lean, pioneering one. It was a bold approach with a high reliance on each and every man's resourcefulness. What he *didn't* bring was also a conciliatory message for those Indians whom he knew would be watching him: They were not putting down roots, but just passing through. Unexpressed was the Americans' chief goal: to complete the crossing before anyone else.

The first day illustrated what they were up against. The combination of wading in swift water and cutting along the densely forested banks made the going deadly slow. By evening they had advanced about "three miles in a line & 5 or 6 by our devious course."

Another problem was the two late additions to the party, the New Granadian representatives José Ramón del Castillo Rada and Bernardo Polanco. Poor replacements for the seasoned topographer Colonel Codazzi, their government had dispatched them to Caledonia with instructions to accompany Strain. Neither man was accustomed to the rigors of a forced march in the wilderness, but more to the point, they were slowing the party down.

Amid much grumbling at day's end, Strain reduced their loads and assigned "assistants" to them. As national guests, they could not be sent back to the ship, nor could they be militarily disciplined. Strain's fate and that of his party rested on managing two men who now knew they didn't want to be where they were—or where they were going.

The party's stopping point was a deserted "Indian rancho" on a small island where several grass huts—judging by the disarray and a smoldering cook fire—had been hurriedly left. Strain ordered four men to stand guard with their carbines, muskets, and pistols beside them, their cartridge boxes belted on.

"I shall never forget the 1st night," wrote Winthrop. "My watch was from 12 to 2 the moon had just risen; it was the type of a tropical night soft & clear, a glow of starlight & from time to time clouds

passing over the moon made everything look strange & uncertain—
every now & then one of the men would think he saw something
moving in the woods which I as often found to be moonshine among
the cacao trees; a dense forest surrounded us from it came all sounds
of insect life, with strange screams of birds, unearthly roaring of
monkeys & occasionally the cat-like mew of the tiger. The party lay
snoring each man according to his own ideas of music."

IN THE WAKE of the New Granadians' difficulties and the raging
fever that confined Midshipman Latimer to the ship, Strain could
sense worry in the ranks. Jungle fears were real. Few put much stock
in the isthmian monsters the Spanish described: the rumored man-
beasts or birdlike air demons whose wings blotted the sun and whose
talons snatched unwary men. But one's exposure to the tropical climate, and how one's body would react to it, was likely to be a daily
(and nightly) anxiety.

According to any ship's physician, the land air was sickly. The
miasma, or poisons that brewed in the jungle soil, were "eliminated"
in the period when the wet grounds dried out. January, the start of
the three-month dry season, was the most toxic time. That was when
the flooded rivers receded, vapors rose, and the atmosphere became
saturated with "more poison than at any other time."

In the Darién tropics, the venomous effect achieved deadly per-
fection. "Whether or not it is the approximation of the two oceans,
and almost constant sea breezes, or the extreme dampness of the
climate; either or both of these causes; in no place have I seen consumption more rapidly developed," wrote one doctor. Ship squad-
rons were under orders in both the British and U.S. navies to rotate
through the Torrid Zone, as they called it, never staying too long lest
they put their company at risk for "malignant ship fever," "slow
nervous fever," or, most notorious of all, "yellow fever." The pro-

tocol dated back to one of the most deadly contagions ever seen: a mid-eighteenth-century outbreak of yellow fever that killed four thousand British seamen in the Caribbean.

For those who had to lay over in equatorial ports, the prevailing theory was that one's "seasoning" came about only after a bout of intense fever. Those lucky few who avoided the fever would still be diminished by the climate. They couldn't expect to perform nearly as much labor as they did in temperate zones.

Soldiers were generally instructed to stay out of the night dew and wear thick insulating flannel against the skin to seal off the hot jungle air. Those who were imprudent and pushed too hard on "wooding and watering" details, overexposed themselves to the sun, or were caught in a "rain shower while perspiring" risked the most deadly grade of fever.

Almost any enterprise, and certainly an expedition hacking its way across the roughest country most had ever seen, put itself at a sizeable risk. An expedition staffed with seamen was reasonably believed to be more at risk. A seaman's health was a simple matter, the old saying went: One must never have lived on land—and must never leave the sea.

Every man in Camp 1 knew someone who had died from tropical fever. Those who came from naval families, such as Truxtun and Maury, could count their relatives among the victims. Most had endured the standard course of treatment: They were bled, purged, and vomited. Others were medicated with arsenic. They knew that where they marched and slept, normal precautions were impossible. Those who hadn't yet been "seasoned" with the fever could only wait and wonder when the paroxysm would strike. Their vulnerability wasn't based on supposition, myth, or Spanish legend. It was in the U.S. newspapers every day. In only the last few years American experience on the isthmus had taken a quantum leap. Just a few hundred miles up the isthmus, between Panama City and Aspinwall,

a trans-isthmian railroad was being completed. And by 1854 some
ten thousand men had died because of it.

THE RAILROAD SPECULATOR was William H. Aspinwall, the New
York capitalist whose Pacific Mail Steamship Company owned the
government-subsidized mail packet line between California and
Panama. The line was attempting to exploit the government's need
and the paying public's desire to get to the Pacific (and hence California) quicker. In recent years the favorite shortcut was Panama.

Passengers would off-load at the docks in Aspinwall, where they
would purchase trip staples (cold fowl, hard-boiled eggs, fresh meat,
bread, tea, sugar, a tin cup, knife, and fork) and switch to native 25-
foot-long *piroguas,* or dugout canoes, for the two-to-three-day trip
up the Chagres River into the interior. Near the summit ridge, at
Cruces, they would off-load again and proceed to Panama via mule
track. The way was arduous and dangerous: "The horrors of the
road in the rainy season are beyond description," wrote Captain
Ulysses S. Grant, then a young officer en route to California. But
most important of all, it was quick. With a waiting ship at the other
side, the trip from New York to San Francisco could be cut to a mere
six weeks.

The downside, said many indignant transiters, were the "shout-
ing naked bogas" who poled the boats; the jarring mule trails where
the beasts sank to their necks in blue-black mud holes; and countryside "reeking with malaria, and abounding with almost every species
of wild beasts, noxious reptiles, and venomous insects known in the
tropics." Accounts from easterners, of which there were thousands,
were regularly published in the leading newspapers. "I have not time
to give my reasons for what I am about to say," wrote a traveler in
the *Providence Journal,* "but in saying it I utter the united sentiment
of every passenger whom I have heard speak upon the subject. It is

this—and I say it in the fear of God and love of man, to one and all—by no means, for no consideration, attempt to come this route. I had rather risk the doubling of Cape Horn a dozen times, or all the dangers and toils of the overland route for a year, than repeat this journey."

But they came. The trickle of emigration before Sutter's Creek became a tidal wave in the late months of 1848. They came from New York, Boston, and other East Coast cities. It was a singular sensation. Never before had so many, of such varied backgrounds and financial circumstances, taken to the sea to travel so far. They weren't only outdoorsmen and gentlemen travelers but farmers, clerks, and carpenters. By the early 1850s up to fifty thousand passengers annually were transiting the isthmus by canoe and mule.

Aspinwall's interocean train line was an elegant and lucrative solution to the rough passage but for one thing. Most thought it was a madman's dream. The climate, the heavy grades, and the engineering involved in bridging the rain-swollen isthmian rivers and laying 50 miles of single-gauge track in pestilent jungle appeared insurmountable. But after a series of near-fatal missteps, including mass labor desertions and a bridge collapse that pushed the company to the brink of bankruptcy, the project began to find its legs. The city of Aspinwall, the Atlantic terminus for the project (and present-day Colón), was formally inaugurated in February of 1852. By late 1853, 20 miles had been laid. Updates appeared in the newspapers, and as the project neared its halfway point the people came and company stock spiked. The passage cost an exorbitant $35—$25 for the rail portion and $10 to walk the rest of the way to Panama City.

It was common knowledge that the railroad was being built on the bones of dead men, but nobody seemed much bothered. The initial labor force was imported from Cartagena, Jamaica, and New York (Irishmen who had survived the potato famine would die by the hundreds in the swamps of Panama). Later a force of a thousand Chinese would be reduced to a few hundred within a couple of weeks, as scores fell desperately ill or "ended their unhappy existence by their own hands."

The work was elevated to a national enterprise. By 1854, the "Yankee Strip" between Aspinwall and Panama City was in full swing and the railroad had reached the summit ridge, a distance from the Atlantic of 37 miles. A mere 11 miles remained to Panama. A trip that once risked life and limb and took anywhere from two days to two weeks had been whittled down to a mere handful of hours. Arriving from New York, a trans-isthmian passenger saw a lush tropical harbor fronted by a 60-foot-high iron lighthouse. Long covered wharves (filled with the shipping of many nations) led to the town proper, where bars, a dozen hotels, and shops with everything from Boston ice to Havana cigars awaited. But for being in Caledonia Bay, it was the global entrepôt of Paterson's vision—a thriving hub situated at the crossroads of shipping lanes, equidistant between the hemispheres.

An isthmus-wide police force, employed by the railroad company to safeguard the transit, was run by a distinctly West Texas lawman named Ran Runnels. His swift and severe retributions, usually in the form of lynching, became legion. On one occasion, in answer to a gold train heist, dawn rose in Panama City with thirty-seven "highwaymen" swinging in the breeze along its airy ramparts.

The isthmus was part of the national lexicon, an extension, it sometimes seemed, of the West itself. With the apparent railroad triumph, the idea of a bigger and better enterprise, a canal at Darién, took firmer hold.

Theodore Winthrop, whose energetic musings captured the mood that first night on the isthmus, knew all about the Yankee strip and Panama fever. He had worked for a year in Panama before taking a berth aboard *Cyane*. His job was in the Panama office of Aspinwall's Pacific Mail Steamship Company, and he had traveled often across the isthmus, at least over the developing railroad route. Just twenty-six, he knew isthmian customs, could speak passable border Spanish, and seemed an important counterweight to those whose youthful imaginations were sure to get the better of them in the Darién wilderness.

In signing up, he was following his nose for adventure—a sense that had been awakened in the last several years with a prolonged trip to California and the Pacific Northwest. A young man of privilege, Winthrop reveled in all the malaise one might expect in a young prince. In 1852, he wrote how he had "seen too much and not enough of life—too much to be unquestioning and indifferent, too little to be desperate or content."

But the outdoors boosted his self-esteem, providing an unexpected outlet for his unfocused talents. An authentic writing voice, never too sure during his undergraduate days at Yale, had emerged. Like the Hudson River artists whose brush strokes leaped across canvas, he found himself unbound in the wilderness. His correspondence with his family overflowed with lush physical descriptions of everything he saw, from the ponderosa forests of the Cascades to the rivers that swept Lewis and Clark to infamy. The Darién exploration offered adventure and then some. He genuinely seemed to feel a calling.

There was a troubling conflict, however. Winthrop's family, and Theodore especially, were close to the Aspinwalls. For several summers Theodore had been tutor to William's son Lloyd at the Aspinwall manse on Staten Island. It was Aspinwall who had fitted him up for a job at the New York and later Panama ticket offices of his Pacific Mail Steamship Company. Aspinwall had sent him off on travels to Europe. When he returned ill from the sea voyage, he was nursed back to health at Aspinwall's house. Winthrop's due to his employer went well beyond the ordinary, a fact that wasn't lost on him.

As everyone knew, the proposed ship canal route directly threatened Aspinwall's vast railroad investment. Winthrop was in a difficult position. He almost certainly held an emotional interest, if not a financial one, in seeing the railroad project succeed. Winthrop might have taken the Darién job independently—he wasn't averse to getting out of Uncle A's shadow—but beginning with his first forays around Cartagena Winthrop began dutifully reporting back to Aspinwall. While letters back to his mother stroll her through stately Cartagena, moonlit nights, and life aboard a drill-happy man-of-war, those to Aspinwall are much more pointed dispatches and suggest a man who never left the payroll.

"Very little information is to be obtained here in regard to the proposed Route; that little is favorable. . . . Lieut. Strain who has charge of the expedition is an able officer & his report will be entirely reliable." Like Strain, who years earlier had struggled to please his scientific mentors in Philadelphia, Winthrop was obligated to masters with ideas all their own. Even if Winthrop wasn't a spy, he probably underestimated his patron's desperation. Aspinwall's other major investment, a brand-new ship named the *San Francisco*, had just sunk in several hundred feet of cold North Atlantic water.

ON SATURDAY THE 21ST the party was under way by six-thirty and making its way up the eastern branch of the Caledonia. A small side tributary, which entered from the south and west, offered a sweeping view of the Caledonia valley. To Strain's dismay he found the valley enclosed by a semicircular spine of mountains abutting the seacoast range and forming a barrier ranging in height from 3,500 to about 1,000 feet. "I could find no opening in any direction," he wrote, "but as Lionel Gisborne had stated above his professional signature to his employers in England, and had promulgated to the world, that the summit level between the two oceans was but one hundred and fifty feet, I was convinced that there must be some lower point which we had not discovered."

Pushing ahead on the main eastern branch, the party entered a fairly large village of forty or fifty houses, again newly deserted. Judging by the densely packed dwellings, Strain estimated as many as 800 inhabitants. On the outskirts were cultivated cornfields and groves of cacao, oranges, and plantain. Within what should have been a bustling village center Strain found a frozen tableau: On low benches fronting the bamboo huts he saw spools of cotton thread and half-woven baskets, everything left behind in a way that reminded Strain of the ephemera on a berthing deck when a sudden squall brought all hands topside.

He led his column straight through the village, but upon coming out the other side met three Indians, one of whom directed Strain to the southwest branch, the quickest path, he said, to the Pacific. Seeing no opening in the cordillera in that direction and "believing he only wished to get us away from their village," Strain declined the advice and opted to stay on the eastern branch recommended by Gisborne.

They continued until midday, when Strain grew concerned their course was bearing too far east, away from the Pacific. The rapid fall of the river was also troubling.

Sent upriver with a small party to scout, Winthrop confirmed the route as impossible. "It was a New England stream in the tropics . . . overhung with drooping palms & rich foliage of vine-canopies . . . but very unfit to sail big clipper ships up," he wrote, estimating the torrent's drop at a plunging 100 feet per mile.

Winthrop, whom his sister kindly described as "fair & delicate looking with chestnut hair & blue eyes," was in his element. His solo trip up the Caledonia saw Winthrop in full song, absolutely joyful in his ascent, and his position in recording it. "More and more lovely & wilder," he wrote in shorthand, "deep blue butterflies . . . deep cool pools overhung with most luxuriant vines . . . if no rain I could while away a life time in one of these dells of love." It was with reluctance that he turned back to tell Strain their route had to lie elsewhere.

Upon retracing their steps and switching to the smaller, western branch of the Caledonia the work got harder. "This is the hardest walking one can do, wading for hours in the stony bed of a rapid river," wrote Winthrop. His shoes and those of others were already fraying, and some of the provisions and ammunition had been soaked as the men lost their footing in the slick-stoned riverbed. "When you add to your own corporeal load you have to carry a knapsack with 10 ds. Prov., change of clothes, pistol, cartridge box, ammunition & carbine all with thermom. at 80 degrees it is wearisome in the extreme. We were glad to come to camp in a charming spot on the W. branch of the river, three miles above junction."

Military custom dictated that the officers and men split into their two messes, or dining groups. Each camp, separated by enough distance to maintain conversation out of one another's earshot, had its own fire and guard. There the differences were supposed to end. When it came to the basics of military life—how much one ate and how hard one was asked to work—Strain felt there should be no difference between the men and those who led them. His view wasn't routinely shared. Years earlier, in the organization of the Mexican boundary exploration, he had argued with his superior officers, noting the bad feelings that might arise from "distinctions" and the necessity of officers submitting to "the same deprivations to which [the men] were subjected."

He had been overruled at the time, but the arrangement at Darién was as he wanted it. Each man received two blankets, one for ground cover and one for protection from the night chill. The food ration was also identical, officer and soldier alike receiving the same staples (hard bread, pork, and rice) in the same amounts. Per day, the men were assured at least a pound of meat, 14 ounces of bread, and an ounce of coffee. A half plug of tobacco, the most cherished commodity, was expected to last them the ten days they would be out. The small stores, dispensed in equal shares daily, ranged from bottles of mustard and pepper to soap and beeswax. Their comforts were no more or no less, Strain could fairly say, than those of the man marching next to them.

On a southern and westward course, Strain was increasingly certain they were on the right track. Earlier in the day he had been intercepted by two Indians who carried a letter from Captain Hollins detailing activities in the harbor. The English survey parties had arrived and were fitting out for their survey.

The letter deliverers, envoys of the San Blas, would serve as guides, Hollins had promised, but there was apparently "deception or misunderstanding." The duo refused to proceed beyond the party's encampment, and almost as suddenly as they appeared they were gone, having abruptly decided to return to the harbor. Strain had no idea what to make of their reversal.

The confusing exchange underscored an obvious potential problem. They had no dependable system of contact to the "outside." Not feeling he could safely spare any of his defense force, Strain had elected not to organize a string of interim camps, or a system of mail-carrying runners connecting his command to that of the ship's. They had no tether. As it turned out, Hollins's dispatch was the last communication Strain would have with the ship for two months.

On the 22nd, their third day out, they began the main ascent of the Atlantic cordillera. Coming to a gorge where they couldn't pass in the riverbed without wetting everything, Strain called off the single-file formation and allowed the men to scramble any which way up the steep hillsides. They were to reconvene in the bed of the stream after the climb, though Strain told all he didn't intend to pursue the river much further, as it was leading toward high mountains and trending too southerly.

On his ascent Strain came across a well-beaten Indian trail, which he was "convinced led to the Pacific side of the cordillera." After he shouted to the others, all gathered back together except Winthrop, Holcomb, the surgeon volunteer Dr. J. C. Bird, J. Sterret Hollins (the son of the captain), the journalist Foster, and a seaman from the *Cyane*. At the customary signal for recall—three carbines fired in quick succession—they still didn't appear. Strain did, however, hear return fire answering his carbines, and figured the missing party was some distance up the river. As he led his group westward along the new trail, climbing higher and higher into the main range, he continued to fire the carbine. He steadily received responses, though fainter. Strain had no doubt Winthrop's party knew where they were and would get to them. Undeniably he was in a hurry.

By 1:15 P.M. Strain's party had ascended three separate peaks—the highest probably 1,500 feet—before dropping down the western slope to an auspicious stream. Evidently he didn't stop long enough to boil tea water, the most common method used to estimate elevation. (According to the arithmetic calculation, each Fahrenheit degree beyond the customary sea level boiling point of 212 degrees equals 549½ feet of altitude.) He knew what he needed to know—the canal couldn't be built here. On the sheer, 60-degree pitches the thick, humid air seemed to push them back. The low light and tight webbing of vines, shrubs, and trees compressed their world to what seemed inches. The gap's nonexistence didn't diminish their achievement: Strain had led the party over the Atlantic Divide and found his way to a stream that, he was convinced—if the maps he had were in any way correct—was an upper branch of the Pacific-bound Savana River.

Disturbingly, the missing party never arrived that night, nor the next morning, though Strain had carefully marked the trail behind him. Long hours passed. Strain decided to wait for the missing party until 10 A.M., allowing them, he thought, enough time to cross the divide if they left at first light. When the deadline hour came and went, Strain jotted a lengthy note telling Winthrop of his intended course and instructing him to turn around and head back to the ship if he didn't get to the note the same day it was written, the 23rd. "Our provisions are getting to be so short," wrote Strain, placing the note in a forked stick, "that we cannot delay any longer out of regard to general safety."

Not knowing their fate, nor why they hadn't traced his signaling shots, gnawed at Strain. The missing men, only two soldiers among them, were vulnerable to Indian attack. On a practical level, Winthrop and Holcomb were experienced woodsmen whom he was counting on. Bird, one of their party, was the expedition's only doctor. With him was the bulk of their first-aid supplies.

Personally, he enjoyed Winthrop's enthusiasm and thought him different from the scholarly gentlemen he had traveled with in the past. Strain didn't believe Winthrop would outright desert, but he couldn't help wondering if he had fallen under the influence of Holcomb and the two had chosen to go their own way, thinking they knew better. Winthrop had an arrogant streak, especially likely to surface when paired with a Connecticut neighbor like Holcomb. Men of their background often had a tenuous appreciation for command structure. They traveled and explored by different rules. Those fortunate souls who chose to put themselves in danger, as young Winthrop did, could just as easily choose not to.

The same morning Strain prepared his note for Winthrop he also sent scouts back up the divide to see if the missing men might have "crossed a lower summit of about 1,000 feet on the left of our path." His scouts saw nothing of the Winthrop party but did glimpse a beautiful river that merged with the stream they were on. It likely emptied at Darién Harbor on the Pacific side—they had to be close.

On such tidings, the day's march began on a high note. The woods rang with work songs and the soaring voice of Seaman Wilson urging his fellow argonauts on. For man-of-war men, customarily kept like "convicts, in profound silence," the moment was unforgettable. To the hymn "Jordan Is a Hard Road to Travel," the response was almost delirious. "Caledonia is a hard stream to travel" went the new chorus.

The travel in and out of the rocky streambed soon became difficult, but more discouraging was the continued evidence of just how unwelcome they were. Freshly abandoned huts were found set ablaze. Lush groves of plantain and cacao had all their fruit stripped. Clearly the Indians were retreating deeper into the interior. Strain's command to "close up" as they marched reflected his belief that an attack was imminent.

On the 25th, two days later, they reached the river seen from the divide and entered the outskirts of Sucubti, one of the largest villages in the interior. It was a place where adventurers had traditionally received cooperation. In the seventeenth century an English buccaneer party had been afforded lodging, provisions, and guides, enabling them to successfully continue across. Even the Spanish, in one of their last expeditions, had found allies in Sucubti.

Strain had heard the "blows of axes" on his approach, but on arrival found yet another vacated village. The axe fells had been delivered to the only substantive item left behind: seven large dugout canoes, scuttled on a nearby shingle beach. The owners had made certain they would be impossible to repair and use.

It was Strain's sixth day on foot. Provisions were low. He recognized the pattern. The Kuna's sacking of their own villages was a survival strategy that had its precedent during the conquest, and usually presaged a bloody battle. The scene at Sucubti was the clearest indication yet of opposition, Strain concluded, and "left the impression . . . that the country would be wasted for some distance before us, and to a point where the Indians would unite in force to dispute our passage." As Strain had observed, no ammunition or clothing had been left behind in any of the abandoned huts.

It was a juncture where Strain might have been expected to turn back and join the other survey parties on the coast. There he could gather more provisions, more intelligence, and guides; as Hollins had advised in a note that never reached Strain, "You can refit for another attempt." He was isolated, beyond sight and sound of the ship. Its evening gun hadn't been heard for two nights.

If not return, he had other options. The village was surrounded by groves of plantains and cacao. If an attack was inevitable and opposition fixed, he could have decided to void his agreement and have his troops help themselves. Heretofore, Strain had zealously kept his word and not disturbed Indian property or possessions. In one instance, Strain prevented one of his men from helping himself to plantains, even though the bunch was hanging from a hut's burning rafter. The Indians' pots and pans were sometimes used but were always returned to the exact positions where they had been found. Strain didn't want to provide the Indians with any reason to abrogate their treaty and "assail his party." If he changed his policy now, he was putting not only his own party in harm's way but also Winthrop's, which was still unaccounted for.

Strain trusted his good faith would win out. Moreover, he saw that they were on the direct route across the isthmus; they had marched to it competently, and "with a rapidity which we could not expect to exceed." With little deviation they had taken the same route across the cordillera as the English buccaneers had two centuries earlier. That expedition, outfitted with three hundred men and supported by Indian porters and guides, had taken five days to get to the village he was in. Strain had taken six.

Unfortunately, their next leg was difficult to plan. As they had approached Sucubti, Strain and his men saw high hills everywhere they looked. They were still amid the river's headwaters, where only a small stretch was visible before the falling water veered off on another bend. The water was barely knee-deep, normally ideal for easy crossings, but almost everywhere they walked they found bouldery debris and deep, violent gashes in the banks that looked like the work of giant dredging shovels. Everyone knew what was necessary to move rocks, trees, and earth. A hard jungle rain atop the summit was probably all it took for the stream at their feet to come to terrifying life and erupt like a passing locomotive, a wall of foaming brown water ripping at everything and everyone in its path.

As they backtracked from the village and dropped back into the gouged-out riverbed looking for a crossing, Isaac Strain reflexively looked to the hills for a low rumble and the flood he couldn't possibly see coming.

7 / DEVIL'S OWN

I know the great secrets which are in this land.

The nature of the land ... causes one to experience bad nights and endure fatigues, for every day it is necessary to face death a thousand times.

BALBOA WRITING TO KING FERDINAND FROM
DARIÉN ON JANUARY 20, 1513

January 25, 1854

8° 50′ N, 77° 45′ W
Pacific slope of the Continental Divide

THE BRITISH EXPLORER Lionel Gisborne had never made it to where the American party now stood, though he thought he had. His mistake started earlier, well before his actual land survey in 1852. It began in Caledonia Bay, where he looked at the shoreline in front of him and began to consider what he would need to find on the isthmus for a sea-level canal to work. He imagined many things: the soft bedrock he would walk over, the flow and volume of tributaries he needed to nourish the canal, but principally he mentally mapped a place with fine, deep harbors on either end (a condition the spacious Caledonia Bay clearly met) and a summit ridge 150 feet high.

After making his quick ascent of the Atlantic cordillera, he followed a stream, then a river flowing from the southwest. "A flat plain extended to the southeast, in the direction of the Gulf of San Miguel, as far as the eye could reach," he wrote. Ascending a bluff with his spyglass, he was rewarded with an uninterrupted view for at least six miles in the same direction, at which point the Atlantic side survey came to an abrupt halt when Gisborne and his partner, H. C. Forde, met several armed Kuna, who escorted the uninvited visitors back to the bay.

Crossing the isthmus between Aspinwall and Panama, the pair chartered another boat and ascended the Savana River from the Gulf of San Miguel, then struck out overland in a northeast direction, crossing low hills, before tracing a small stream east. From a point nearby they looked northeast in the direction of Caledonia Bay and stood with Balboa-like wonder looking at what they had previously seen, only from the opposite side: the same flat plain, no intervening hills. Believing they were soon to be harassed again, and certain that the formality of walking the terrain between the two points was unnecessary, Gisborne concluded they had either walked or seen the entirety of the route from Caledonia Bay to the Gulf of San Miguel.

His subsequent map showed the depths of the canal's proposed harbors and segmented the route across to reveal the mile-by-mile topography. Beginning on the Pacific side of the isthmus and ending on the Caribbean, the letters *A* through *K* corresponded to a thick black line representing the canal. The first half of the route traced a narrow but widening river valley to the midpoint of the isthmus, where it hurdled a low mountain pass before descending into an even broader valley. Both valleys would be remade as a vast unnamed freshwater lake designed to support and replenish the canal. The final few miles flowed through a gap in the otherwise contiguous coastal mountains. From one end of the isthmus to the other the Caribbean coasts were darkened by the bristled, ink-black circumferences of tropical peaks. The pass at Caledonia Bay, the one that Strain now concluded did not exist, stood out as a clot of white.

It was an astonishingly inept piece of work. Hurried as he was, Gisborne misread the isthmus spectacularly. His first error was in fixing the longitude of the desired endpoints of the canal. Even the most minor mistake in longitude near the equator is lethal for the simple reason that the gradient gaps are largest. Thus, Gisborne had managed to grossly misplot the position of Port Escoces and the mouth of the Savana River, putting the former at a longitude 7 miles too far west and the latter 10 miles too far southeast. He had miniaturized the width of the isthmus dramatically. Not only had his view failed to overlap by many miles, a later U.S. government analysis concluded, "but Gisborne's line of sight didn't bear upon the points he supposed," namely, the canal's hypothetical endpoints at Caledonia and Fuerte del Príncipe on the upper Savana. If one dutifully followed Gisborne's coordinates one would never leave the isthmus since the route never actually touched either shore.

Gisborne's errors also accounted for Prevost's problems. He charted his north-northeast course using the two terminal points he felt were correctly oriented to each other, Caledonia and Fuerte del Príncipe on the Savana, the ones Gisborne had misplotted in both latitude and longitude. Consequently, Prevost's course was 60 degrees north of what it should have been. Had he succeeded in making it to the Atlantic, he would have ended up on a beach 30 miles away from his intended target, Port Escoces. Prevost's belief that he was only hours from the Atlantic shore was wrong. He hadn't even crossed the divide, and many more mountains barred the way. When he turned back his hardest work lay ahead.

Gisborne produced a map that put mountains where they weren't, recorded heights that never were, and misplaced almost every meaningful geographical point on the Isthmus of Darién. His conclusion about the height of the dividing ridge, a mere 150 feet and maybe lower, was based on a sequence of inductive assumptions, each more inaccurate than the last.

The fascinating thing was that Gisborne wasn't a fool, hadn't intended to mislead anyone, and in fact was deeply wary of the previous gaffes of overeager Darién explorers. Prior to his exploration he wrote "that scarcely a single fact relating to this Isthmus can be relied on; the writers seem to vie with each other in a series of contradictions, laying themselves open to the same charge of want of consistency by their obstinate and one-sided view of the particular scheme they have made their hobby."

He knew how to use surveying equipment, and had a high threshold for jungle discomfort, but he had been done in by his own irresistible fantasy, one that ripened like sun-stroked fruit as he looked upon the deep green Darién from a lovely anchorage in Caledonia Bay. The survey he produced was the survey he subconsciously wanted: the survey the world wanted. With remarkable ease he exchanged critical thinking for the visionary kind, an ever so slight shift where human desire reshaped all that was seen, and all that wasn't, into a picture of perfect proof. Observer's bias was an impairment as baffling and insidious as infectious disease. Gisborne's "virtual blindness to facts" wasn't unusual—scientific men of his time saw the legs of industry striding down the darkest tributaries of the Amazon and up the sheerest, snowcapped Andean peaks—but hints of his susceptibility might have been noticed earlier. In the pages of his Darién book he vividly forecast the enormous will of nineteenth-century science, saying that before long his readers would experience the universal application of electricity, an enlightened time when "electricity will replace the pen, if not guide articulation, and will convert night into day."

That Gisborne was on the mark might be seen as confirmation of his unrealized brilliance. He was a visionary, just not a very good engineer.

SHORTLY AFTER STRAIN'S party left Sucubti on January 25, they were stopped in their tracks. Almost like a dream, five Indian men emerged from a curtain of green, directly upon their riverbank path. Given the soldiers' near certainty that an attack was imminent, it was almost a miracle no panic shots were fired. A surprised Strain was himself going to his sidearm when he realized they were not being engaged. He also recognized the party's leader.

He had been aboard the *Cyane,* a part of the treaty-making grand council that agreed neither to contest nor assist the Americans. But now, almost unaccountably, recorded Strain, "he offered to guide us to the Savana, and then provide us with canoes for our descent to Darién Harbor." Perhaps the Indians, seeing that his party had passed respectfully through their villages, had finally been won over. Or perhaps the man was simply an enterprising sort who wished to collect on the lieutenant's generous monetary offer but could do so only in the absence of his peers.

It was only three days across, Strain was told, a bit of news that certainly supported his decision to advance. The leader, who spoke some Spanish, also confirmed what Strain seemed to suspect but wouldn't let himself believe: that they were not on the Savana at all, nor a tributary of it, but rather the Chucunaque (pronounced "chew-koo-NAA-kay"). Once again, Strain's instincts were tested. His maps didn't show the Chucunaque River anywhere near their present position. On Cullen and Gisborne's maps it was dozens of miles to the east, separated from the Caledonia watershed by an unbroken range of mountains. Did he trust his fellow explorers, whose work had been endorsed by one of the most respected engineers in Europe, or those before him, who only moments ago he suspected might be poised to attack? At least temporarily he cast his lot with the newcomers. He ordered the call to march and for the first time in six days fell behind, placing the route-finding in another's hands.

For the day's duration they tramped in a westerly direction through cocoa and plantain groves, and over several hills, before finally arriving at a deep ravine. Their Indian guides insisted on returning to their homes but promised to come back the next morning with provisions. Troubled by their abrupt departure and still half wondering if they were walking into a trap, Strain took laborious

precautions to protect the camp against a night attack. In the morning the chief guide returned (with a largely new party, it turned out)
and led the expedition across two ranges of mountains, 800 and 600
feet high, respectively. No less anxious, Strain ordered Truxtun to
notch prominent trees along the route in case they were abandoned
and needed to find their way back.

Their trek was turning out to be nothing like the anticipated long,
level stride across open plain. Strain's belief that the worst topography of the isthmus was behind them proved painfully untrue. Ridge
after ridge offered a virtual free fall to a stony streambed. It was as if
the land were a well-veined leaf, a later explorer wrote, each vein a
watercourse and each space between them some malicious, saw-
toothed incline. The slippery reddish-yellow clay made firm footing
impossible. What little stamina they didn't spend toiling upward,
they wasted scrambling to catch themselves from falling. The simple
act of putting one foot in front of the other required unrelenting
concentration and self-discipline.

At the worst moments, Strain's junior officers had wondered if
the route was no route at all but an effort to prove what one of the
Caledonia chiefs had impatiently warned of: that the hills were
everywhere. The hills were God's design, Truxtun and Maury had
heard the old chief say, and such a design was evidence of what was
and wasn't intended on the isthmus. No gap existed, no soft spot
where God's will might be divined differently. They had interpreted
his protests as obstructionist. He would say anything to get rid of
them. The more the Indians had objected to the purported "discovery," the stronger the suspicion became that something was being
kept from them. There was still that feeling, that they were being
duped.

The blistering dawn-to-dusk pace felt spiteful. Their guides
passed across the same grinding landscape with an unfathomable
lightness, almost never stumbling or appearing to tire or get thirsty.

In observing his own sweat-soaked body and those of his hobbled men, Truxtun had ample evidence of an acclimatization gap neither he nor anyone else of a northern constitution could satisfactorily explain. Justly or not, agonizingly long stretches had passed without water. In scaling the high interior ridges they were drawn farther and farther away from the riverbed, a course that accentuated the party's gloomy feeling of isolation.

Eventually they came to a clearing where they passed beneath lush orchards bearing plantains and bananas. There were papaya, mango, and orange trees, and great fields of sugar cane, the fibrous stock of which is as sweet as candy. The cacao trees were over 30 feet high with nearly seamless stretches of large, bright-green oval leaves forming a dense, embowered shade. The rough, rust-red pod, within which was the edible bean, hung in great profusion, a shower of fruit growing every which way, even out from the bare trunk. In some cases the ripened plantains lay on the ground rotting in the damp. Other survey parties who followed Strain onto the isthmus would remark on the immense refreshment made from a plantain-rich "grand stew & roast." At Strain's insistence, as well as that of their guides (who hadn't returned with fruit as promised), they passed by.

As they struggled down the day's final descent, they encountered a new Indian contingent of five men. In Strain's estimation they almost certainly represented the Chucunas, or Kuna Bravo. Unlike their San Blas brethren, who escaped centuries of incursions by migrating over the Atlantic Divide to the coastal margins of the isthmus, the mainland Kuna had kept on the move in the interior, clinging to their ancestral home along Darién's rivers. The territory of the "wild Kuna" was vaguely delineated but long known to extend to the Gulf of San Miguel, along the tributaries of the Chucunaque. They traded with the San Blas and shared a similar tribal organization but were wholly independent. They were also culturally distinct, having successfully eluded the Spanish missionary influence.

Survival through appeasement didn't appeal to them. When Balboa crossed the isthmus in 1513, supported and guided by a thousand coastal Kuna, the inland chief Quarequa courageously rose to oppose him. The Spaniards routed him. Ever since, his descendants and those of the neighboring *cacique* Ponca had either fought or simply burrowed their way deeper into the endless folds of forest.

The Kuna Bravo, wrote an English colonel a decade earlier, were "exceedingly fierce and warlike . . . and of astonishing muscular power . . . and although in a savage state of darkness and ignorance, still of an intelligent and generous nature." They were expert naturalists, hunters and foragers, and none had a better understanding of jungle survival.

Then, as always, they had refused to permit strangers to pass through their country. Part of the reason was sovereignty—it was their land—but a finished road across, much less a gaping canal, threatened their control of a productive trade route. Dry goods and tobacco were delivered from one coast to the other solely by the Chucunas, the only ones truly familiar with the way across.

The leader, who chose not to offer his name, addressed a long speech to Strain. He refused Strain's request to pass through their territory, but precisely why, or whether he might actively resist the Americans' passage, was unclear. Strain's guide, who might have translated some of the remarks into Spanish, declined any involvement at all. Strain pleaded. How could he conciliate if he couldn't or wasn't allowed to understand? He appealed directly and indirectly, using hand gestures to prompt the Chucuna elder to also appeal. Without explanation the Sucubti interpreter shook them both off.

Strain thought he made out one key word: *chuli,* "no." It was just as likely he heard *dule,* a word that sounds similar and translates to "Kuna person." As with the previous council aboard the *Cyane,* Strain was more or less respectful, but when it was over he explained they were determined to proceed. "They offered no direct opposition," recalled Strain, noticing his translator's troubled expression. "But from that moment the conduct of our [original] guides underwent a change."

The march of the day, about 12 miles in all and ending at a major river, was the most excruciating yet. Some of the party were "thoroughly broken down" and Strain mercifully called several halts toward the end of the day. The seamen christened the ravine Devil's Own.

The New Granadian commissioners were in the worst condition, but little better was Edward Lombard, Strain's longtime friend. His thankless task was to pipe his silver boatswain's whistle each morning to rouse the men to the day's march. Perhaps to erase Strain's earlier doubts about his fitness for the passage, he had overextended himself during the seven days they had been out—at the high dividing pass near the Atlantic, he volunteered to shimmy up a tree to reconnoiter the countryside. He was already fatigued when a severe scorpion bite dropped him to his knees in Devil's Own. Lacking medical supplies, Strain's only treatment option was dosing Lombard with brandy—an antidote almost worse than poison for poor Lombard, a strict temperance man.

Lombard's "attack" was the only one of its type, but at day's end most of the men had been marked. Trekking in and out of rivers was causing fungal infections and circulatory problems in their feet. The white bottoms were bloodless, wrinkled, and tender, a condition later described as "warm-water-immersion foot." Walking was so agonizing, some had tried to march on the edges of their feet, seeking out scraps of foot tread that wouldn't make them wince each time their shoes, or what was left of them, struck the ground.

Itchy brown and reddish patches of fungus appeared where their haversacks rubbed against their backs, or high on the leg extending from the crotch. Others recorded bewildering symptoms of parasitic afflictions; certainly the most lurid of which was a searing pain on the epidermis of the penis head. Each brush against flannel felt like splintery glass.

Evening hours were spent stripping chiggers and ticks from their bodies, and the open fires burned dusk till dawn—not to keep off the insects, which couldn't be kept off, but to discourage what the party believed were the jaguars howling on the camp periphery.

In the morning when the men awoke, some found themselves weak and disoriented, their night clothing saturated with blood. The culprit, a vampire bat, excised such a tiny piece of flesh, and bit so surgically, a sleeping man almost never stirred. An anticoagulant in the bat's saliva produced a steady trickle of blood that flowed freely all night long.

AT SUNSET ON THE 26TH their camp was an island in a wide, unnamed river. Strain thought it the Iglesias. It was the only large river that ran off toward the Gulf of San Miguel from the Chucunaque, the river he supposedly had been on two days ago. He continued corroborating his position with the Gisborne maps, figuring that the engineer's errors were isolated to the Atlantic side of the isthmus, where his survey had been much briefer.

Close as they were, they were also dangerously low on provisions, Truxtun reported. Several of the men, each of whom was responsible for his individual food ration, had run out. Their ration was adequate for an average shipboard day but not a day in the jungle where they were man-hauling gear and expending up to 8,000 calories a day. They were already losing weight and starving for calories. According to the standard formula, they were likely losing anywhere between one and three pounds a day.

Strain asked the officers to sacrifice their food, "which they had more carefully used," and redistribute it in equal portions. The result, besides some of the first grumbling from his subordinates, wasn't demonstrably better: Collectively, they had one day's worth of provisions left.

The fruit they were surrounded by—easily digestible and loaded with carbohydrate, fluids, and essential vitamins and minerals—was their obvious salvation. Plantains, one of the most nutritious, carbohydrate-rich fruits in the world, was an almost perfect endurance food. Except it was off-limits. "The plantains and bananas were abundant in the vicinity of the camp," a pained Strain related, "but the Indians would neither sell nor give; and as I felt bound by my promise made to the chiefs . . . [I] await a greater emergency before supplying the party by force."

That evening Strain's guides announced they couldn't bring him the rest of the way and were going to return to Caledonia Bay immediately. No amount of persuasion could convince them otherwise. Their place would be taken by the Chucunas, who would guide Strain the remaining two days to the Savana River. They would also supply them with canoes to reach Darién Harbor.

The next morning the Sucubti guides left, but before doing so they refused Strain's request to deliver a letter to Captain Hollins. Having originally said he would bring Hollins verbal word of the shore party's whereabouts, the old Indian leader told Strain he had reversed his plans and would be going elsewhere, not getting to Caledonia until the following month. Strain, who had done his share of posturing back at the New York Ethnological Society on native peoples and their mind-set, was mystified. What were the guides' motives in caretaking for them this far? he openly wondered. A supposed personal interest in his and his party's safe passage—a reason the guide offered—was impossible to reconcile with what was happening. They were being left to the "most hostile and perhaps the most numerous [tribe] on the whole isthmus," Strain later wrote, and they were being refused much needed food—though there was a surplus of plantains and bananas everywhere they looked. As if to further distance themselves, the Sucubti refused to accept "recompense for their services," a disappointed Strain noted. Whatever good faith once existed was no longer. Before Strain had a chance to formally say goodbye, he added, they vanished into the forest.

Five Chucunas, the promised substitutes, made their dramatic appearance the same morning, "armed with their bows and steel-pointed arrows, which they use only in war." They were likely from Morti, a nearby village (though it was unseen by Strain) at the easternmost end of the Chucuna territory.

A few hours of hard travel took the party far afield of the river, at which point the Chucunas disappeared too. Strain waited an hour before deciding their guides—whom he said he suspected of treacherous intent—had "abandoned us." He ordered the party to retrace their steps to the river, where he called a "war council." Attended by his officers, in addition to the New Granadians, it was a military version of an open hearing, allowing the opinions of others to be expressed in an atmosphere approaching true democracy. The issue on the table wasn't whether they should return, but the route they should take forward. Should they pursue a compass heading in the same westerly direction their guides had been leading them—the supposed two-day route to the Savana River—or should they work their way down the river they were on, which, by the maps laid out before them, eventually emptied in Darién Harbor and the Gulf of San Miguel?

It was January 27 when Strain unfurled his maps on the ground and traced his finger up and down the isthmus. "The question the council was called upon to decide, was whether it was most expedient to march through the forest direct for the Savana, and thus incur the danger of perishing from thirst either in the march or among the mangrove swamps, which we were aware fringed its banks for more than forty miles above Darién Harbor, or to adopt the more cautious course of a tedious journey by the river on which we then were, and on the banks of which we expected to meet white inhabitants above the point at which the mangrove swamps and brackish water would be found," recorded Strain. "No proposition to return to the ship was made, and I believe that every one felt that nothing but a transit from sea to sea would satisfy the world as to the impracticability of the project for constructing a ship canal, and make our work complete.

"We had no guides, but we had on the other hand seven days hard march between us and the ship, and had, moreover, every reason to expect Indian hostility on our return. The moral effect of a retrograde movement upon our own party whose pride revolted at the idea of a failure, had its influence upon the decision. We had served out our last provisions; but up to that time we had always found plantains on the bank of the river, and had every reason to believe that the supply below would be ample for all our wants; for after the flagrant treachery of the Indians, we felt ourselves no longer bound by the stipulations made on board the *Cyane*."

Truxtun, Maury, Boggs, and the rest of the council voted unanimously to follow the river they were on. Strain brought the decision to the men. He knew they didn't wish to retrace their footsteps through Devil's Own; he also knew there was a natural bias to stay with the river, which provided water and a passageway. It had to end up in the Pacific eventually. It offered a sliver of sky.

The forest was much more uncertain. No different from their settler forebears, the majority saw the woods as the "most troublesome of growths." To allay their fears of hunger, Strain emphasized they would be free to help themselves at the orchards they passed. They had yet to fire a single bullet in the pursuit of a meal, he stressed, and several of the officers, himself included, were expert huntsmen. Finally, said Strain, a few days without food wouldn't be a terrible hardship. He invoked his experience in Brazil and added that strong men could live three days without food and still be comfortable.

Even eight days without food wouldn't make for much suffering. For the seamen volunteers of the *Cyane,* unaccustomed to traveling in the bush, much less living off it, it might not have been a point worth making. They really had no choice. Desertion, a regular event in foreign ports, was hardly an option in a hostile tropical wilderness. Survival lay with the group, with Strain. The order to march was given. Single file, they commenced.

Of course, the Indians had neither confirmed nor denied the river was the Iglesias, a name they undoubtedly didn't recognize. They had generically identified it only as *río grande,* or "great river." The "great river" was the Chucunaque. Two days earlier Strain had been on a tributary, the Sucubti. Unknowingly they were casting their lot with a tropical river described by a writer as one of the "most torturous known to geographers." The geographers might have characterized the river correctly, but only out of dumb luck. In point of fact the river wasn't *known* at all.

There was another thing. At the time of their council they were only five miles from the track Prevost's party had cut four weeks earlier (they had been even closer when in the woods where the Indians left them). They were mere hours from the open, well-marked *Virago* path and perhaps only a day and a half from the British food depot on the upper reaches of the Savana. Of course, Strain had yet to learn of Prevost or the track he cleared. Had he known, he certainly wouldn't have ordered the course of march he did. In going downriver, he was headed in the exact opposite direction.

8 / CHUCUNAQUE RIVER

There are no herds of ungulates, no cascades of or-
chids—just a thousand shades of green, an infini-
tude of shape, form, and texture that so clearly
mocks the terminology of temperate botany....
After just a fortnight on the trail, our passage began
to take on the tone of a dream. The Darién turned out
to be less a piece of terrain than a state of mind. Lost
in a forest, it is not the absolute number of days that
matters but rather the vast uncertainty that consumes
every moment.

AUTHOR AND ANTHROPOLOGIST WADE DAVIS
IN A MODERN ESSAY ABOUT A TREK THROUGH DARIÉN

R. USUCUNANTE

R. MORTI

Sassardi

Plantation

DEVILS STM.

R. ASNATI

Asnati

Plantation

CAPT PREVOSTS ROUTE

R. SUCUBTI

R. SUCUBTI

Sucubti

LA PAZ

Fort
ncipe

R. LARA

ennets
Rancho
GRENADIAN
PRESIDIO

R. TUYRA OR CHUCUNAQUE

R. SAVANA

R. ARCTI

R. YLESIA

R. CHICO

DARIEN HARBOR

La Palma

Chapigana

January 27, 1854

8° 51′ N, 77° 58′ W
Upper Chucunaque

I N THE BOOKS STRAIN POSSESSED there were few historical references to the Chucunaque. Neither Cullen nor Gisborne had reached the river, and though they offered plausible descriptions, their prose was brief and too general to be helpful. The Spanish had supposedly explored the Chucunaque valley, and even built a fort on its upper portion, yet their maps showed the river's source, course, and position well off. Even the Chucunaque's published character was inconsistent with what Strain saw: It was described as a "precipitous river, with numerous rocky falls."

Instead the riverbed fell along a comparatively mild grade. The writhing meanders were characteristic of a powerful floodplain river where the fall line is negligible and the channel wanders the full width of the soft valley floor, carving a path of least resistance around boulders, treefalls, and the flood debris of innumerable mountain tributaries. Unlike most rivers, where the sinuous meanders mirror one another, the Chucunaque was all chaos, the product of the freakishly large volume of rain that fell on the Darién each year. With an annual rainfall of over 200 inches a year, the Atlantic Divide is one of the rainiest regions on earth. Eventually Strain would conclude that the switchbacks doubled the length of the river, meaning 70 miles of isthmian gain took some 140 miles by the course of the river.

But when Strain was starting out on January 27, his biggest concern was the river's depth, not its length. The high water forced them to leave the bed and clear a path along the overgrown banks. Over the next four days they advanced down river anywhere from 5 to 10 miles a day. It was slow going, to be sure, but they couldn't be far and food was abundant.

Between fishing, bird hunting, and foraging deserted plantain and banana groves, there were few complaints at camp each night. On a full stomach, and with the reassuring presence of the wide coffee-brown river beside them, a mood of optimism prevailed. Even the nightly infestation of mosquitoes and sand flies was treated with humor. In the expedition log kept by Samuel Kettlewell, the officers christened an early river camp the Camp of the Mosquitoes Elephantes.

On the next day, their twelfth since leaving the ship, they found themselves lost. They had attempted to shorten their route by running compass courses across the bends of the river. What was a reliable technique on most rivers proved a disaster on the Chucunaque. In one of its improbable jogs, the river abruptly veered east and stayed east on one of its longer bends. One day turned into two and then three as Strain led the others through swamps and a viny understory booby-trapped with bands of *pinello*, a pineapple-like bush with slashing, swordlike leaves. They had gotten used to picking up what they needed as they went. Along the cultivated banks of the upper river the supply had been unlimited. But in the heavy, snaring bush, there were no plantations.

Water was also distressingly scarce, and by the second day Strain was taking emergency precautions. They marched under severe water rations, and to ensure the supply wouldn't be raided, he ordered the last remaining canteens put in the officers' possession. Morale sank. Finding Strain by the watch fire, Kettlewell asked him to name the camp. Noche Triste, replied Strain, "sad night." The next camp, little better, was dubbed Sorrowful Camp.

Lost and suffering, the party's pace nearly stalled. One day only two miles were made, Strain lamented. Ironically, that estimate was probably high since the only way mileage could be accurately tallied was with a surveyor's tape, something he was without. Prevost had discovered a startlingly large overestimation error in his own travels. For every three miles they *believed* they had traveled in Darién forests they had actually only gone a third of that.

In the beginning the greatest distress seemed psychological. Just the mere fact of being away from the river, which the party saw as their salvation and Strain called "their guide and support," was troubling. In subsequent days the physical symptoms began to show. Lombard and the Granadians were failing—the former, Strain thought, from a kind of nutritional shock. For several days the party had subsisted on an almost exclusively vegetarian diet which, in Lombard's case, was a dramatic change for a veteran who had lived his whole life on a shipboard ration of red meat and hardtack. Whether from malnourishment, dehydration, or an infection of his scorpion sting, he showed worrisome signs of mental unbalance. In one instance he gloomily wandered off into the forest on an unexplained and apparently undirected absence for hours.

Even Truxtun collapsed after relieving an exhausted Strain from his trail-breaking duties. In consequence of the fatigue problems Strain announced a new strategy: From now on pairs of men would work jointly in cutting the track. The rest of the party, which heretofore had stacked up miserably behind the leaders, was encouraged to rest. At a point when sufficient headway had been made and a lengthy path cleared, they would march. The illusion of steady headway might be enough to uplift the men, Strain hoped. After an hour the overtaxed trailbreakers would be replaced with a fresh pair. The weary night watches, no longer seeming necessary, were also eliminated.

At midday on February 2 Strain decided to reverse his course, heading east-northeast, if only to regain the river and relieve his party's growing desperation. In the absence of plantation fruits, Strain continued to forage for edible wild plants and educate the party about their usefulness. The arboreal items weren't mere curiosities, he insisted, but worthy staples in and of themselves. Thus the *trupa* palm, a ubiquitous species with an egg-shaped nut, was announced as having a "refreshing" acid pulp and a kernel of an oily but highly nutritious nature. Strain said he had satisfactorily fed himself on nothing but the palm fruit for an entire week in the Brazilian jungle. The men ate the fruit, but their skepticism wasn't much diminished. Even among well-fed men the idea of subsisting for any length of time on berries and nuts smacked of fantasy.

On February 3, they finally stumbled upon the lost river. Strain saw it first, passing word on down the line. The relief—the men let out a booming round of cheers—was intense. Their prospects, which seemed to fluctuate by the hour, rose again. When Truxtun, their best fisherman, took to the riverbank he landed six catfish. That night with the moon glow spilling over the river portal, there was a sense, Strain wrote, they had dodged their last threat and were nearing the borders of civilization.

The jungle, for the first time in days, didn't feel like an adversary. Winthrop wasn't present, but at another time he captured the fleeting mood perfectly: "The admirable compensations of Nature are nowhere more perfectly perceived than in a tropical night. The day may have been remorseless, but the night is a kind restorer. It is not only a change to the senses, not merely a different temperature, not merely that the crushed air revives, and the atmospheric particles which have been bullied by the staring sun into a shrinking isolation, now awake to sociality and glad circulation, rushing here and there like children released. But there is also a spiritual effect in the tropical night." Winthrop was right. The dreamy moonlight—at least as it illuminated the reclaimed river—was the sweetest balm any of the men could imagine, sweeter than food or water. Hope, knew Strain, soothed the harshest sores.

THOUGH STRAIN DIDN'T know it, Winthrop was fine. He had made it back to the ship not long after he and Strain's party had lost each other on January 22. The separation had troubled him, just as it had Strain. His opportunity to be part of the historic crossing party was all but lost, and for that he blamed Strain. He had heard the lieutenant's "recall" shots but incorrectly believed they were coming from upstream. Part of his rationale was that Strain had originally told them to reassemble in the streambed once they had ascended the steep ravine. He had no inkling, he said, that Strain was looking for another trail or that he had given up on the Caledonia streambed. As a consequence, he, Holcomb, and the others headed upstream, continually expecting "every moment to overtake the rest of the party." They didn't stop until they reached the summit a day later, at which point, lacking provisions and a compass, they were forced to retrace their steps back down the ravine all the way to the harbor beach.

How each party might so differently interpret the direction from which their signaling shots were fired didn't make much sense. Strain said he heard return fire come from upriver. Winthrop said he heard Strain's shots "tending up the stream & above us."

Both men couldn't be right, and the fact that each thought the other knew where they were but had chosen to disregard the other deepened the misunderstanding. There might have been an innocent explanation. Ricocheting off the trunks, branches, and leaves of dense understory, loud noises in the jungle often appear to be coming from several different directions at once. Modern naturalists have discovered birds who routinely use the scrambled acoustics to lose predators. Gunshots, a reliable way of locating one another in northern forests, weren't at all dependable at Darién, where low-frequency sound waves (like blowing into a conch shell or thumping upon a tree's buttress root) were far less likely to be distorted. It was simply a language nobody knew.

Winthrop returned to the ship on the 24th—about the same time Strain had reached Sucubti and was beginning his passage toward Devil's Own. On January 25, a day later, Winthrop hastily left again. Under orders from an alarmed Hollins, Winthrop marched directly to the canyon where he had last seen the others. Another contingent was dispatched with him carrying orders to trace the eastern branch of the Caledonia—the one Strain and Winthrop had written off—to try again the route popularized by Gisborne. With the joint English and French party off investigating the same route, Hollins feared their rivals knew something they didn't. One of the *Cyane*'s junior officers, Lieutenant Charles Fauntleroy, led the return group.

"When we arrived at the forks of the river," Winthrop wrote, "the Officer in command of the main body, who had been instructed to detach certain men &c with our relief for Strain allowed a personal jealousy to interfere with his duty & diminished our number & stores. He is the only man aboard ship who I do not regard as a friend and him I can only treat with bare civility."

On January 25 Winthrop set off with Holcomb, Dr. Bird, and four men. The rest of the extremely well-armed party, eleven in total, went with Fauntleroy. Winthrop carried extra shoes, cutlasses, blankets, and food, all critical needs for Strain and his party, but how many men and how many more supplies were held back, he never specified. Nor did he detail which was the greater priority: the rescue or his own crossing. Winthrop's orders were curiously worded, calling for him to seek Lieutenant Strain but also to "cross over to the Pacific if possible by an unexplored branch of the River Caledonia."

A day later, the 26th, Winthrop's party arrived at Strain's camp on the other side of the divide and discovered his January 24 note explaining his future course. Amazingly, they were only forty-eight hours behind them. Feeling it would have been useless to follow Strain's course down the stream—which Strain had speculated was a tributary of the Savana—Winthrop and Holcomb elected to cut a diagonal on their course, "thinking that we might fall in with traces of the party." They didn't, despite hard travel that day and the next over a series of thickly vegetated ridges. On the 27th they reached the 3,000-foot summit ridge where, by clearing away trees, they saw the *Cyane* bearing north by east some 12 miles away.

A lengthy descent brought them to an encouraging southwesterly flowing torrent. "Here we camp feeling absolutely certain that it is a branch of the Savana . . . [and that we are] almost certain of soon overtaking our party," Winthrop recorded. The next two days brought "wild and romantic scenery" and another major river but no traces of Strain. The new river wound to every point in the compass, but generally ran parallel to the line of the isthmus, flowing between the ridges. Having "reached a point beyond which it was not safe to venture without risking our lives," they turned around on the 30th. Provisions were dwindling dangerously, and they were simply unwilling to gamble on the options before them. It was one thing to descend the river in a canoe, Winthrop thought, but pursuing the torturous overland line along the river's banks was madness.

Another possibility—traversing the dense forests and lofty hills to the west—required seven to ten days of strenuous trail clearing. They had already endured plenty, including driving night rains and the bullet ant's painful sting. The former had Winthrop "in chills for an hour and a half." The ant he described as a species "as spiteful and venomous as emancipated niggers." His notes are unspecific, but the landmarks he mentions suggest they followed the unmapped and un-explored Chaiti River valley out of the mountains and had indeed, as Winthrop suspected, merged with the Chucunaque.

He saw no sign of the lost party because Winthrop's route brought him *downstream* of them. Unknowingly they had leap-frogged ahead. The day of the 31st, as Winthrop hurriedly retraced his steps back upriver, was the day Strain's party had veered *away* from the Chucunaque in their disastrous attempt to find a shortcut around the river's bends. Winthrop, with his supply of blankets, food, and shoes, probably missed intercepting Strain by only a few hours.

Winthrop returned to the *Cyane* on February 2, "used up" and unable to prevail upon Hollins to send out another relief party. News was fresh of the *Virago*'s disaster, and the English, French, and American commanders were debating how to respond to the mur-ders. There were four major vessels and some nine hundred men now standing by at Caledonia Bay. In addition, Colonel Agustín Co-dazzi had arrived with two hundred convicts to serve as a trail-clearing work party. Several attempts at finding the gap had thus far failed, and as yet nobody had found their way over the divide except for the newly returned Winthrop and the missing Strain party.

Ultimately, Gisborne's plan won out. He persuaded the joint leadership, including Hollins, to hold off on any new mission until he and a small, newly assembled party had a chance to cross. Gis-borne said he had managed to gain the confidence of an American-educated Kuna named Robinson. The latter had not been part of Strain's grand council aboard the *Cyane*, nor had he been known to the Americans until after Strain's party had begun the crossing. Gis-borne had succeeded in assuring Robinson that a retribution mission was not planned; he and everyone else understood that the murder of the *Virago* crew was a tragic misunderstanding. In exchange for £100 sterling, Robinson said he would lead Gisborne safely across.

Gisborne argued that any additional parties might "excite" the Kuna, causing them to doubt his peaceful intentions and oppose his crossing. With his success, he said, lay the best prospects of gathering intelligence on Strain's whereabouts. Hollins agreed to withhold further rescue attempts until he heard back from Gisborne. The Englishman left on February 7, but the expected quick confirmation never came. As late as February 25 there remained no definitive word. True to his word, Hollins refrained from sending anyone else across the isthmus. Winthrop had been the last, best chance.

Onboard Winthrop's moods changed as rapidly as the passing tropical clouds. On the day of Gisborne's departure he wrote a colleague in New York: "The canal is impossible—the Isthmus is a great mass of Mts. and all the representations of the English Engrs. upon which these expeds were sent are totally false . . . you can speculate in P.R.R. Co. [Panama Railroad Company] or anything else, with perfect certainty that no Darién Canal will disturb you." Two weeks later, with rumors spreading that his comrades had been devoured by wild beasts, he wrote despairingly: "It is a strange feeling for me to contemplate the possibility of the loss of our whole party & to think that if Holcomb & I had not been separated from them, there was much more chance of their safety. Why should five out of the 27 have been saved by the merest accident & the remainder perished, as we fear, by the most dreadful of deaths. Life is of very little value to me, as I shall never accomplish anything in it, but there is something very desperate in the tho't of a death in this wilderness."

UPON RETURNING TO THE river on February 3, Strain came to an unhappy conclusion: They were likely on the Chucunaque, not the

Iglesias, as he had previously thought. His maps had grossly misplaced its location on the isthmus, but the twisted course and inexhaustible length could make it no other. Presenting the bad news to his party, Strain softened it with a solution: They would build a boat, something he had successfully done years ago on the Paranapanema in Brazil, despite not having "a single nail, screw, or any oakum or pitch." A large dugout canoe, the best option, was impossible without a cutting axe (theirs had been damaged), so instead they would fashion planks from a few medium-sized trees, joining them with wooden wedges and clamps. With their comparatively large labor force, they could craft a serviceable launch in only a day or two, Strain promised. Not surprisingly, the footsore men heartily endorsed the plan and went to work.

Strain's instincts were impressive. At a critical time, he found a project to unify the party, one that a working seaman could appreciate and feel well suited to. Modern jungle experts regularly cite the importance of broad themes, not quick fixes, in successful survival leadership: firm but nimble thinking, sensible planning, and strong group dynamics. Though Strain had not had the benefit of any formal training, his strategies were strong. He had successfully adapted much of the party to a vegetarian diet and was following a river downstream, a course that increased the likelihood they would find settlements and rescuers.

As a commander, he had endeared himself to the men by simply working as hard, if not harder, than anyone else. To date he had led the party most of the way while consistently carrying 20 to 30 pounds more weight and eating less. In the Indian country he kept many of the late watches too, seemingly requiring less sleep than the rest, who frustratingly reported feeling "seedy" and unrefreshed in the morning. None of the men faulted his principal decisions—to accept the guidance of the Sucubti Indians and to proceed down the Chucunaque. His decision to put the choice of a river or overland route before the greater group showed common sense and a willingness to build consensus. The latter tactic, one of the most important skills in a group survival situation, was something the younger, more solo-minded Strain might have easily disregarded.

The expeditionary objective—crossing the isthmus—was not on their menu of choices. The spirit was unabashedly in the manner of Balboa's second crossing, which is far less popularly known than his South Seas expedition. On that trip Balboa successfully crossed a second time, portaging the planks and materials of a Pacific exploring fleet he hoped to build. The men followed without reservation, in part, it was said, because Balboa himself carried the heaviest of the hand-hewn planks on his own back. Shortly after they arrived a flood swept away their provisions and most of the man-hauled lumber. Many of the details are lost, but modern historians now place Balboa's fabled shipbuilding camp on the lower Chucunaque, perhaps 50 miles below where Strain's smaller but no less daunting endeavor was under way.

ALMOST AS SOON AS THEY started, Strain seemed to recognize he was asking too much from his weakened party.

Crafting a boat from scratch required immense manual labor. Over the course of a day Strain oversaw as his party progressed— two planks 24 feet long were split out and partially hewn. But the pace was deadly slow. Their tools were woefully insufficient, their failing state apparent in the way the tree felling exhausted them. Even a rudimentary vessel would likely cost them weeks, not days.

When news came a day later that someone sighted a stand of balsa trees nearby, Strain altered his plan. Balsa wood was light and especially buoyant. Derived from a tall tree with smooth gray bark, *balsa* was a Spanish word meaning "raft." Strain built a raft. They only needed to arrive, after all, not explore oceans.

The biggest advantage to a raft was the speed and relative ease with which it could be assembled. No clamps or wedges were necessary for splitting the timber. The disadvantage proved to be their limited supply of balsa. The wood-collecting parties came up short. Their 10-foot-long raft, with logs bound to one another using plaited bark strips, was far too small to support the entire party.

Strain gave preference to the most feeble; the rest of the party followed by the riverbank, scouting for more balsa as they went. With Truxtun placed in command, the raft pushed off at 4 P.M. carrying the two New Granadian commissioners, engineer Boggs, Kettlewell, and one of the crew of the *Cyane*.

Only a few hours later Strain heard the distress blast of a firearm and rushed back to the river. A bank-to-bank logjam blocked their passage. Two massive trees had fallen across the Chucunaque from opposite shores. Evidently the seasonal floods had either undercut the behemoths or simply scoured free the little soil that supported them. Debris was everywhere.

There seemed to be no alternative but to abandon the raft. The deep water made disassembly difficult, and the scarped banks were too steep for them to carry the logs, even light ones, up and over the impasse. Breaching the deadfall with machetes might take days. Decades later an American expedition equipped with motorboats and dozens of laborers would need several sticks of dynamite to crack open a passage through a similar obstruction.

The river's character stepped forward: the slashing bends, the maddening propensity to dam itself. Sometimes the river volume trickled to almost nothing. At junctions with her larger tributaries, the Chucunaque might easily appear the lesser of the two, beginning a new round of doubts about the river's true identity.

Another option had been teasingly taken away. Strain said he couldn't risk any more raft descents, much less ones that serviced his most infirm marchers, until he was more certain what lay ahead.

They would have to march. The party's other trials, which had been temporarily overridden in the raft-building enthusiasm, came back with a fuller, more demoralizing force.

Two days earlier they had run out of tobacco, and already they were fighting the aftereffects: spiking anxieties, increased hunger pangs, and low energy. A seaman could perform astoundingly well with few inducements and no luxuries, but withholding tobacco from him seemed like a punishment. Strain began to see a rash of careless and even undisciplined mistakes. The worst was nothing more than a petty offense, but the ramifications were huge. A seaman had taken the company's fishing hook without permission—Truxtun, an expert fisherman, had been the only one allowed to use it—and clumsily mangled it. Freshwater fish, the lower Chucunaque's most plentiful and accessible food source and an item Strain counted on to sustain them in what increasingly appeared to be the widely uninhabited country ahead, were now beyond their reach.

An officer's journal extract on the 6th: "Proceeded down stream about a quarter of a mile, when finding a place to camp, built a fire and spread our blankets in the mild moonlight. We all feel down-hearted to-night, being without anything to eat, and not having eaten enough each man for the six or eight days to make one good meal; our clothes all in pieces, and nearly all almost shoeless and bootless. Have no idea where we are, nor, of course, when we shall reach the Pacific. The sick almost discouraged, and ready to be left in the woods to take their chances. I would freely give twenty dollars for a pound of meat, but money is of no use here."

Over the next week the suffering worsened. They hadn't seen a banana or plantain plantation in weeks. Apparently there would be no more until "civilization," however far away that might be. Thin soups were made from whatever small game Strain shot. "We sustained life principally on the acid covering of palm nuts," Strain wrote. They ate them by the bushel, the plum-sized, dark red fruit appearing in bunches anywhere from five hundred to four thousand in number.

The palm variety, as Strain knew, offered superb benefits: the waxy flesh was substantive and had a high content of oil, protein, and vitamins. Reasonably refreshing in taste and highly filling, the fruit was seen as a godsend. For men whose haversacks were empty of provisions, its sheer quantity reassured.

But the daily gorging—one of the camps was happily called Nut Camp—was beginning to reveal disturbing side effects: The extreme quantity of consumed pulp overtaxed their digestive systems, which couldn't process the fiber overload and left many with extreme constipation. The oil's deceptively harsh acids dissolved their tooth enamel, the hardest substance in the human body. The salvational effects of the *trupa* were (like everything else) illusory, only a teasing procrastination before much more intense privation.

February 12: "Want of proper food began to tell severely upon the physique of party," wrote Strain, "and each day out marches became shorter. Halted early in afternoon, on account of the debility of the Granadians, not having made more than 2 miles."

With Lombard in deep distress, and the party reduced to firing rounds into trees to dislodge high clusters of unrecognizable fruit, Strain felt everyone edging to the point of no return. He organized a collection party to find wood for a small raft. An advance party could proceed quickly to the villages downstream and return with canoes and provisions for the rest of the party. The river, wider and less banked on the section they were now following, appeared less liable to throw up a barrier. Balsa couldn't be found and hadn't apparently been seen since the 6th, but a similar species was cut and brought to the water's edge. Strain found the wood shared almost the same specific gravity as water. In other words, the timber floated, but only by itself. The tiniest additional weight submerged the log. Another possibility, shredding the bark off the *parama* tree and fashioning a thin-hulled, bathtub-shaped native craft, he dismissed out of hand. To Strain's mind, the craft were almost guaranteed to overturn, thus wetting their ammunition and rifles—the two things that gave them the best chance of survival.

That night, at Camp 24, they foraged a plant that looked teasingly like wild spinach. It had large leaves, triangular with toothed edges. Debate over its suitability ended, Strain recalled, when one of the party said that hogs ate it and "if it was good enough for hogs, it was good enough for men." It was true that the young tips and leaves of pigweed, or lamb's quarters, were edible and often boiled as a potherb by early colonial settlers. But they had misidentified the plant. Shortly after supper the entire party suffered terrible waves of nausea, then fits of vomiting.

A decision had to be made. Many were sick, weak, and severely hobbled. In looking ahead to their prospects, Strain recognized that their survival depended on a fast march. They would never reach help at the rate they were going, with ailing individuals determining the pace they could go. The only way to protect the party as a whole was to send the strongest ahead to get help and have the rest follow as best they could.

Strain had wanted to keep the group together in part because of his concerns about an Indian attack. They were clear of that risk, he knew, but he also had a personal bias. Two of the most ill men, Boggs and Lombard, were personal friends. He had convinced Boggs to come with him. It was a last hurrah for Strain's former Springfield, Ohio, classmate, since he would soon be leaving the Coast Survey for a far more settled life. He was engaged to be married. Lombard he hadn't been able to say no to. And the New Granadians represented another level of anxiety: They were diplomats whose health and safety had been entrusted to him.

On the morning of the 13th "I called the party together, and stating my intention to advance in person in search of canoes and provisions, called for volunteers," he wrote. Of the half dozen who responded, Strain selected Avery, Golden, and Wilson, "whose appearance seemed to promise the most physical endurance." Wilson was a landsman; Golden an adventurous young seaman who served with Strain on an earlier cruise; and Avery a tough outdoorsman who had cut his teeth on the Atrato, a similarly intractable river valley to the east.

The remaining party was put under the command of Truxtun. Maury, who hadn't seemed to suffer a single bad day since they had been out, was the second in charge. Ideally Maury would have gone with Strain. But the feverish Truxtun had struggled, and by keeping the fit Maury with him Strain was ensured a strong command. If Truxtun faltered and became gravely ill, Maury was a successor the men could accept.

Strain believed the party he left at Parting Camp was far from helpless. Despite their hardships and exposure, the majority could get along. Nor were they without resources. Their firearms were almost all in good condition and their ammunition abundant and dry. Strain left behind the best compass and the double-barreled fowling piece.

"I did not leave exhausted and dying men to recruit their strength with a few days rest," wrote Strain, who kept two carbines, two pistols, Avery's Sharps rifle, two machetes, and a pocket compass. He believed the party would rebound with both rest and food, as it had done before. He scouted the nearby woods and found them filled with palm nuts and small game. The nearest settlement, he predicted, was less than a week away. He expected Truxtun to lead a steady march once the main party felt restored. Their progress would keep their minds focused and hopeful, Strain thought, while the advance party could take on the burden of a breakneck pace. The logic was sound.

On the day the group split, Strain and his three volunteers tallied

18 miles in the day's march, easily the most ground covered in a single day for the trip. Tellingly, the same stretch took the main party four agonizing days and left them in a condition Strain wouldn't believe possible. Truxtun, Maury, and the journal keeper Kettlewell dubbed their stopping point Hospital Camp.

9 / LIFE and DEATH

In the tropics there is no gradual transition from dark to light and from light to dark. The sun rises and sets with alarming haste.

FROM *TROPICAL NATURE*,
BY ADRIAN FORSYTH AND KEN MIYATA

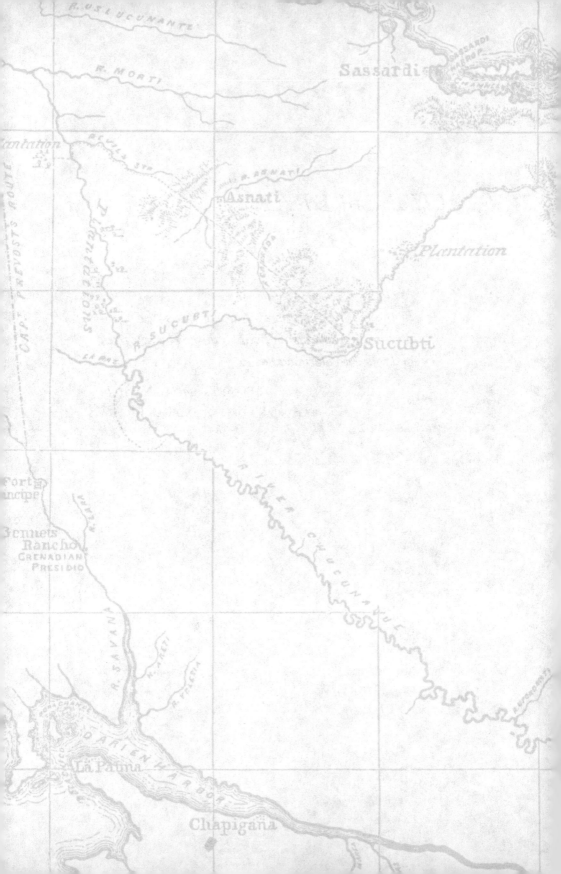

February 17, 1854

8° 28′ N, 77° 54′ W
Hospital Camp

A S HE WALKED ALONG the high riverbank, Truxtun could
see by the machete-cropped vegetation that Strain had come
before him. It was easy to understand why he had selected
the site: The shoreline looped out, offering a wide clearing and an
unbroken view down a long stretch of river. The effect was liberat-
ing, as though they were astride a big body of water and had a little
breathing room between them and the draping, double-canopy forest. Tendrils of late afternoon sunshine spilled to the forest floor, the
light rushing through the gap in the tree ceiling like water over a
falls. Truxtun and Maury were reminded of an equally striking over-
look at the beginning of their river descent—Camp Beautiful, Strain
called it.

The officers and men began to separate for their different camps
when Maury discovered a note Strain had left behind. Truxtun, the
new acting commander, drew the group around him to read the message word for word:

Dear Truxtun—We encamped here the night we left you [Mon-
day night]. *Look out for a supply of palm-nuts, as they appear to*

grow scarce as we descend. We are off at once, and hope to make
a very long march to-day. This river appears to me more and more
like the "Iglesias," and I have strong hopes of popping out sud-
denly in Darien Harbor. You may rely on immediate assistance, as
I will not lose one moment.
    Your friend, I.G.S.

Truxtun didn't even finish before the party erupted in a booming
round of cheers. For the seventeen men left behind, the end of the
ordeal seemed imminent. Once in Darién Harbor, Strain would be
able to get help and supplies from the *Virago*, which the party knew
from previous discussions in Cartagena would be waiting to assist
any of the exiting survey parties. A perpetual lookout began, each
man training eyes and ears in a downriver direction awaiting Strain's
return. A few days later their vigilance seemed rewarded. When a
loud blast exploded somewhere in the distance, several of the men
identified the noise as a ship's cannon, a report meant to assure them
that Strain was safely on board the *Virago* and on his way back.

But the days collected without further word, and the realization
began to settle in that he hadn't popped out in Darién Harbor. In the
meantime they hadn't moved. In part they expected to see Strain,
which made their own progress less than critical. But they were also
recovering. The four-day march to their present position had pushed
many to their physical and emotional limit. Just two days before being jolted back to life with the reading of Strain's note, Kettlewell
warned in the journal, "The necessity for the advance of Captain
Strain becomes the more evident as we proceed, and is displayed in
the frequent breaking down of the men, the slowness and constant
halts during the march, and the increasing suffering, attributable to
our diet of acid nuts, the fibres of which, remaining undigested, produce painful effects."

Now, after rallying momentarily, they sank again. The abrupt changes in fortune were maddening, striking at moments when they were least anticipated. A heaven-sent day in which they spit-roasted a wild pig would be followed by several others where nothing but nuts and berries were turned up. Men found themselves revived one day, prostrate with sores and nausea the next.

The inability to find food, specifically game, was mystifying. The wild lushness of the jungle seemed, by logic, a worthy indication of a surrounding bounty. But the truth was that the understory, particularly the lowland understory of the Chucunaque, was home to comparatively few large game creatures. Winthrop had recorded a plentiful supply of game during his rescue bid, including "wild turkeys, a deer, monkeys, ducks, and tracks of wild hog, tigers & tapirs," but he had been on the mountainous Atlantic slope where the wildlife disbursement and ecological character of the jungle was nothing like the lower Chucunaque. Even the ubiquitous palm nuts had, as Strain warned, grown increasingly scarce.

Though they continued to hold out hope and hunt both day and night, the anticipated game jackpot didn't exist. Any native game was either well obscured in the "visual confusion of the forest" or beyond firing range in the highest canopy.

On February 23, after a week of triage at Hospital Camp, caregivers such as journal keeper Samuel Kettlewell were almost as weary as the sick. His day's entry read: "Holmes still unable to walk. [Seaman Benjamin] Harrison had a chance at a piccary, but unfortunately his cap missed. . . . Harrison slept out in a ravine during the night to watch for game, but obtained nothing."

Almost daily firearms were heard, raising hopes that someone was looking for them. Sometimes the blasts were muffled, other times more indistinct, like the crack of a musket. Always they responded by blasting back with return fire, at which point the communication would end. The sound they mistook for Strain's signaling wasn't gunfire but falling timber. The giant lowland trees, shallow-rooted and often hollowed out and rotten due to the work of saprophytic fungi, termites, and wood-boring beetles, fell so steadily a later Navy explorer was reminded of a distant battle he could not see.

On February 26, ten days after they arrived, the party broke camp and marched (as Strain had always intended them to do). The day was a disaster and ended only a half mile after it began. Truxtun's decision to let his men stay so long at Hospital Camp had backfired. Almost certainly he had done the humane thing, but they had lost the necessary, highly metronomic rhythm of the march. By allowing them to pine for Strain, he realized, he had diminished his own authority. They had lost much of their will to go on.

Kettlewell, in the official log, tried to put the best face on the effort. "Although the distance attained was small, an object was gained in removing the party from a camp which had been so long occupied," he wrote. The new camp, Hospital Camp 2, was sited well below a major rapid, "the noise of which would have intercepted the sound of guns, which we still hoped to hear from Darién Harbor."

The sick now suffered from a range of bug-borne diseases and infections. In a prolonged exposure scenario where individuals traveled through high-risk tropical wilderness without protective repellent, adequate night shelter, or internally taken prophylactic medicine, contracting a mosquito-spread illness such as yellow fever or malaria was almost guaranteed. Early-stage malaria, symptomatic as fatigue and body aches in as little as a week, was widespread. The severity of the symptoms would have varied, but the sequence of chills, fever, and sweating was common to all—as was the disease's signature habit of seeming to dim only to reoccur.

Boils had also appeared on several of the men, an indication of infection, and skin fungus was common. Scrapes and cuts, unavoidable in the thorny underbrush, couldn't be kept clean or adequately covered. Others reported a strange worm of sorts embedded under the surface of the skin, and covered over like a blind boil. "As to the manner in which it was deposited no information could ever be obtained," wrote Kettlewell, "but it appeared to grow rapidly, in some subsequent cases attaining the length of one inch, and was extremely painful, especially when in motion."

Their tormentor was the botfly, a larval parasite transported by mosquitoes. Getting under their skin, either through a fresh bite or existing sores, the larvae is initially unnoticeable but becomes larger and extremely painful as it fattens on human tissue. River bathing produced the most excruciating episodes because the maggot, which employs a snorkel-like apparatus to breathe, feels its air supply shut off and begins to writhe, using its sharp anal hooks to mobilize. They had likely been carrying around the botflies for weeks, their famished bodies more than adequate for the needs of parasites. Crude attempts at removal, while psychologically satisfying, did them more harm than good. The portions of the maggot they couldn't excise with either their fingernails or knife blades rotted beneath their skin, leading to still further infection.

By March 3, and in the continued absence of Strain, the group's discipline began to falter. He had been gone nineteen days. Quarrels began to break out over the few scraps of food they were able to forage, and several men, apparently urged on by the mutinous New Granadian commissioner Castillo, formed a plan to flee and return to the ship. Separate of that plan, Lombard and William Parks were discovered missing. The two seamen slipped out of the camp early in the morning without permission, taking with them blankets and their cooking utensils.

"It was supposed that they intended to desert, and attempt, by following up the river, to regain the *Cyane*," wrote Kettlewell in the day's journal. Lombard's idea was actually quite a bit more desperate. They wouldn't retrace their steps immediately but instead would hide in the vicinity of Hospital Camp, waiting like vultures until their shipmate Holmes died. When the party left, they would sneak back and dig up the corpse, using his flesh to nourish them for the long trip back.

The turn to cannibalism, given the sustained level of suffering and the dwindling food supply, wasn't unanticipated. Shortly before departing the main party, Strain had warned them that when the journey was concluded they should have nothing to regret or blush for. "That, rather than any disgraceful expedient should be resorted to, for sustaining life, I would willingly see every man of the party dead at my feet."

Strain, Truxtun, and others were familiar with the gruesome story of the whaling ship *Essex,* an intrigue that had gripped the nation some decades earlier and was fresh again in people's minds with the publication of Melville's *Moby-Dick* in 1851. There were innumerable stories of shipwrecks on distant foreign shores where men had survived on the bones of others. But more vivid and current was the harrowing story of the Donner party. In 1847, only six years earlier, members of that transcontinental, California-bound party had resorted to an "outrage against human nature" after becoming pinned down in the high Sierra snows.

Though the Donner party was a civilian-led enterprise, the doomed expedition offered some eerie parallels. They were a large migrant party who found themselves misled by an irresponsible promoter (whose supposed shortcut through the Utah wilderness proved anything but) and failed by assorted rescue missions. Lacking strong leadership, the party seemed quick to give in to the famine. When the suggestion was first made of "one dying so the rest could live," they had been three days without food. That almost noble-sounding proposition was followed by murder and a gluttonous butchering of the dead. It was an appalling story, with the letters and diaries of the expedition appearing in every newspaper of every capital city, from America to Europe.

Of course, in the purely biologically driven jungle the act of cannibalism was a rather ordinary occurrence. Myriad insects devoured their young or their mates. The biological imperative of the scorpion or lion was not shaded by questions of morality or the way a species was supposed to behave. The word *cannibalism* originated from the Spanish name for the Carib—Caribales or Canibales—a West Indian tribe whom seamen feared as man-eaters. Cannibalism and the jungle environment seemed to go hand in hand.

Naval men were quick to point out that the human incidents had been limited to merchant vessels or whaling ship wrecks, whose crews were perceived as morally inferior to government lads. To anyone's direct knowledge a Navy-led expedition had never resorted to cannibalism to save itself. By the mid-nineteenth century "the custom of the sea" seemed a relic of the past, at least among the first nations. Strain and others expressed revulsion for obvious reasons, but partly because self-preservational excess violated the hierarchical framework they had faith in, the one in which man and military stood atop. Resisting animalistic behavior in the name of discipline and duty was what separated them from everyone else.

And yet in 1853, sailing amid the ice floes of King William Sound in the Canadian Arctic, Dr. John Rae would shock the world anew. He had finally learned the fate of the long-missing Sir John Franklin expedition, whose vessels *Erebus* and *Terror* had sailed from England in 1845 to achieve the elusive Northwest Passage, only to vanish a few years later. The search for Franklin's party and its celebrated leader would prove to be one of the "most protracted, far-ranging, and physically demanding in the history of exploration."

As late as the early 1850s much of London society clung to the hope that their ingenuity and will had spared them. But late in 1853, Rae reported he had solved the mystery. Some thirty bodies had been found by native Esquimaux, he related. Some corpses were partly buried, and others were either in the tents where they had expired or under a boat they had overturned for shelter. Sir John Franklin, the leader, had died weeks before the remainder of the party arrived at their desolate death camp. In his absence, Rae was sorry to report, the others were "driven in the extremity of hunger to the last acts of maddened human beings," forestalling their own demise by living off the flesh of their dead comrades.

Lombard and Parks were seamen, not officers, and Lombard had seemed to be tottering on the edge of insanity for weeks. Their partnership had evolved innocently enough: They had been taking to the woods regularly, they said, to pray for the survival and return of Strain. As days passed and prayers went unanswered (and Holmes lay dying), fear took root. The morning they fled they were looking for a place to camp when they lost their way. The notion of what they were up to seemed to unhinge them even more than they already were. After a few hours they began firing their guns for an answer, suddenly desperate to be found. Upon recall the twenty-two-year-old Parks quickly confessed.

How Truxtun would react might well have been a mystery to his men. Previously he had made kind gestures toward the men and their predicament and hadn't overtaxed them. He somehow seemed closer to being one of them than he was to the towering kind of sea captain Melville described, the one whose deepest bray you only hear in the "height of some tempest." But Truxtun recognized that his command was at a crossroads and he was swiftly losing control. The men, scared and suffering, were in a state where a mutinous turn might not be so far-fetched. It was the signal moment for Truxtun, and he knew it. Before the entire expedition party he told Parks and his co-conspirator Lombard that he would answer any return to the "horrible proposition," or hint thereof, by blowing their brains out. If the men were looking for just a hint of tolerance—the kind of weak reply that might open the door to anarchy—they didn't get it.

THE FOLLOWING DAY, March 4, Holmes sent for Truxtun at an early hour, his speech low and slurred. He had a dark complexion with black hair and a small build. He smelled of rot, and his dark hazel eyes had sunk into his skull. He looked like an old man, not a twenty-one-year-old. Unable to rise, he soon lost consciousness and died a few hours later. He had been among the first volunteers from the ship's crew. According to the journal, "his left foot, which had been pierced by a thorn many weeks before, was in a condition which threatened decomposition, if it had not already taken place." The field autopsy was that the puncture led to an indistinct disease, which in tandem with malnutrition resulted in his death.

His burial took place in a small clearing near the river. Because they had only hatchets, knives, and an axe, the survivors scratched a shallow depression in the matted ground and piled the body over with smooth, well-formed river stones.

Holmes's death, the party's first one, shattered the fragile group psyche. For several it was the "stress switch," a modern military term for the moment when prolonged physical suffering and psychological overload finally overwhelm their victims. The corpse, along with the increasing length of Strain's absence, was the surest evidence that the mission the men had signed on for was hopeless. In that instant the discomfort became unbearable. Their will to complete the crossing had steadily diminished, but now the darkness seemed to swallow them.

Truxtun lay awake the night of the 4th agonizing over what to do. Feeling he had no option, he decided they had to turn back and head for the ship. At minimum it was 50 miles, but the plantations were theoretically within reach. With neither Strain nor food to look forward to, he wouldn't be able to persuade the men to march downriver. To stay, especially in the morbid presence of Seaman Holmes's gravesite, was certain to invite more breakdowns and perhaps outright opposition. If either he or Maury became physically debilitated, there would be little to prevent whatever imperative the men chose. They needed to go immediately.

He stored the note he wrote to Strain inside a detonating-cap pouch and hung it on the cross over the stone grave.

MARCH 5, 1854, NO. 2 HOSPITAL CAMP

Dear Strain—This is Holmes's grave. He died yesterday, March 4, partly from disease and partly from starvation. The rapidly failing strength of my party, combined with the earnest solicitation of the officers and men, and your long-continued absence, have induced me to turn back to the ship. If you can come up with provisions soon, for God's sake try to overtake us, for we are nearly starving. I have, however, no doubt of reaching the plantain patches if the party be able to hold out on slow marches, and reaching them, I intend to recruit. Since you left I have been detained in camp eighteen days by the sickness of Holmes and the Spaniards.

I trust I am right in going back, and that when you know all more fully, you will approve of my conduct in the course, the more particularly as even the palm-nuts and palmetto are no longer sufficiently abundant as we advance for our sustenance, and as I am now convinced that something most serious has happened to yourself and party to prevent your return to us. After long and serious deliberation with the officers, I have come to the conclusion that the only means of securing the safety of the party, of saving the lives of several, if not all, is at once to return in the way and to the place of provisions.

With the kindest remembrances and best wishes of the party for your safe return to the Cyane, and a happy meeting aboard, I am, yours truly,
    W.T. Truxtun

To Captain I. G. Strain, U.S.N.
In charge of the Isthmus Darién Party, etc.

Truxtun's homeward strategy met with unanimous approval and instantly supercharged the camp. The party was eager to get under way but was forced to wait the remainder of the day for the return of a small hunting party. Their late arrival brought disturbing news. They reported that Parks was once again missing. He had left the detachment early in the day with the understanding he would bring a large supply of palmetto back to camp. Nobody had seen him since. Assuming he was lost, Truxtun had the carbines fired to signal him back. There was no response. The apparently contrite Parks had fooled everyone and deserted again. Truxtun counciled with the rest to see if they wanted to delay leaving for a day with hopes he would again come to his senses and stumble back to camp, but the decision was unanimous to leave as scheduled at dawn.

On March 6, the boatswain's mate, Lombard, lustily piped the familiar "up anchor for home" call to begin their new course. The homeward turn, Melville wrote, made "every man a Goliath, every tendon a hawser!" True to form, the Darién party burst out of their camp with renewed vigor, covering a long rugged stretch in two hours instead of the two days it took when they had no idea where they were or when "we shall reach the Pacific." The discovery of nuts and the killing of a marmoset prompted Kettlewell to write, "Providence smiling graciously on our return." By day's end they had made seven or eight miles.

The following two days featured considerably less progress, as

Castillo, the New Granadian commissioner, repeatedly broke down and required assistance. At midday on the 8th, they reached the camp where they had split with Strain. According to the day's journal, "At 1.30 . . . we left the Parting Camp. Miller was permitted to throw away his carbine, owing to his inability to carry it. . . . A tree was finally met with which produced a species of the palm-nut, the covering of which resembled mangoes. As it was too large to cut down, as many as possible were obtained by firing into the clusters. Revived somewhat . . . the party reached No. 3 Return Camp at 4:50 P.M."

On the 9th only a few more miles could be gained. The debilitated couldn't keep up, causing halts of two or three hours at a time. Truxtun permitted several to discard their firearms either because they were faltering or because those they had been ordered to assist were. A crane and woodpecker Maury shot—in Strain's absence he had taken over the role of chief huntsman—were given to the ailing. The restorative effect, once dramatic, was barely discernible.

On March 11, after a breakfast of "pulsely" water (a thin soup made from a potherb) and acid-nut tea, Castillo temporarily collapsed. He was brought back to his feet with a dousing of cold river water and the raw flesh of a freshly killed dove, but soon the officers reported their own difficulties. Apparently their intentionally undersized rations had started to weaken them. Truxtun and Maury decided they would have to be a little more selfish in the future. From future kills they would give the meat to the men but keep the blood for themselves.

On the 12th, Castillo fainted minutes after the march began and was dead by the meridian hour. Before burying him, a ring, a lock of hair, and the rest of his belongings, presumably including a copy of his fateful orders to "accompany the first party which took the field" were transferred to the junior officer, Polanco. There was no obvious contributing cause of death, no thorn puncture such as Holmes's to remark on, but his skeletal frame was plain evidence of extreme starvation. After a brief ceremony—Truxtun wanted to keep the party moving—Castillo's body was placed in a hastily dug shelf along the riverbank.

Minutes later they lost the river and were forced to camp away from its banks for the first time in weeks. On the 13th, without breakfast or water, the march resumed. They were only a half mile along, and not yet back at the river, when Polanco's collapse forced another lengthy halt. They were still dozens of miles from the plantains. A council of war was called to discuss if "the life of one man who could not survive many hours should be regarded before the lives of the fourteen now remaining." It was unanimously agreed to abandon Polanco. Both Holmes and Castillo had mercifully expired, but Polanco was conscious and aware of the consequences of being left behind. He attempted to follow, the journal duly noted, but collapsed shrieking as the party trailed off into the forest.

They were fourteen now. Hours later they found themselves back at the river, but at an expected and unwanted place. Before them was a portion of river they had already walked and the disturbing sight of Castillo's partially exposed grave. That night the misery grew: Several men vomited after boiling and eating the roots of a potato-like vegetable.

On March 14, the Kettlewell journal marks the damage: "Left camp at 7.30 a.m. After marching about half an hour, Edward Lombard who had delayed the party very much yesterday, threw himself on the ground . . . and begged to be left to his fate. . . . Miller, a landsman belonging to the *Cyane,* who suffered intensely from a bad ulcer, wept bitterly during the day's march. He declared it to be his belief that he would not march on the morrow."

They were barely inching along. Upon arriving at Return Camp No. 9 they were down to a double-barreled fowling piece and carbine for the fourteen of them. Several suffered from botfly, or woodworm, infestation (Truxtun had three, including one on his neck), while Boggs and Maury, two of the group's leaders, were repeatedly doubling over from a batch of poisonous berries. Meanwhile, Lombard continued to plead for his abandonment, but Truxtun coaxed him on, privately wondering if his true aim was to double back and cannibalize the decaying corpse of Castillo, or the left-for-dead Polanco.

On March 15, almost two months after they had left *Cyane*, Truxtun allowed Lombard to make his case before the entire party. According to Kettlewell's journal, Lombard declared his inability to march any further and his earnest desire that the others go on without him. Before granting the request, Truxtun put the matter to a vote. Again the others unanimously decided they had no choice but to leave him. In the course of ten days Truxtun had put to vote the leaving of Parks (who remained absent and was presumably dead), Polanco, and now Lombard. The votes, the last of which was done in the presence of Lombard, were extraordinary. It was a strategy that might have reflected Truxtun's uncertainty in his own leadership but more probably reflected an instinctual understanding that their survival depended on group unity and that their biggest threat was their own mutinous impulses. Among those casting a voice vote weren't just officers but the landsman Robert Miller and a black seaman, Roscoe Johnson.

At Lombard's request, he was left a survivalist's kit: a pot, hatchet, knife, and a fire to sit by. The boatswain's mate's silver whistle, the property of the U.S. government but his mainstay for the last eight weeks, was also left to him. Conceivably he might have found the strength to march back to the dead bodies behind him. The matter was beyond his control, Truxtun had decided. Kettlewell recorded Lombard's last wishes, then offered up a prayer. With nothing more to be done, "his last comrade tearfully wrung his hand, fell into the ranks, and the word *forward* was the last human sound that reached the ear of the dying man."

Reaching the memorable river bluff they had christened Camp Beautiful on the outward journey, the party stopped for a couple of hours. They were twenty-one camps from the beach. At day's end the journal noted: "Mr. Garland still suffering severely, and applying cold water. Mr. Boggs very sick; and Miller's thigh much excoriated . . . we have remarked for some days the cloudy state of the atmosphere, and rain has fallen at intervals, but not in such quantities as to excite uneasiness in regard to the approach of the rainy season. . . . The weather now reminds us of Indian summer at home."

Over the next week the marches grew progressively shorter—and those able to work for the party, either gathering nuts or hunting game, became far fewer. Boggs and Miller continued to receive extra attention and assistance, the latter's ulcer showing signs of spreading. His cuts weren't healing, another sign of advanced starvation. Nighttime offered little relief, with the swampy heat and growing numbers of mosquitoes; they also battled inflammations caused by chiggers, a mite-sized insect that causes violent fits of itching. To start each day's march the officers were reduced to threatening the sleep-starved men or kicking them awake.

The hunger had led to exhaustion, malaise, and physical deformities (sunken eyes and attenuated limbs), but also strange waking hallucinations. Maury and Truxtun, walking at the front of column, would engage in long, detailed conversations about imagined Philadelphia society banquets, effusively describing not only the food courses of the feasts but the woodwork of the serving table, the color and texture of the spread, and the pattern of the china. Incongruous as it sounded (and demoralizing as it seemed for famished men to fantasize about food), the behavior wasn't at all unusual among starving men and has since been described by psychologists as an exotic and wholly involuntary mind-body survival strategy.

Thrown together by circumstance and crisis, Maury and Truxtun worked well together, somehow managing to drive the march onward. Separately they surely would have cracked, but together they managed. While Truxtun kept close tabs on the men and led the march, Maury wandered afield, almost singlehandedly keeping the party alive with his sharpshooting. The extra effort required to walk and hunt was too much for the rest, and Truxtun marveled at not only Maury's stamina but his willingness to provide for the others.

In a different way, Truxtun had stood up just as tall. With the fate of the party in his hands, he had turned his back on orthodox military strategy. In going upstream he had elected to go away from the places where he was supposed to find help: the Pacific coast region and the villages near the river's mouth. In countermanding Strain's order to follow behind him he risked his career. Even if he chose correctly and survived, he could expect the humiliating spectacle of a court-martial.

Truxtun and Maury sustained each other. They delighted in the smallest, most trivial victories, a quality experts associate with success in group survival situations. They talked, laughed, and found humor—and, one would imagine, sanity—in even the most macabre moments. In an episode memorable to both, Truxtun snatched a toad from the underbrush and, biting off and discarding the head, ate the remainder whole. Coming up from behind, Maury shook his head and needled his well-bred companion as being "something of an epicure." Smiling, Maury picked up the head and swallowed it.

It's fair to say neither anticipated their budding relationship. They came from families who had fiercely different views of what the country stood for and where her brightest future lay. Maury's family were slave owners; Truxtun's proudest moment at sea had been his capture of a slave ship off the African coast. In a few years' time Jack Maury and William Truxtun would find themselves on opposing sides of the divide, facing off at places soon to be famous: James River, Fredericksburg, Hilton Head. In Darién, they were in a different world. Northerner and southerner, they simply walked on.

On March 22 they had been gone from the ship sixty-three days. The Kettlewell journal sparely recited the day's misery: "Left 14 Return Camp at 6:30 a.m. After marching a few yards Mr. Boggs became excessively ill, and was unable to move. Soon after Mr. Maury shot a bird, which was cooked for him."

The infusion of meat and a long midday rest didn't revive Boggs. After another abortive attempt to march, Boggs once more had to be waited for. With everyone's condition worsening, the principal officers huddled together and agreed they would have to leave Boggs, since he appeared to be days away from death and was showing no capacity for recovery. His pulse was weak, his heart rate slowed by the starvation. "It is now," says the journal, "becoming a point involving life and death to reach the banana plantation. . . . Mr. Kettlewell was deputed to speak seriously to Mr. Boggs without delay, and prepare him for being left."

The party was readying to leave—Boggs had apparently anticipated the judgment and had already communicated his last requests to Kettlewell—when Truxtun suddenly doubled up and became violently sick. With their leader unable to march, the party halted for the night. Boggs, moments from certain death, got a reprieve.

The next morning, the 23rd, Boggs and Truxtun were slightly better, but others had failed during the night. Philip Vermilyea, a twenty-eight-year-old seaman from New York, was abandoned when the march staggered to a start at six-thirty. They left him with a tin pot, some nuts, a blanket, and a hatchet. There is no mention of there being a vote about whether to leave him. Apparently there was no question. The luxury of helping one another was gone. They had to make the plantations.

But even without Vermilyea their advance plodded. An hour later Vermilyea caught up to them, having found renewed fight in the fear of dying alone. With all but Maury and Kettlewell unable to go on, the party made another camp a short distance away. Erroneously,

Truxtun estimated they were within a long day's march of their supposed salvation, the upriver plantations. In truth they were seven
camps distant.

Few could get up and move. Maury and Kettlewell, who would
soon be collecting firewood and cooking and caretaking for the
others, were among the handful who kept to the pre-supper routine
of washing at the river. The camps, once painstakingly organized
with blazing fires and nightly watches, were primitive, with the space
separating men and officers now down to a few meaningless paces.

In the vicinity of one another were the officers Truxtun and
Boggs, both of whom expected to be left behind in the morning.
Wrapped in the quiltlike counterpane his Springfield family had insisted he take, Boggs had been frail for weeks, more a victim of cumulative wear and tear than any one poison. Truxtun's illness had
come on hot and hard, like Panama fever, an umbrella term covering
a broad category of flash fevers that toppled the body in hours, not
days, often from dehydration. It's unclear whether he had already
made his arrangements with Maury or simply was waiting until
morning. Obviously he believed Maury, Kettlewell, and a few others
still had a chance to survive by leaving him and the others behind. In
the family genealogies he would join those Navy men like his father
who died before his time. It might have occurred to him he was a few
years younger, though, and hadn't even gotten around to leaving a
son behind.

Several seamen, a little ways off, were also awaiting Kettlewell's
return from the river to relate their last requests. John Henwood,
Robert Miller, and Benjamin Harrison, all volunteers from the
Cyane, believed they were finished. And finally there was Vermilyea,
who had barely risen that morning and certainly wasn't capable of a
marathon push of several dozen miles. Even if Maury killed a crane
or a peccary, an improbable bounty, their chances for recovery
weren't likely to improve. Starvation was a cumulative agony where

a point of no return existed. Deny the body's organs long enough and even the heaping bowls of Maury and Truxtun's fantasy feast were of little use. Their discussion of other alternatives didn't last long. Sending Kettlewell and Maury ahead for the plantains was out of the question. The distance was too great, and even if they miraculously reached the fruit trees they could only carry so much food back.

The journal entry for March 23 was apparently cut short that night, a sure sign of complete distress. Keeping the ship's log was a military duty, and nothing short of death justified a blank page. But on this night, the incomplete entry was merely due to a strange and unforeseen occurrence at dusk.

It was so unexpected that neither Maury or Kettlewell could believe their eyes and ears. First there was a blast that sounded like a musket, probably a tree fall, but then moments later they saw dugout canoes rounding the bend carrying both Indians and white men. Maury stared extra hard, the way he did when he shouldered his fowling piece. Then he erupted. "I see Strain!" he shouted up the bank to his distant partner, Truxtun. "I see Strain!"

10 / PACIFIC

Difficult works are attempted for the sake of Heaven, for the world's sake, or for both. The first are tasks undertaken by the saints. . . . The second are performed by men who navigate the boundless ocean, and journey through distant countries and changing climates, to acquire what are called the goods of fortune. And those who brave hazardous enterprises for the sake of both God and man are stout soldiers.

MIGUEL DE CERVANTES SAAVEDRA,
THE ADVENTURES OF DON QUIXOTE

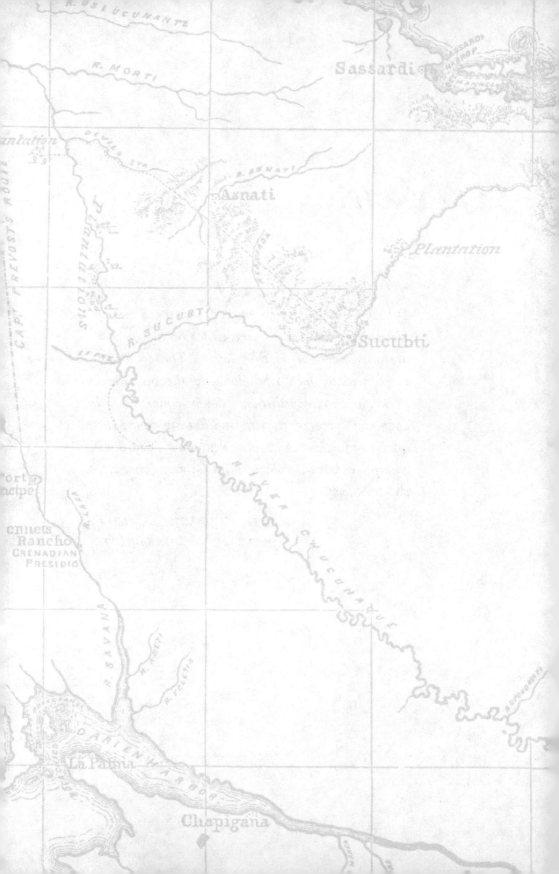

February 15, 1854

8° 27′ N, 77° 52′ W
Chucunaque

FOR THE MEN STRUGGLING their way to the river's edge—
and for Strain, drawing deeper with each paddle stroke to receive them—the impending reunion was nothing short of a
miracle. Since leaving with Wilson, Golden, and Avery on February
13, he had marched, rafted, and canoed 350 miles, some 275 of them
in the last fourteen frenzied days.

When he had set out some six weeks earlier, Strain fervently believed he would salvage the Darién expedition, not simply rescue it.
If he could find his way to a frontier village or persuade an Indian
fisherman to guide him, he might see the Pacific in days. He knew
he'd traveled dozens of miles along the course of a major river that
ran to the Pacific; he also knew the string-thin width of the isthmus.
The experience he likened to a grinding mountain ascent where a series of false summits precedes the true peak. Only one more push
might be necessary. Their target was preciously near.

On February 13 he'd advanced so fast and far that he'd written
Truxtun of his imminent hopes for "popping out into Darién Harbor." In fact, no sooner had he penned the note than he found all directions barred by dense undergrowth. The high, near-vertical

riverbanks made a crossing to the other side unthinkable. Instead they burrowed "head foremost" into the stormy tangle, hacking and pushing until they had won 200 yards of forward gain. Their target, a more open stretch of forest, turned out to be a bottomless swamp. Strain could faintly see the river but couldn't raise his sinking, mud-stuck boots fast enough to get to it. Consequently he gave the order to turn around and try another route. Seven hours after starting on the morning of the 14th, he, Golden, Wilson, and Avery had clawed their way back to the river, exhausted, drenched in grimy perspiration, and famished. They hadn't eaten or even taken the time to forage. They had begun the day convinced they were in a finish-line sprint and would soon be rewarded with the view of an awaiting man-of-war amply stocked with the "luxuries of spirits, fruits, molasses, and tobacco."

But at day's end they were barely farther along than when they started. Nightmarishly, their all-out effort had netted them a half mile of forward progress. With neither the strength nor the resources to suffer through a repeat experience, Strain once again looked to the river's treacherous but beckoning current. Their best hope, he decided, was to build a raft and use the falling Chucunaque to deliver them from the belly of the jungle.

By 10 A.M. on February 15, they had assembled a primitive two-man raft, lashing the rough-notched logs to one another with woody vines hacked from the forest. The lianas were a pet peeve: They dropped like rescue lines to nowhere from the canopy, or raced in ever tightening spirals up trunks hundreds of feet high. When they ensnared ankles or shoulders, as they had the day before and so many before that, they were virtually inescapable. Some were thicker than their own legs. Bulling through almost never worked. Instead the march stopped and whomever was caught had to slowly back up and reverse the steps that had somehow produced the Gordian knot. Being able to excise a few climbing vines from the billions that crawled under, over, and seemingly through them—especially with a view to aiding their progress—was one of the more emotionally satisfying things they'd done in days.

Strain and the landsman Wilson piloted the dinghy-sized raft, with Avery and Golden following as best they could along the banks. Made of mere driftwood, not balsa logs, the makeshift vessel floated poorly. Brown river water rushed over the deeply drawn sides, flooding the logs and submerging the surface beneath several inches of water. To the quick, foliage-obscured glances of the men onshore, there appeared to be no raft, just river, with Strain and Wilson having achieved a kind of divine buoyancy in and of themselves. The illusion was quickly dispensed when they got a better view. They were sinking.

Strain navigated the precarious descent from the bow, where he could eyeball the hazy, dark river surface for obstructions. He employed a crude, clublike paddle for both offense and defense, alternately forward-stroking in slack sections or bracing with it against deadfall. In shallower sections, he and Wilson were on and off the contraption constantly, thrashing through the waist-deep water and hand-grappling their way through viny entanglements. Their hardships were in striking contrast to the little reptilian wonders scooting around them. The "Jesus Christ" lizards strode *atop* the stream surfaces, exchanging one bank for the other with teasing ease. They walked on water—a marvel and taunt all at once.

After expanding the platform with more logs, Strain brought aboard the beleaguered Avery and Golden. Their relief was short-lived: The added weight caused the raft to burrow deeper and steer more erratically. In the early afternoon a bone-jarring collision with a submerged log rent the raft in two, nearly throwing them all off in the process. In the throes of snapping vines and chaotic shouts Strain managed to throw his leg out, spanning the two newly shorn halves of his raft until he gradually eliminated the watery gap in between.

Hours later the repaired and rebuilt raft skidded to a halt on the shoaly river bottom; Strain and his men had to untie the logs, then portage the dismantled raft a quarter mile downstream, where it was once again reassembled.

The river, much to Strain's disgust, was proving to be neither a shortcut nor a labor saver. In parts it was barely a trickle, and yet he could tell by the high eroded banks that the water level was sometimes dozens of feet higher. He could only imagine the sweeping rise of the Chucunaque in the high-water months of May and June. But he was navigating the rain-nourished river at the peak of the dry season, an ideal time for overland travel but not this unanticipated part of the expedition, a river trip. Dozens of mountain tributaries were nothing but dry, sun-baked boulder beds. February and March couldn't be a more difficult time of year for what Strain had in mind: a nearly 150-mile source-to-sea descent. The water level was just enough to camouflage the boulders and deadfall they needed to see. The gouged-out depth of the bed and the newly exposed vertical walls made portages impossible. Hazards were everywhere.

The following day a hard noontime downpour—a sometime event even in the dry season—briefly kick-started the current. But the sudden pushiness beneath them was hard to handle, and all afternoon they washed into snags, including one that took two hours to work themselves free from. Nearing sunset they had safely negotiated the worst of the rapids when an attempt to bypass more shoals drew them into a patch of fast water. The pinwheeling raft raced into a sprawl of overhanging branches and thick, woody vines. Wilson and Avery, laden with their anchor-like packs, were knocked overboard in deep water. Strain and Golden hung on but couldn't prevent the raft from careening off onto another snag, where it teetered wildly, its ends shoved around by the slapping current. In the course of a frantic effort to hack themselves free, Golden's machete slipped from his grip and sank to the river bottom. For a few moments it appeared they might all drown.

Finally the raft sprang free and drifted harmlessly into an adjoining eddy. Wilson and Avery were already on the hard clay shore, each splayed out and panting for breath. Wilson, who had nearly had his leg broken in the initial collision, was the worse for wear. Like many man-of-war men, he couldn't swim. Avery had somehow got a piece of the flailing, panic-stricken man and deposited him ashore.

They had saved themselves, but the episode had depressing, far-reaching consequences. The water had wet "nearly the whole of our ammunition, and all our friction matches and tinder," wrote Strain. Without fire or firearms, they were without their primary survival tools. With cruel swiftness, the last three days had pushed them to their absolute limits. For days they'd been the sun's target, exposed and drifting with not even an awning to shield themselves from the searing heat; now they passed the night cold and shivering, unable to spark a fire, and forced to bed down in their river-soaked clothes and blankets. They had been away from the ship a month and had been lost and hungry for most of those days. But the night of February 16 would stick in all their minds as the most dreadful to date.

Strain had navigated tens of thousands of sea miles, some in uncharted waters that had never seen a man-of-war. He'd explored wild rivers in Indonesia, Madagascar, and Brazil. But without an adequate craft, nor the kind of river knowledge possessed by local boatmen, he was helpless. The Indian navigators, guided by centuries of ancestral experience, had river eyes. They could slalom between the unseen shallows, or pole off the lurking deadfall as if guided by the most expert of nautical charts. Conversely, Strain was running the river blind.

They lost much of the day in an attempt to sun-dry their gear. Faced with the possibility of squandering what was left of their ammunition in another river mishap, Strain decided to abandon the raft on the very next day, the 17th. It was a rather abrupt decision but no doubt the right one. They couldn't afford to jeopardize their survival staples, fire and firepower. A century later, the U.S. military would institute a jungle warfare and survival school in Panama where the infamous final exam was a fifteen-day outing without food or water. At the outset officers were allowed to choose a single tool to aid their survival; invariably they picked matches, aware that one of the greatest dangers in the equatorial jungle wasn't the extreme daytime heat but the damp evening cold.

For the next two weeks they used their machetes like scythes to open a trail on the untracked and overgrown banks of the Chucunaque. When English pirates and Balboa's boatbuilding expeditionaries explored the upper Chucunaque valley, they had likely done so along regularly used Indian trails that then crisscrossed the low divides between the tributaries. In the ensuing centuries the Indian presence had largely disappeared with the exception of migrant fishing parties. Those cleared trails were jungle again. None had apparently attempted the punishing riverside route Strain followed. Utterly unaware, he was committing himself and his men to a stretch likely never walked by previous explorers.

Scientific visitors a half century later would make a wholly unexpected discovery when surveying this same territory. They classified most of the Chucunaque watershed as "lower humid zone," meaning the terrain supported a diverse and plentiful amount of tropical flora and fauna. But the lower sections of the river where Strain now found himself were intriguingly different. From Yaviza at the lower end of the river, a tongue-shaped strip of "lower arid zone" extended up the Chucunaque for some 30 miles. The area was an almost mutant rainforest habitat. The sort of biomass one expected to see in the lowland neotropics was either anomalously missing or drastically diminished in volume. The name "arid zone" spoke for itself. It was a comparative desert embedded in the teeming jungle. Hospital Camp was the upriver portal to the region. But Strain was in the heart of it. Superimposed on an ordinary topo map, the shaded dead zone almost perfectly mimicked the larger shape of the isthmus itself.

Strain noticed the relative lifelessness of the region on his afternoon foraging trips, but he didn't identify a new river zone or anticipate more desperate days ahead. The emptiness wasn't that dramatic, and besides, the growth along the river, where he principally traveled, was as lush as ever. With their concentration and energies used up on busting open a crude hole, the future was rarely further away than the green wall in front of their faces.

Repeatedly the party bogged down, with each of the four suffering breakdowns of one type or another. On the 17th, shortly after the rafting problems, Strain found himself feverish and chilled—the combined effects, he thought, of leg sores that had been blistered in the river sun, then ripped raw by the spiny undergrowth. More probably he was enduring the first wave of malaria, whose signature fever and chills occur as attacking parasites devour red blood cells and rapidly multiply in the bloodstream.

The following day, February 18, Avery halted his march after only a few miles because of extreme nausea. A bout of agonized vomiting was followed by repeated dry retching. The seamen, Strain later recounted in the journal, were demoralized to the point of lying prostrate and sobbing on the jungle floor, refusing his pleas to take a turn breaking trail until Strain threatened to either flog or abandon them.

There were no villages, deserted or otherwise, and no fish-drying racks such as they'd seen farther upstream. There appeared to be little to no human visitation to the area. That feature alone was hard to fathom; it was difficult to believe that a river of such size, so close to the Pacific, would be so untrafficked. Every few days the men heard shots, which they initially mistook for Truxtun's party, thinking they might be gaining. But each time Strain's men returned fire there was no answer.

Saturday, February 25: "Set out at 8 a.m. and found bad walking all day, both in the forest and on the beaches which we met," wrote Strain. "In the former we had to cut our way, while the beaches were so steep that we had sometimes to cut steps to crawl along, and even then we were in constant danger of falling into the river, which I did on one occasion."

Inconsistent rations seemed to almost exacerbate the suffering: There were a few memorable strikes—some "little-neck" clams were discovered at one point, and Strain took a wild turkey at another—but the feasts were strangely disappointing. Expecting to be sated, they complained afterward of being only hungrier. On February 26, two weeks after they had separated from the main party and Truxtun at Parting Camp, Strain shot and killed a large monkey, the biggest meat jackpot to date. Slaughtered and hastily cooked up in an overstuffed tin pot, the animal provided 5 pounds of red meat per person. After consuming their entire portions, the men begged Strain to boil the skin too.

As the overland trek dragged on with no sign of their Pacific destination, and having again to subsist for long stretches on hard nuts or palmetto, the hollowed-out, dull ache in his stomach began to obsess even Strain.

"This was the second time during the expedition that I really felt voracious," he wrote on March 1. "I found myself casting my eyes around me to see if there was nothing that had been overlooked that could allay my hunger. Without a fire, which at this time we never lighted unless we had meat to cook, we laid down and slept."

Frustrations piled up. Several days earlier Strain had spied a large wild hog, which had almost providentially wandered into their camp.

The massive, 300-pound animal would have fed them for weeks, but Strain's shot merely wounded the pig, enabling it to escape. In lamenting the episode, Strain explained that he had aimed at the hog's broad body and not the head (which would have killed the beast instantly) because he lacked the confidence to squeeze off a precise shot. His slender, walnut-stocked carbine was the best in the party, yet it now required two men to fire it, wrote Strain, "one to take aim and pull the trigger, and the other to pull the cock back, and let it go at the word, invariably destroying the aim." In the perpetual dampness the forged metal mechanism had rusted to a state of almost total uselessness. The increasing frequency with which he missed—Strain said he saw and misfired at turkeys on several subsequent occasions—was a haunting reminder that their ammunition stores weren't likely to hold out much longer.

Shot by missed shot, he feared he was further sealing their fate. His tortured frame of mind was like his grandfather's, who decades earlier had wondered why he couldn't find the spiritual strength to rouse his weary frontier congregations. "In the forenoon delivered a sermon," wrote the Rev. Isaac Grier in a 1792 diary of his three-year wilderness mission, "But not with that warmth . . . that Love to God and Souls of Man with which the gospel ought to be preached." Unable to provide simple sustenance to another sort of congregation, Strain found himself facing his own demons.

It was becoming increasingly difficult to subsist on the acid nuts, which were harder to find and less ripe when they did so. Attempting to bite down on the hard kernels was an excruciating form of agony. The acid had eaten up almost all their protective tooth enamel. The exposed underlying layer was like an open nerve, and everything that bore on it—heat, cold, but especially the gnawing acid—caused sharp tremors of pain.

Every night they dutifully set stakes in the clay shores of the river, expecting to see in the morning an indication of the Pacific's tidal rise. Strain continued to correlate his position in relation to the Iglesias, the river he still believed he had to be on. On the 23rd, he recorded that they passed a small stream coming in from the northeast. According to Gisborne's map, which he'd brought along, a stream running the same course was shown four miles above the Iglesias's mouth, and another was 11 miles from it. Two or three rapids with a drop of some 12 feet probably explained the absence of tidewater. Yet another sharp booming sound was also heard on the 23rd, an indication that Darién Harbor—the place where the *Virago* was expected—was near. In fact the river they'd actually passed, the Ucurganti, was merely a major unmapped tributary of the Chucunaque. They were as far from Darién Harbor as they'd ever been— actually farther, due to the river's wayward jogs.

By March 2, they had almost come to a standstill. Crossing several deep ravines—their course of march being southerly—they were forced to slide down the slopes, then notch footholds in the opposite sides in order to make the ascent. The journal notes, "Our bodies . . . literally covered with wood ticks, and . . . obliged to pick them off morning and evening." Hobbled by foot sores and fatigue, the crippled Strain found himself barely able to sustain the march. The ticks gorging on them were not merely a disgusting nuisance but parasitic disease carriers. Strain had no boots left and had been lately relying upon a moccasin he'd made from an old leather legging—a primitive form of protection at best. His only hope was to try another raft. The river, increased by tributaries, seemed freer from driftwood, and deeper in the bends. Seamen Golden and Wilson helped collect the wood but said they'd take their chances grinding along the banks. Still spooked by their last attempt, they wanted nothing to do with another river descent.

Strain and Avery launched on the 3rd, with Golden and Wilson attempting to keep in contact by marching as close to shore as possible. The raft was even more improvised than the previous version, with six half-rotten tree trunks lashed to one another with strips of monkey skin and liana vine. The next two days seemed endless to Strain, whose future was utterly tied to a river he didn't know and couldn't predict. He didn't even know the time. His pocket chronometer had failed weeks ago, only days after he'd left the main party. "It almost appeared to me that time had refused to register the tedious hours which we passed in the wilderness," remarked Strain glumly. "On some occasions almost all men become to a certain extent superstitious."

Hours drifted into days, with both he and Avery falling into a daydreamy state in the soupy heat. Attempting to pull them back into the present, Strain bombarded his companion with personal questions—about his travels, about his upbringing, anything that might keep him engaged. He even sought to amuse Avery by reciting from memory a few of the more famous passages in Cervantes's *Don Quixote*.

Though he tried desperately not to, Strain, like Maury and Truxtun, didn't merely wish for food, he experienced it. The detail was sumptuous, baroque almost: the gilded creamy white flatware, the polished silver serving trays, the curls of steam leaking from dozens of dishes of jellied venison, pâté chaud, and capon in cherry-wine sauce. Ornamental dishes abounded. Some he'd seen, others he'd only heard of: the "temples of history" and "pyramids of liberty" made of flaky pastry, noble swans and flying birds atop pedestals, waiting to be carved. He was in the Astor House or some luminous place like it, adrift in female loveliness and men of intelligence and eminence, the beat of the endless banquet kept by countless toasts, the black-coated orators seemingly aglow.

Strain was virtually a prisoner of the visualization for days. In the 1980s sports psychologists would look at such vivid mental experiences and investigate the impact they had on the body. They found mental imagery had a profound capability to enhance physical performance. Olympic-caliber athletes were encouraged to closet themselves away and train their minds to re-create their event—say, a downhill alpine ski run. If they did it well, they could experience their task with exceptional detail layered in, building what scientists called "muscle memory." When the time came to compete, the mental preparation had starved the experience of its debilitating stress. Of course, Strain's visualizations weren't voluntary but rather an elaborate coping mechanism against a more complicated stress, that of starving to death. Doctors can't fully account for such hallucinations, but Strain, Truxtun, and Maury's minds might have been trying to do roughly the same remarkable thing: sate themselves with nothing but virtual food.

ON THE EVENING of the 4th, having scavenged a half-eaten iguana for supper, Strain noticed a heavy rushing sound, like that of a river break. Looking up the Chucunaque, his eyes settled on a spot that they'd lazily floated over hours ago. Now there was a mini rapid with current breaking over the nearly exposed bed. It was the ebb tide, he realized. The contracting Pacific was recalling its estuarine waters, part of the same massive tidal action that drops the water line some 17 feet at Panama City.

Strain wasn't going to tell the others until he was sure, but Wilson and Golden erupted minutes later, yelling, "Oh, Captain, here is tide! Here is tide!" They had arrived at the reach of the Pacific. In a fairly remarkable coincidence they'd met her waters on the occasion of Strain's thirty-third birthday. Unfortunately the day marked another, less celebratory milestone: the first death of the U.S. Darién Exploring Expedition. On March 4, Truxtun was burying George Holmes 50 upstream miles away and hatching his desperate plan for a retrograde march. At the moment Strain had reached the Pacific his men had decided to turn and walk away from it.

ANOTHER FOUR excruciating days passed on the river. They were
aware there might be many more. The extent of the Pacific tide was
unknown. On the Hudson River, Avery unhappily recalled, the Atlantic tides extended a full 150 miles from its mouth. They had descended only 20 river miles since discovering tidewater, and could be
weeks away.

On March 9, and with the prospect of help seeming no less remote, Strain gave his place on the raft to Golden and set out with
Wilson to look for food in the forest. Four cartridges were left. By
day's end he had three, having shot a partridge that the ravenous,
nearly delirious Wilson devoured raw. It was 3 P.M. before they were
back to the river, at which point a disconsolate Wilson looked up and
spotted their raft, unmanned and floating idly in the main channel.
Not only were Avery and Golden nowhere to be seen, but their blankets and spare arms, the pathetic extent of their belongings, were
missing. Strain's mind raced: If they had found assistance, why
wasn't there a note from the pair? If they'd been assaulted, a scenario
that seemed far more probable, why was there no blood or some
other sign of a struggle?

Even if an ambush awaited them, they had no choice. Time was
their overriding adversary. They were down to a paddle, a few
wretched scraps of clothing, and a dwindling supply of nuts. Late in
the afternoon Strain and Wilson clambered aboard the ghost raft and
started off downriver on the receding tide.

It was impossible not to notice the dramatic change in the river. It
was as if the Chucunaque had finally submitted to forces bigger than
itself. The river, writhing and contorted for the vast majority of its
course, fell almost straight now. The main channel was nearly 10 feet
deep. The bottom-lying debris, which caused havoc in the clearer
shallows upriver, was safely interred deep below the surface in soft,

flocculent mud. Even without the flushing rains of spring, summer, and especially fall, any buoyant object finding its way into the Chucunaque here had a good chance of being drawn all the way to the sea.

The ebb tide might draw a captive item past Yaviza, then down the wide Tuyra River to Darién Harbor and the vast Gulf of San Miguel. From there, it would likely get blown out into open ocean by the prevailing offshore trade winds, tracking counterclockwise along the north equatorial gyre, an oddly shaped Pacific current that is virtually horizontal.

Unlike the far larger Northern and Southern Hemisphere gyres that sweep past vast expanses of coastline on their broad circular treks, the north equatorial sticks to Darién's latitude line with little deviation, pushing due west across the widest part of the Pacific, then back again. In a manner of speaking, something adrift in Darién never went anywhere but Darién, never left—at least not for long.

Strain's inability to control his destiny, or that of those depending on him, was a tormenting thought as he drifted for the next half hour. Then he saw a track along the left riverbank—no, it was a clearing like those he'd seen weeks ago on the outskirts of Indian villages. The activity from below began to take visual form—a little stream on the same bank, a pair of unidentified canoes rushing toward him. According to an account that would later circulate among the men and find its way into print, the captain "sat across the logs and hailed as though he trod the deck of a man-of-war." If the approaching men had been as familiar with *Don Quixote* as Strain was, they might have thought him a ghostly counterpart. If he wasn't delusional, he was a fool. Strain was in no condition to bring a fight to anyone.

Fortunately, he was in the hands of rescuers. They'd been dispatched by Avery and Golden, who had been intercepted hours earlier by the same boatmen, then brought downriver to Yaviza, the main village in Pacific Darién. Strain and Wilson beached their raft on the exposed mud bank (undoubtedly to be reclaimed by the river on that evening's flood tide) and transferred to the large dugout canoes. Two miles later the old ruins of an ancient fort came into view on the right bank, then a grass-hut settlement.

It was near dark on March 9 when Strain stepped ashore at Yaviza, the old Spanish frontier post. The peep and whoop and general bedlam of chorusing frogs was deafening. Their noisy nightly march to the riverbank was every bit as predictable as a ship's evening gun. Strain wore the Panama hat he had started out with, in addition to a scrap of blue flannel shirt and his improvised moccasin. After he collapsed on the beach, the two boatmen shouldered him the rest of the way. At some point his hosts placed a pipe into his hands. He'd remember the tobacco as a life-sparking force surpassing all else, even food. He hadn't smoked in five weeks.

The four-man U.S. Darién Exploring Expedition's "advance party" had arrived in a less than triumphant manner, but they arrived in good order and with due discipline. They still had the revolvers and rifles they'd started out with. Some hadn't worked in weeks, and the march would have been less burdensome if the men had abandoned them, but they retained them for this moment, wrote Strain. They represented "the emblems of an organized party" and assured the world that the Americans had done somewhat better than merely survive the wilderness.

An eyewitness who met Strain within his first twenty-four hours of arriving at Yaviza described him as "almost worn to a skeleton— perfectly naked, and his body covered with sores from the insects that penetrated the skin." He weighed 75 pounds, or about half the body weight he'd begun the expedition with. His ravenous body had first devoured its stores of fatty tissue, which would have accounted for a precipitous drop in his body weight fairly early in the expedition. As the weeks continued the weight loss leveled out, but the internal damage spread. In the absence of its normal fuel, the body had turned on itself, consuming half his lean muscle mass. Every major muscle was in the process of being consumed, including the heart.

Strain said he was so weak he found it impossible to write. Both his immune and circulatory systems were crashing, reducing his ability to fight infection and fatigue. Yet he had marched only hours earlier, and his ability to think seemed unaffected. There was no physiological accounting for his stamina; the starvation, combined with disease and exposure, should have stopped him. But perhaps it was simpler. Mentally he never gave himself the choice. For reasons that might have reached to Roxbury, Pennsylvania, or São Paulo, Brazil, or the border lands of Texas, Strain intended to finish the crossing. The guns he carried were proof. His foolish burden was his daily reminder.

Incredibly, Strain declined to eat or rest until he'd organized the formation of a relief party. At 8 P.M. on the 10th, within twenty-four hours of his arrival, Avery departed with four canoes, an abundance of provisions, ten native boatmen, and an interpreter to relay instructions to them. The cool evening and flooding moonlight seemed auspicious. Strain stayed behind. His priority was to intercept the *Virago* for provisions, money, and a passage to Panama for his party. He made arrangements to set out at first light.

11 / BATTLE ROAD

*Their appearance was fearful, their visages attenu-
ated to the last degree, and their hair had grown to
an enormous length.*

FROM THE REPORTS OF BRITISH RESCUERS

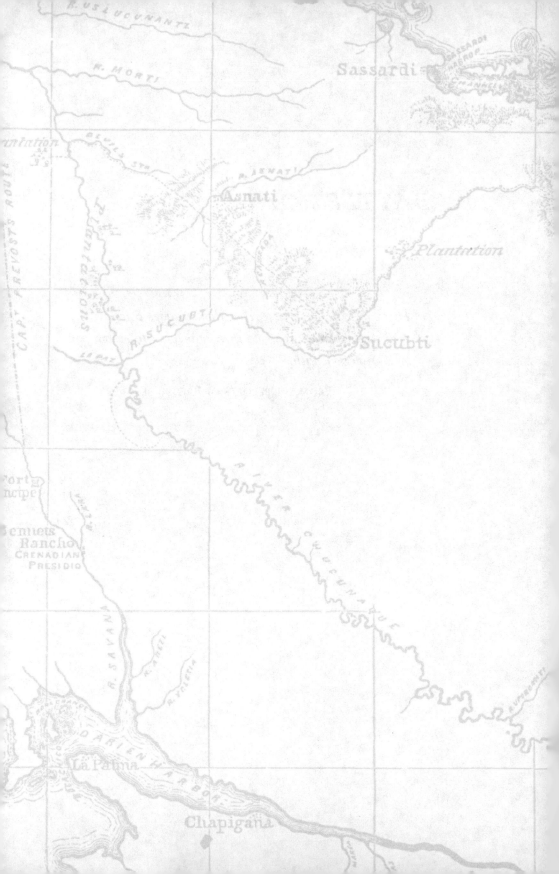

March 10, 1854

8° 10′ N, 77° 45′ W
Yaviza

WITH THE RELIEF EXPEDITION under way, Isaac Strain's
doings over the next twenty-four hours suggested somebody who truly believed the worst was over. He began
to contemplate what they'd been through, and between bouts of copious and unrelieved food consumption, get his old bite back. He
grumbled about the corrupt local help, invoking the sort of dour
view of the population's industriousness that was altogether typical
of nineteenth-century travelers to the tropics. "The people here
sleep at night," Strain quipped, "and rest during the day."

Meanwhile, he began to mentally log a number of general observations, many of which found their way into his journal once he'd
restored himself enough to write. He remarked on the turbulent local history and the dramatic Cerro Pirre, a handsome sentinel peak
rising sharply from the valley floor. "After our long confinement in
the forest, where our view was constantly limited by the forest
growth," he wrote, "it was an intense pleasure once more to see high
land and enjoy a distant view."

Situated on the right bank of the river, Yaviza was the New
Granadian–controlled capital of Darién. The several hundred

inhabitants were the descendants of Caribbean slaves who had worked the nearby Spanish gold mines. They grew plantain and maize for subsistence, and each winter cut from the nearby forest trees that they formed into rough planks and shipped to Panama in exchange for clothing and spirits. "During my protracted journey in the wilderness," recalled Strain. "I had frequently, in the spirit which actuated Alexander Selkirk [the model for fiction's Robinson Crusoe], wished myself once more in a position to be cheated, and if I had selected from a minute map of the world, I do not believe that I could have had any wish so thoroughly gratified as at Yavisa [*sic*]." He was once more a traveler on a grandly colorful adventure.

His demeanor attested to what he later admitted: He had no idea how destitute those he'd left behind were. Truxtun's party had assumed the worst about him, but he foresaw nothing of the sort for them. They'd been separated twenty-four days, a long time, but because he'd almost been overtaken by Truxtun's party on the first day, he supposed them to be comparably healthy. Unlike Strain's advance team, they didn't have to break trail. When he reached Yaviza, Strain said he expected Truxtun to be no more than "two or three days behind."

After a spate of maddening but predictable delays Strain paddled six miles to Santa María el Real, a village of six hundred inhabitants near the mouth of the Tuyra River, where he swapped his small canoe, the only one he could acquire in Yaviza, for a much larger cargo-carrying *pirogua*. Three hired boatmen along with Wilson, Golden, and Strain set out for Darién harbor and the *Virago* on the 11th, about twenty-four hours after Avery's departure upriver on the Chucunaque. Paddling and drifting with the Pacific-bound ebb tide, then anchoring to hold their position during the heavy incoming tide, it took twenty-four hours to reach the village of Chapigana. None of the three Americans was able to sleep during the journey, said Strain, either because of "intense pain" from botfly infestation or their unquenchable appetites, "which it appeared no amount of food could satisfy."

At Chapigana Strain, Golden, and Wilson were assisted across the sharp-stoned beach to the home of Andrew Hossack, the same Scotsman whose association with Edward Cullen had begun the canal speculation at Darién. Strain learned that the *Virago* had already left for Panama, not to return for a week. There were no provisions available in any of the nearby villages, Hossack told him; his only hope was to proceed up the Savana River some 40 miles to its junction with the Lara, where he'd find the depot supervised by Gisborne's Atlantic and Pacific Junction Company. Because of violent trade winds blowing across Darién Harbor, a massive sheet of water some 15 miles across, Strain was told he'd have to wait until morning before he'd find a crew willing to help him make the journey.

Strain's time with Hossack was brief, but he came to understand for the first time the fuss that was being made over his party's disappearance. In Hossack's possession were a number of Panama and Aspinwall newspapers. The articles described the months-earlier Prevost disaster and the intense distress over Strain's whereabouts. One of the lengthier reports, though it bore the anonymous signature of "AMATEUR," was from Theodore Winthrop's pen. On March 4 Winthrop wrote of the "loss, we fear, of Lieut. Strain and his party, in all twenty Americans, and two gentlemen from Cartagena."

The news clearly took Strain by surprise, and though the reports about him were easily dismissed he couldn't definitively allay fears for the eighteen he'd left behind. Strain dictated a note to Hossack, who agreed to pass along the word of his safe arrival on the Pacific, and his expectation of seeing the rest of the party in a day or two.

Strain's two companions, Wilson and Golden "were in a fearful state," reported Hossack, who dispatched the note to the *Panama Herald* five days later, on the 16th. The lieutenant himself had suffered "beyond all expression, as his body is all ulcerated and eat up with bush-worms; the clothes torn off his back, wandering through the wilderness without any pantaloons, and arrived here bare footed."

As for the rest of the party, he not only "supposed them all to be living," said Hossack, but believed they would soon be able to prosecute further explorations of the isthmus. In what the editors naturally supposed to be a gross misunderstanding, Hossack wrote that the lieutenant was planning to recross the isthmus to Caledonia Bay—once he recovered the rest of his party, got them medical aid, and recruited their strength—"and from thence commence his surveying operations." The proposition was never mentioned again, not in Strain's post-trip government reports nor in the popular articles to come, so it might have been a misunderstanding—Hossack wasn't beyond a little flamboyant storytelling himself. But there was also an unmistakable element of Strain in the errant, quixotic notion, the part of him whose tolerance for suffering seemed to stray beyond the bounds of normalcy, or even duty. (Ironically, rather than calm fears Hossack managed to inflame them by appending the news that "11 of his party are either killed or starved," a rumor that had come to him after Strain had departed.)

Before daylight on the 13th, Strain set out for the English depot in a large cargo canoe Hossack provided. The Savana was a wide river, a mile and a half between its low, swampy, mangrove-lined banks, but after 10 miles the river narrowed and began to turn on itself. Large forest trees replaced the mangrove scrub at the water's edge. With three of Hossack's boatmen expertly paddling, they reached the depot late the same day. Strain's eyes drew up the river's now steeply sided banks to a large canvas tent with the Union Jack flapping above. Beside the tent, on the east bank, was a large thatched rancho, the starting point for the ill-fated Prevost trip.

William Bennett, the supervising naval engineer, hailed Strain like a long lost brother, offering him supper, provisions and "a supply of money and sufficient quantity of his own clothing to supply the whole party." Bennett also offered to pilot the provision boat himself, sparing Strain the rough return trip to Yaviza. When Strain insisted on going himself Bennett had a bed put in the well of the canoe so he could rest. Stunned at the lieutenant's macabre physical deformity, Bennett couldn't help thinking Strain was more dead than alive.

Over supper, Bennett reiterated what Strain had heard in Chapigana: that he'd been assumed dead. There was more news, though. A month earlier, the same day Strain had separated from Truxtun on the Chucunaque, Lionel Gisborne had arrived at the exact spot where they now sat. He'd found an Indian guide to lead him across the isthmus, accomplishing what he claimed was the only authenticated crossing "since the Spanish Milla went across with the Indian chief Ruclenchi in the last century." The reason the *Virago* had hurriedly left San Miguel, Bennett added, was to deliver the Englishman to Panama, where he intended to make himself available for interviews and begin a new round of survey work.

The blow had to have been gut-wrenching—up until now Strain had assumed he and his men were first to cross—but he made no remark, either in Bennett's presence or on paper. With genuine gratitude for his host's assistance (he left in his temporary care the ailing Golden and Wilson), Strain started back for Yaviza at five o'clock, arriving at Chapigana after midnight. The next morning he obtained a very large canoe, with an awning, "for the accommodation of the party whom I expected to meet at Yavisa." When the tide turned he and his boatmen launched again, variously drifting, paddling, and anchoring in the course of the Tuyra until they reached Yaviza on the evening of the 15th.

Of course, neither Truxtun nor anyone else from the expedition was there to meet him. There was, however, a letter dated March 13 from Avery informing Strain of the progress he had made and of his expectation to overtake Truxtun "on the day on which the letter was written." According to Strain's journal, he spent that night and the next in "sleepless anxiety."

Evidently they were not now, nor had they ever been, close behind. Avery was already beyond the camp where they'd built the raft on the 2nd of March. Strain had been seven more days in reaching Yaviza from there. "I could obtain no canoes or men," wrote Strain, who had been urged to follow without delay, perhaps to help Avery coerce the boatmen who were threatening to turn back. But Strain was torn. He still had no information on the condition of the party, nor an understanding that they'd reversed course back toward the hazardous Indian country. The letter had assured him that Avery and his partner, a trusted New Granadian official, would proceed no matter what, with or without the boatmen. If he went back up the Chucunaque, he'd sacrifice his opportunity to contact the *Virago*. Though rumored to be en route to the Chucunaque for their relief, somebody needed to make certain the *Virago* arrived soon. If on schedule, she should have just been steaming into Darién Harbor.

Strain decided to stay the night in Yaviza and wait for news. If no update was forthcoming in the morning, he'd reassess. "By following up the river I was placing myself in a position where I would be powerless," he wrote.

At 4 A.M. on the 17th, Avery returned, bursting into the night-black house where Strain was staying. "My first question was, 'Have you brought the party?' " recalled Strain. "He replied: 'I have brought one; I have brought Parks.' "

Avery had reached Hospital Camp 2 three days earlier (shortly after dispatching his first note to Strain), where he'd found Holmes's grave, the primitive cross astride it, and Truxtun's emotional plea for help. He'd attempted to continue upriver but after encountering a logjam the next morning chose to abandon the rescue bid and return to Yaviza for more men and instructions. Understandably the discovery of Holmes's grave had done little to encourage Avery's already tentative party. Though he'd offered double pay and other inducements, the majority of his work party refused to go on. When Avery turned back for Yaviza he'd been no more than a day's travel from Truxtun's poor men.

As they had returned downriver, Avery continued, he heard a holler on the right bank and upon landing found Parks. He'd been on his own since March 5, the day the rest of the party set off without him. It wasn't clear from his incomprehensible telling whether he had deserted, as Truxtun assumed, or simply lost his way, but he'd been away from the river for much of that time, he said, and only the night before had he stumbled upon the river again. He had drunk some six quarts of water, he said, but wasn't sure when he last ate, having long ago exhausted his supply of palmetto. Wood ticks covered his body, and he acted delusional, repeatedly calling Avery "Captain Strain." Avery oiled Parks's skin to relieve the sores and carefully parceled food and water to him in small doses, aware of the lethal consequences in allowing him to overindulge. It was a miracle he was alive.

By daylight Strain had hired five canoes for another ascent of the Chucunaque. It had never occurred to him that those he left behind would reverse course and march for the ship. For the first time Strain feared what those from Caledonia Bay to Washington, D.C., did: a rout.

Strain elected to use the canoe he borrowed from Hossack to paddle for the *Virago,* from which they were ensured assistance and provisions (apparently the majority of those that had been purchased for the aborted Avery attempt had been smuggled off by the boatmen). Strain knew from Bennett that the *Virago* was scheduled to be back in the harbor, but moments before he was to get under way, he received another jolt. Parks, who had arrived only two hours earlier, was dead.

"I was shocked," Strain wrote in the journal. "I had left him but a few minutes before, apparently asleep, and though delirious he appeared strong, and was no more emaciated than the members of my own party." Leaving Avery behind to make arrangements for Parks's funeral and to canvass the nearby villages for as large a rescue force as possible, Strain launched back into the Tuyra, making 18 miles before the flood tide forced them to tie up to the bank. The harbor was a full day away, and if the *Virago* wasn't in the harbor, which was a distinct possibility, Strain figured he would keep going to the English depot, where he'd request men and arms. Fortunately, the *Virago* was already under way, responding to the rumor that eleven more men, this time American, had been murdered.

It was early afternoon on the 18th. An inspired Strain memorably described the *Virago*'s approaching paddlebox boat as ascending the river "with all the rapidity obtainable from oars and tide." In charge was Lieutenant William C. Forsyth, and in his command were a party of nineteen, including four officers, thirteen "blue jackets," and two marine artillery. At least two of them had been on Prevost's crossing: George Julier, the tree climber, and Dr. William Ross, the *Virago*'s assistant surgeon. "I now felt that my party were secure from danger," wrote Strain, who was immediately transferred to the paddlebox boat for the short cruise back to Yaviza, arriving about 9 P.M.

The exact British orders are unknown. Part of the survey plan had always been to map the Chucunaque, so their response wasn't purely humanitarian. They were, for example, forbidden in the course of the relief expedition from straying at any time from the river proper, a directive that was likely the result of "the disasters of their previous expedition into the country," Strain guessed.

Yet a genuine bonhomie developed. Bennett had volunteered for the relief expedition, and according to Strain was prepared, if necessary, to disregard the orders and accompany Strain into the bush.

Later, the Americans would write of the "worthy tars" who came
to their aid, the noble action of their commanding officers, and the
deep feelings in their hearts—ones that might someday extend between their respective governments, "mother and daughter, after all."

The united British and American relief expedition left Yaviza at
11 A.M., having finally acquired three lightweight canoes for the portions of the river the paddlebox boat wouldn't be able to navigate.
Powered by fourteen oarsmen, the paddlebox boat had made 18 river
miles on the relatively direct course above Yaviza. But too many obstacles were scattered ahead. "It wasn't so much from the general
shallowness," wrote Dr. Ross, whose journal detailed the trip up the
Chucunaque, "as from the commencement of rapids and the numerous snags and trees which obstructed our passage."

The English were getting a quick lesson in the peculiar nature of
the river. In fact, the Chucunaque's unpredictable, vaguely predatory character had made itself known the first night out. "About midnight an immense forest tree," Ross remembered, "growing close to
the water's edge, and whose roots had been denuded, by the current,
of the surrounding earth, became loosened and fell with a tremendous crash into the water, just clearing by a foot or two our boat."

Other than the sentry, Strain had been one of the few awake,
pondering the state of things, he said, when he heard the now familiar explosion of fracturing timber, looked up, and glimpsed the "dark
and swaying form of a tree" slowly topple in what seemed at first to
be in their general direction, but then directly for their small flotilla
moored at midchannel. As he watched helplessly, the tree exploded
onto the waterline like cannon shot from the heavens, ripping off the
stern of one of the canoes tethered to the paddlebox boat. The noise
raised everyone from their beds, most of the soldiers believing the
party was under attack. Avery, who'd been sleeping in one of the
dugouts, had been spared by inches.

Humboldt had once written how slowly tropical forests were

"made to disappear by fire and axe," and in fact Strain's party had wasted its axe on the trunk of one of those steel-hard trunks. But one of the many paradoxes of the Darién was that the same trees, so resistant to the hand of man, seemed to fall all by themselves with no trouble at all.

AT 2 P.M. ON THE 19TH the English, the New Granadian boatmen, and Strain left the paddlebox boat, beginning the second part of their journey in assorted sizes of dugout canoes. Left behind was a guard of eight, plus Avery, who was suffering, and Wilson, who had returned with Bennett but was also failing. The longest of the canoes, some 40 feet, was given to Dr. Ross, who was preparing the craft to be a floating hospital. Forsyth commanded the next largest, while Bennett had his own. Near the lead Strain paddled himself in a smaller, slenderer version. Two more dugouts were manned by the New Granadians.

Battling against an ebb tide and assorted river obstructions, the party stopped at sunset, having made only three more miles. "The remainder of our journey up may be briefly condensed by stating that, during the next four days," began Dr. Ross, "we ascended the river a distance of sixty-seven miles—that it had a most torturous course, with reaches approaching almost every point in the compass . . . that its banks were wooded by forest trees and beautiful flowering plants close to the water's edge, among which were conspicuous palm, mahogany, and cedar trees . . . that it had in general high banks, bearing evidence of having been recently subject to the torrent of the river in a very swollen condition."

Ross said their travel through the wild river country was far more fatiguing than what he and the Prevost party had endured two months earlier up the isthmus. They paddled almost without rest, and whatever halts they did take were to drag the cumbersome boats across shallows or over trees. In one or two instances, where fallen trees stretched from bank to bank, they spent hours digging a canal around the roots in order to slip past.

"Meanwhile we were by day exposed to the intense heat of a vertical sun," continued Ross, "and, at night, to heavy dews and rain, which completely saturated our blankets, and added to the annoyance of millions of the most voracious musquitoes I ever met with."

Ross's detailed journal entries possess the elements of a standard government reconnaissance, noting mileage, course, and character of the river. Along the entire route a series of levels was taken and recorded. He included commentary on the "warlike" Indian inhabitants, whom they did not see, along with tidbits of natural history ("This river abounds in alligators") and the pleasant taste of the "sweet water."

During the same time period Strain's observations were a good deal more personal and agonized. Evidence of his own hardships (on the 21st they came upon his abandoned raft and the paddles he'd hewn with a machete) came first, then those of the main party. On the morning of the 22nd, they reached Hospital Camp 2 and Holmes's grave.

Seeing the crude pile of stones with one of his men beneath them shook Strain. He couldn't decide what was more disturbing: being left behind in the unmarked wilderness or being buried thousands of miles from one's own shore. He recalled the words Truxtun had left—"for God's sake try to overtake us, for we are nearly starving"—and felt his mind drift away to the palm and white-sand beach they had landed upon two months earlier. Perhaps theirs had always been a death march, as every crossing was. Holmes's remains were part of a historic trail of bones left behind by the Kuna, Spanish, English, and now Americans. Bones formed the topography of the isthmus, beginning at the beachhead of Caledonia and trailing up every riverbed and down every mountain slope. How many more was the only question.

Initially Strain was encouraged to find two regular camps with paths cut between, all by the book, but as they paddled farther up and inspected the return camps the disorganization became dramatically more pronounced. The worn-out belts and cartridge boxes discarded on the riverbank were a sign some had become too weak to carry full loads. Elsewhere, old scraps of leather, cut from their belts, were scattered about. Strain figured they'd been used as patches for their boots. The scattered quills of a buzzard, a vile scavenger, suggested they had reached the demented point of eating anything. Finally, a system of bankside crosses, which had been prearranged so Strain could identify Truxtun's position when he returned for them, had ceased altogether. Obviously they had given up on him.

On the morning of the 23rd, Strain was informed another body had been found. It was Polanco, the New Granadian junior officer. His skeletal remains, clothed in a linen undershirt and blue flannel, were exposed and lying upon the mounded outline of what seemed to be his own grave. At first Strain thought he'd been dug up by wild beasts, but the theory didn't square with what he saw, as the grave showed no signs of being disturbed. Upon Forsyth's supervision, the body was exhumed, revealing the corpse of the senior New Granadian representative, Ramón del Castillo Rada. Later, in hearing the survivors' stories, they would reason that Polanco, rather than being left to die in the Darién wilderness by himself, had found the strength to get to his feet and stumble several miles downriver so that he could die in the company of his late countryman. Before departing, Forsyth had Polanco's remains buried in Castillo's grave, marking the site with a wooden cross.

A few miles along, the fleet of canoes was stopped again, this time by a mammoth blowdown that stretched from bank to bank. It would have to be cut in two. The New Granadian boatmen, by far the most adroit at navigating the river, informed the officers that the river was only going to get worse, the portages more protracted. The shoreline closest to the river was miserably overgrown, meaning they would either have to slash open a trail through the clumped vegetation or wander farther from the Chucunaque in search of more open terrain. Distressingly, it appeared the Truxtun party might have opted for the latter. It had been hours since the last sign of a river camp. Whatever the case, the New Granadians didn't have the heart for going one step farther.

One can easily imagine Strain's fury. Their insolence, and perhaps the months of frustrating obstacles and misunderstandings, pushed him to the snapping point. He looked like a messianic vision, all bushy beard and billowy white oversized clothes. Without the boatmen, he knew, their chance of success fell steeply. Nobody else knew the river or how to handle the boats on it the way they did. Trying to regain his composure, he told them that they had volunteered for the rescue, and by turning around were jeopardizing soldiers' lives. He had been granted the authority of military discipline, he added, brandishing a six-shooter. They didn't have the option to leave; if they chose to turn around, they did so only upon the risk of extreme punishment, if not death. The eleven boatmen walked away to consult among themselves, then returned with their own ultimatum: They would continue on, but only until day's end.

They'd lost much of the morning, but late in the afternoon there was some good news: The scout boat, navigated by one of the New Granadians, had come across a campfire only three or four days old. In short order several more camps were uncovered, only a few miles apart; obviously the group was in great distress and barely able to maintain the march. Finding a trail of abandoned items—canvas haversacks, fragments of clothing, carbines—Strain began to fear the worst. It was possible they'd lost their discipline entirely, he now believed. He wondered how the breakdown would occur, who would suggest the ghastly solution of eating their dead "so that others might live," and what the horror would look like when he and Her Majesty's officers came upon it. He had eagerly anticipated their reunion for days. But the terrible thoughts of what was around the bend, and what he would do when faced with it, made him dread the discovery almost as much as he craved it.

Another campfire was found, then another; the latter was still warm. Urged on by the thrill of the chase, the boatmen dug their paddles deeper. They were excruciatingly near. Forsyth and Strain repeatedly ordered the muskets to be fired, waiting for an answer. Just before sunset a faint return was heard, "from the right bank of the river, a little in advance," recalled Ross.

Moments later the scout boat reported the smoke of a fire. Firing from his own musket, Strain rounded a wide bend to the sight of five of his men on a shelving beach. His nightmare seemed to have been realized: He was looking at the only survivors.

Reported Ross, coming onto the scene moments after Strain: "Several people were seen emerging from the woods, and crawling down the steep bank. They proved to be of the lost party, and a more wretched set of human beings were never beheld: so emaciated were they, that, clothed in their rags, they appeared like spectres; some had retained their arms and blankets, while others, scarcely able to drag along their own bodies, had thrown theirs away. . . . they were literally living skeletons, covered with foul ulcers and phlegmons." Their hair, matted and wild, fell to their shoulders.

They had been separated thirty-eight days. Thirteen of the eighteen remained, and most of those, reported Strain, were in a "state of the [most] extreme debility from starvation and fatigue," and were almost without exception "invalids." Ross, the English physician, observed that "in nearly all, the intellect was in a slight degree affected, as evinced by childish and silly remarks." They were in shock. They had, several said, given themselves up for lost.

The excited shouts from the river—from Maury, then Strain— lifted Truxtun out of his malaise. Only moments earlier prostrate and glassy-eyed, he was among the first to struggle down the riverbank and reach the water's edge. Rushing toward Strain and throwing out his arms in a sobbing embrace, Truxtun broke down. For the last week, as the men began to die off and the plantations never got closer, he had felt himself physically and mentally give way. The following day he would have granted the command to Maury, then watched the men disappear in the direction of the ship without him. He would have been left in his final hours to contemplate not only his own frailty but his unsuccessful decision. In the presence of Strain he surely felt he had been graced with his deathbed confessor: "My God, Captain," were his first words. "Did I do right to turn back?"

There was a prevailing myth among seamen about those long shipwrecked, then discovered. They often dropped dead moments after their apparent delivery, it was said, their weakened hearts unable to withstand the thunderstruck feeling of seeing the people they'd wished and prayed for standing heaven-sent before them.

Upon first sight of the survivors, the rescuers seemed every bit as vulnerable. The full weight of Strain's decision to go ahead was graphically displayed at the camp where the scene resembled the horrid aftermath of a battle. Many of the men, one of whom Strain could not even recognize, were so weakened they could speak no louder than a whisper. Only a few could rise. But there was no unseemly begging, Strain remembered, and several minimized what they'd been through, attempting to comfort Strain and shield him from the painfully obvious: the devastating human cost of the crossing.

At least three of the living could never have made another march, said Strain; two were near death. Philip Vermilyea, who'd been left behind earlier in the day but had managed to regain the group, was among the worst off. Vermilyea asked Strain to shake his hand, "and apologized in a feeble voice for not being able to raise his arm from the ground."

Little better was the engineer, Boggs, who was resting on his counterpane; it was an heirloom, Strain knew, imbued with fine needlework and prized by the pioneer families of Springfield who carried them on their long journeys west. Strain told his "old and true friend" from home that it was over, that they "had all of us now" and would soon be on the Pacific. Before he knew it, he'd be back home, back in Springfield, out of his filthy rags and into a wedding coat and a black bowler. Weakly returning the optimism, Boggs replied, "I do not think that I shall die now, Captain; but it is fortunate for me that you have arrived, as I should not have been able to go on to-morrow."

Not more than three or four could have reached the plantain fields, believed Strain, "and none could possibly have regained the ship." Had they been even two days later, the whole of the party would have perished, Ross suspected. Strain's fears that they'd resorted to a "disgraceful expedient" in order to sustain themselves proved unfounded. They had done nothing shameful, he said, nothing untoward; they'd simply marched until they couldn't. Looking at the grossly disfigured victims scattered about, the British officers would later marvel at what they described as the "party's discipline." They had not panicked, not risen in opposition to their commanders and turned to an option, hideous as it was, few could have blamed them for. Starvation was a physiological condition but also a psychological one in which the fear of starvation was nearly as debilitating. They had no prize to drive them forward. Another party, lacking strong leaders and a well-coordinated plan, might have given in. There were incidents in everyone's memory. But the Americans appeared fully resolved to do the next day what they had done each preceding day: those who could walk, walked. Those who couldn't would have to be left behind. Their behavior resounded with extraordinary purpose: Like the ice-bound Shackleton party sixty years later, they seemed convinced that they were engaged in something far bigger than themselves and that, perhaps, their story would survive.

Strain put the party in the charge of Ross, who demanded that nothing be given to the survivors except what he ordered. The men were ravenous for food but even more desperate for tobacco. "I cannot but look upon [this] as a curious physiological fact," wrote Strain. "It was general in the main body, and was also the first thing asked for by myself and other members of the advance party, upon our arrival at Yavisa."

Triumphantly dubbed Camp Recovery, Ross set to work removing botflies, dressing wounds, and oiling their skin (the oil hastened the removal of the wood ticks by loosening the parasite's feeding grip; once dislodged, they could be picked off whole). His personal interviews determined gross physiological malfunctions due to malnutrition and their dependence on palm nuts; in one unfortunate case, he duly noted, the constipating effect had lasted some twenty-five days.

Sentries were ordered to stand guard over the party, both to respond to their medical needs and because Ross feared they might rip into the stores and fatally gorge themselves on the molasses, sugar, and tobacco suddenly in their midst. Strain himself had done as much at Yaviza. Though he knew the extreme danger of overeating, he'd been utterly unable to deny himself what his body ached for. Consequently he suffered from hours of crippling stomach pain and was fortunate he hadn't killed himself. The doctor's refeeding prescription was simple if unsatisfying: a weak soup, with rice and bouilli and a small quantity of port wine and water. No tobacco.

On the morning of the 24th, and in spite of the doctor's careful regimen, "many of them could not move and had to be carried into the canoes." The survivors kept to the same general diet for the next three days, gradually receiving small rations of soft biscuit, molasses, and sugar. Haircuts and a thorough wash had the "effect of reviving them amazingly," the doctor reported. On the 26th they reached the paddlebox boat, where one of the party got into the safeguarded food stores and had what Ross described as an epileptic fit, a reaction to "over repletion."

Shortly after they arrived at Yaviza on the 27th Vermilyea succumbed, becoming the expedition's sixth fatality. The next morning he was buried adjacent to his shipmate Parks in a service attended by Bennett, the British relief party, and the small number of Americans who were deemed healthy enough to attend.

Efforts to revive Boggs were frustratingly unsuccessful. He'd endured the rugged weeklong river journey back to Yaviza, and another day's worth of canoe travel to reach La Palma, a small grass-hut village near the entrance to Darién Harbor. Strain made arrangements for him and the rest of the party to stay in the village, which he thought would better aid their recovery than the confining berths of an overheated ship. Ross and Dr. Henry Trevan, another of *Virago*'s doctors, agreed to make daily visits. All were still in a very debilitated state, the doctor reported in early April, but were recovering. The exception was Boggs.

After a week Strain left the party in charge of a much-improved Truxtun and along with two others embarked in a 40-foot-long open boat for Panama City, some 90 miles away. Notorious for its suffocating calms and a bullying vertical sun, the transit up the Pacific coast was torturously slow. "It is warm on the desert of Sahara; it is warm in the cañons of California; it is warm on the sands of the

Great Salt Lake Valley; it is warm, very warm at the Newport Ball. . . . But if you wish to know what the word Hot means,—if you wish to experience the sensation of having every drop of your blood baked into brick-dust,—be becalmed in a bungo in the Bay of Panama." Such were the words of Theodore Winthrop, who made the same trip a few years earlier.

Strain arrived five days later, on April 13. Three days later he took mules, then the partially completed railroad across the isthmus for Aspinwall and his long-anticipated reunion with the *Cyane*'s Hollins. The local newspapermen pronounced him fast recovering from the effects of his journey and looking fully competent. Twenty-four hours later he was back in Panama, where he chartered a sloop and sailed for Darién Harbor. If the *Virago* wasn't ready to leave—boiler repairs were delaying her—he intended to transfer the party himself in the sloop. The passage took four days. He found the party newly clothed in "duck and serge," outfits that their British counter-parts had sewn from *Virago*'s stock of cloth. Everybody was much improved, but for Boggs, who was "sinking very rapidly." Fortu-nately the *Virago* had been repaired and was ready to go.

On the 23rd of April the entire party was back in Panama, with the majority continuing across the isthmus to meet the *Cyane* at As-pinwall. Strain and Maury stayed behind with Boggs, whom they rushed to the city's American hospital. On his trip across the isth-mus, Strain had brought back the crew's personal mail from the *Cyane*, including a letter from Boggs's fiancée. Strain and Maury read it aloud, hoping to spark a miracle recovery, but on the same day, about 11 P.M., Boggs finally let go.

"It is a melancholy reflection," a Springfield newspaper reported a few months later, "that this estimable young man should have been permitted to reach the borders of civilization where medical attendance and comforts could be had in abundance, only to lie down and die—that just as the day was dawning upon his despairing and

trying circumstances, impenetrable darkness should suddenly en-
shroud him. But the ways of an all-wise Providence are inscrutable
and past finding out." Naturally everyone assumed the grief-filled
sentiments were Strain's own.

Before he could leave the city Strain was tracked down by several
of the resident American gentlemen. His safe arrival had been cause
for jubilation, and before he departed, an assortment of newspaper
publishers, merchants, and ex officio dignitaries pressed upon him a
Panama chain, a world renowned piece of goldwork only crafted in
Panama. It was a slight token, the gentlemen wrote, of their appreciation for Strain's "noble conduct . . . and of your personal exertions, which were the means of rescuing your party from the jaws of
death." They hoped the famous lieutenant would do them the honor
of attaching the chain to his expedition compass.

On the morning of the 24th, Strain and Maury mounted mules
and hurried back across the isthmus to reboard the *Cyane*. They arrived at 9:30 A.M. on the 25th. The party was safe, their health immeasurably improved and stable. Boggs would be the last and final
member of the U.S. Darién Exploring Expedition to be buried on the
isthmus. Ten minutes after Strain boarded the *Cyane* all hands upped
anchor and made sail to royals and flying jib. On barely a whisper of
wind, they were once more under way.

12 / CROSSING LINES

In judging the Darién Expedition many will pronounce it to be a failure . . . but let those who so judge, surrounded by the comforts of home, remember that this has been a sealed book for beyond a Century. [It] is now open for others to read.

LIONEL GISBORNE

April 16, 1854

9° 20′ N, 79° 55′ W
Aspinwall, Panama (Navy Bay)

WORD TRAVELED BY MAIL packets and electric wire. On April 16, Captain Hollins telegraphed the Navy Department with the message, "Lieut. Strain & party are safe." National newspaper headlines, replete with exclamation points and extra-bold, oversized type, screamed the joyous news and a rapt public devoured the thrilling details of how the brave Darién men had overcome unimaginable suffering to emerge from the jungle. For weeks newspapers in Panama and New York had covered the building drama and luridly speculated on the party's fate. Their deliverance was viewed with all the more gravitas since the men were long presumed dead. In San Francisco and New York grateful residents mobbed the docks to thank *Virago*'s crew while city leaders threw open to them "all the public places of amusement."

But the excitement tended to obscure the obvious next question: Why had it taken so long to find them? Why hadn't one of their own, or even one of the other expeditions, found them weeks if not months earlier? Men-of-war occupied both sides of the isthmus, with a slew of parties wandering through the interior, on and off, for months. The isthmus wasn't *that* big.

In fairness, a rescue was an unwieldy affair in a place such as Darién. There was an intense array of wilderness dangers and logistical
headaches. There was no such thing as changes on the fly. Help
might be sent, but whatever was done might be irrelevant before it
even got under way. Depending on where one was, a message traveling a few dozen miles as the crow flies might take days or weeks.
Meanwhile, the highly active isthmian press inflamed every rumor,
leaving rescue organizers something else to think about. The seemingly best strategy for getting anything done—small parties with native guides—ran counter to the understood rules of engagement in
hostile territory, which was to rush in a siege force prepared for Ar-
mageddon. A nineteenth-century jungle rescue took a leap of imagination, willpower, and a lot of luck—something perennially in short
supply in Darién.

Still, the American rescue actions were hard to figure. Theodore
Winthrop had gone out looking for Strain on January 25 and returned to the ship on February 3. The ship had stores and two hundred men at its disposal, but the next U.S. officer-led relief expedition
didn't set out for another month. In fact, on the 1st of March,
Winthrop submitted his letter of resignation to Hollins, and four
days later, on March 5, he sailed home aboard the steamer *George
Law*. His fellow volunteers Holcomb and Bird were with him.
Hollins assured him, said Winthrop, there would be no further attempts to rescue the Strain expedition. Though the captain had no
hard information, the entire expedition had apparently been given up
for dead. The search, he said, was over.

Only it wasn't. On March 3, the eve of Winthrop's official release
and two days before he left for good, Hollins informed the department that he intended to "clear up the mystery," outlining a major
search and rescue he planned to oversee himself. After being stalled
in Caledonia Bay for weeks, the ship was now anchored off Aspinwall, and Hollins said he and a few officers would make the transit to

Panama, where they would lay the groundwork for a Pacific-based rescue mission.

The misunderstanding between Winthrop and Hollins couldn't have been more gaping. Either Winthrop made the whole thing up, which is unlikely, or Hollins deceived him in order to hasten his exit and get on with the rescue himself. Winthrop's stated belief, that a sudden change of mind overtook the commander days after he left, simply wasn't true.

Undoubtedly Hollins was mightily exasperated. He had little experience in the tropics and possessed none of the physical attributes required for a successful dash across the isthmus. His barrel-shaped torso was like that of many sea captains of his era: well adapted to weather and wind and anything the sea could throw at him. But big bodies suffered faster and harder than any others in the jungle climate, something he well knew. Even his experience was all wrong. He was a veteran of war, not adventures. Hollins had never explored a thing.

There was another frustration too: his February pact with the *Espiégle*'s commander, George Hancock. It had come back to haunt him. He had agreed to hold off his own relief efforts on account of Gisborne's trip across the isthmus. Gisborne had asked the *Espiégle* to enforce a kind of isthmian exploration blackout, at least until they had heard he was safely across, thus averting a scenario that might agitate the Kuna. He was, after all, unprotected. For weeks Hollins had been handcuffed. On February 25 he dispatched a note to the *Espiégle* voicing his anxiety, it now being three-plus weeks with no word. The English commander, while sympathetic, firmly reminded him of the prior agreement and said that he expected to hear from Gisborne shortly. Even if he was inclined to violate the pact and set forth a relief party, Hollins was outnumbered, two ships to one. The search-and-rescue mission stood indefinitely stalled.

Potentially, Gisborne *was* the best chance for a rapid rescue, as he himself argued, but his mind was elsewhere. From the first moment he had arrived he had suffered one embarrassment after the other. First the Americans took off preemptively, snubbing his supposed "command" of the exploring parties. When he had set off, on January 24, he, Cullen, and a French-English exploring party of forty-four had encountered Winthrop, who was returning from his mix-up with Strain. The published route had been examined and didn't exist, he was told. "They received our statements with much surprise," remarked Winthrop. Gisborne charged off anyway but returned after nine days of ineffectual wandering, never having made it over the divide. Obviously there had been a terrible mistake.

Gisborne had further reason to be mortified—Edward Cullen. The doctor told anybody who would listen that Gisborne was out of his league. Cullen, the discoverer of the Darién route, thought he should be at the lead of the next pioneering party. In early February, with the news finally reaching Caledonia Bay that Prevost's men had been murdered, Gisborne put aside the petty squabbling, realizing there was an even bigger threat to his survey. It was entirely possible his mission would be delayed or even canceled if his government demanded redress and pursued the Indian assailants militarily.

Gisborne needed to act quickly. On February 7 he opted to take a pass on the military might of his nation and others, deciding that the only way to examine the route was to put himself and a small unarmed party in the hands of the Indians themselves. The party consisted of only himself, Lieutenant St. John of the Royal Engineers, two porters, an Indian guide, and Robinson, the American-educated San Blas Indian who had only recently returned from a long sojourn in Washington, D.C. Notably, Cullen was left behind with orders to stay put.

Gisborne followed the valley of the Caledonia to the foot of the cordillera, where he crossed by an "Indian track to the River Sucubti." Unable to obtain canoes at Sucubti for the descent to the

Chucunaque, he reluctantly proceeded overland, striking off in a northwest direction. At the village of Morti, a place Strain had been led *away* from, the chief allowed Gisborne two canoes to descend the Morti to its junction with the upper Chucunaque. From there, the same point visited by Strain, he ascended the river two miles to the point where "Captain Prevost's track from the Savana struck it." Concluded Gisborne, "We followed the track and arrived at the Savana within the tidal influence of the Pacific in a day and a half, or five days after leaving your ship." Due to the presence of the thirty-year-old Robinson, the Gisborne party was cordially greeted at the villages, invited to sleep in huts, and provided with food.

Gisborne had accomplished the crossing with minimal trouble, arriving on February 12. Yet it would be some time before the parties in Caledonia Bay would learn of it. After receiving communications dated February 8 from the Sucubti and February 10 from Morti, an anxious interval of fifteen days followed. The *Espiégle*'s Hancock didn't get word until February 28, by which point Hollins had already sailed for Aspinwall because of low provisions. Word might have come much sooner, in half that time, if Gisborne had made a point of it. But before notifying the *Espiégle* of anything, Gisborne launched another exploration, this time retracing Prevost's track back toward the Atlantic. The tributary that Prevost thought would deliver him to the Atlantic within a day was actually on the Pacific side of the divide. On that portion of his exploration the Gisborne party became exhausted and decided to return to the Savana, back-tracking along the easy "Prevost Road" rather than climbing over the cordillera to Caledonia Bay. Gisborne didn't dispatch Robinson with the confirmation news until the 25th, two weeks after he'd safely made it across. Thus the delay.

Later, Gisborne would claim he had made every effort to learn the whereabouts of Strain's party. True or not, Gisborne hardly prioritized the rescue effort. It wasn't until he'd made his Atlantic-to-

Pacific crossing, then retraced Prevost's route in the other direction (and came back) and been delivered to Panama by the *Virago* (to recross and do some more exploring on the Caledonia Bay side), that he enlisted the services of Captain Marshall and Lieutenant Forsyth to go looking for Strain.

Marshall was apparently weighing a punitive action when Gisborne interceded and more fully explained the delicacy of the situation and that the Indians had promised to apprehend and punish the murderers. His opposition wasn't entirely altruistic. Gisborne was still planning on exploring—new hostilities would put him in harm's way. Moreover, the public clamor to do *something* had reached a fevered pitch at Panama, something he realized shortly after arriving. And there was another reason to go where Strain was: Nobody had ever surveyed the route up the Chucunaque. A British reconnaissance would give him a thorough profile of the isthmus at Darién, encompassing virtually all the territory between the Gulf of San Miguel and Caledonia. Even if he flubbed in his earlier work, he'd be able to present the stockholders of the Atlantic and Pacific Junction Company with the most complete exploration ever done. His reputation might be spared.

One who increasingly saw it as his life's work to sabotage that reputation was Edward Cullen. Abandoned at Caledonia Bay, he had become, in Gisborne's long absence, the scapegoat for the doomed Strain expedition. Winthrop's statements had made it extremely clear that it was his misrepresentations that had fouled the U.S. effort. Days turned to weeks, and the longer Strain was gone, the more Cullen was vilified. He vowed to do something.

His appeals for a role, any role, fell on deaf ears. Captain Hancock was seemingly as disgusted with Cullen as everyone else and checked him at every turn. When Cullen attempted to board a schooner for a visit to Carreto—apparently he had in mind a desperate rescue attempt—Hancock stopped him, refusing him permission to leave the vessel or land ashore. Livid, Cullen slipped into a canoe in the early morning hours of February 23 and boarded the English survey vessel *Scorpion* in hopes of finding a more favorably disposed environment. A heated exchange of letters followed throughout the day. Hancock reminded him of his improper conduct. Cullen told the captain to stick it, he was a private gentleman. Hancock had Cullen removed "by force"—in this case, armed marines—and returned to his quarters on the *Espiégle*.

After a talking-to, Hancock came away with the impression that the doctor was apologetic, "abject even," and that was that. In fact, he was so satisfied he allowed the doctor to return to the *Scorpion* while his ship, the *Espiégle,* made a brief passage to Cartagena to meet the European mail. The doctor gave his word he would "hold no communication with the mainland" nor do anything without informing the captain of the *Chimère*, the French warship. But shortly after Hancock sailed, Cullen raced into overdrive. Hardly the cowed subordinate, he immediately fired off a letter as a "representative of the Atlantic and Pacific Junction Company of London," objecting to various things, requesting all original letters together with the sketches and plans that Gisborne had forwarded from the interior, and finally calling a consultation to "consider the best steps to be taken for the . . . sending across in one body, to the River Savana the largest number of men that can possibly be spared from each of the ships." He copied the entire fleet.

A day later, and not bothering to alert the captain of the *Chimère,* the resourceful Cullen found himself another canoe and delivered himself up to the U.S. ship *Cyane.* As far as Hollins knew, Cullen was on official English business, not a runaway. At the very least he appeared to be the one person who had any intelligence at all about the whereabouts of Strain, telling the commander that the Indians placed him on the banks of the Chucunaque, "only three days walk from Caledonia Harbor." On February 25, the *Cyane* sailed for Aspinwall with the doctor in tow. If Cullen was hoping for a safe sanctuary on the mainland and a chance to lead the glorious, long-delayed rescue, he sorely misjudged.

The Strain expedition had been absent more than forty days, and the most recent reports suggested they had been killed by Indians or died of hunger. Pulling in on March 3, Cullen found that his timing couldn't have been more dismal. If there had been any discussion of involving Cullen in a rescue effort from the opposite side of the isthmus—which Cullen later claimed there was—it was quickly dropped. The U.S. citizens of Aspinwall were outraged, and as Cullen later noted, it was all he could do to "escape from Aspinwall to avoid a lynching about Strain's reported loss." For three days he remained in hiding before sneaking aboard the *North Star*, a steamer bound for New York.

Indefatigable as ever, Cullen got off a letter when the vessel reached the States. Addressed to the editor of the *Panama Herald* and published on April 1, Cullen congratulated his colleague Gisborne on his safe crossing, something he'd learned of only hours before fleeing Panama. Regrettably, the English engineer was still off the mark, he wrote. The true pass, the lowest one, was a few miles to the west, across from the Channel of Sasardi. *That* was the gap he'd been talking about all along. And as for the American sufferings, Cullen was adamant. Had the *Espiégle*'s commander allowed him to launch his rescue when he wanted—instead of locking him up—he'd have gotten to Strain's party six weeks earlier. Had Cullen been in charge, nobody would have died.

At least on the latter point, Cullen might have had an argument. They were more than three days away, and Cullen knew the interior no better than anybody else, but he did appear to have won the trust of the Kuna who lived on the San Blas islands. Clearly the inhabitants of the isthmus were the only ones with both clear information

on the whereabouts of Strain and an understanding of how to get to
him effectively.

Hollins, recognizing this, had the right idea in enlisting Cullen,
just rotten timing. Once they arrived in Aspinwall and realized that
the notion of a Cullen-led anything was untenable, Hollins evidently
decided to lead the search himself. Now knowing that Gisborne had
returned and he was free to do as he pleased, the commander crossed
the isthmus to assemble his party and start in after Strain. When he
got to the other side, however, he had a change of heart. A tax dispute was brewing; Hollins hoped to mediate but was unable to persuade the Panamanian authorities to suspend a 10 percent tax on
American shipping. Hollins abruptly returned to Aspinwall on
March 11 in order to protect the vessels planning to resist the duty.
Suddenly the job of finding Strain fell to his subordinate, Lieutenant
Fauntleroy, the same Fauntleroy who had withheld men and food—
apparently out of some dislike for Strain—when Winthrop's party
left Caledonia on its one and only search-and-rescue effort.

Fauntleroy was prepared to accept an invitation to join the *Virago*
rescue mission, but a day later demurred, deciding instead to form
his own party. New intelligence, Fauntleroy wrote Hollins, suggested a dramatically different tack. A man from Chepo, accompa-
nied by an Indian from up the river, had come to Panama to tell the
governor they shouldn't be held culpable for the terrible fate of the
lost American party. According to the men, eleven of Strain's command had been devoured by wild beasts. Given the new accounting,
Fauntleroy now favored going forth among the friendly Indians on
the Chepo River, where he'd rely on villagers to lead him to Strain.
The revised plan also provided "an excellent reason for declining to
accompany the *Virago* party," which he'd have to assist as a mere
subordinate—something that was bound to cause deep discomfort in
Washington.

The plan was ludicrous. Fauntleroy had no experience and could enlist no help. A crucial written proclamation from the governor, absolving the Indians of guilt and guaranteeing their safety, never materialized. The Chepo men who had come to Panama vanished. For the next twelve days, from the 14th of March until the 26th, Fauntleroy and an associate from the Swedish consulate ascended the Bayano, a river about as far away from Strain as one could get in Darién. They met no one with any information and returned sick and exhausted. Almost comically, the night he stumbled back to Panama, the 26th, was the night word reached the city that Strain and a portion of his party—thanks to the heroic efforts of the *Virago*—were safe.

In the interim, Hollins had launched a second rescue expedition, this one taking place back at Caledonia Bay and resembling what Cullen had envisioned weeks earlier. On the 23rd the *Cyane* had finally departed Aspinwall, the taxation dispute resolved and all the steamers cleared from that port. On the 28th, after Strain had safely arrived at Panama but before Hollins had heard about it, two officers, ten seamen, and an Indian guide departed for the headwaters of the Chucunaque. They had progressed over the divide and 12 miles down the course of the Sucubti before getting Hollins's recall order on the 31st. Strain was safe. The news had come to Hollins on the 29th, brought to him by a schooner hired in Aspinwall. "Glad tidings have reached me this evening," wrote the U.S. consul, G. W. Fletcher. "Thank God Lieut. Strain and his party are safe."

Availing himself of the chartered schooner, Hollins dispatched Dr. George Peck, the ship's surgeon, to Aspinwall. He carried a note telling Strain that the *Cyane* was continuing on to Cartagena, where he and his men were to meet them. Almost two weeks later, on the 11th, Hollins changed course again, having gotten a return note from Peck. Evidently their condition was much worse than anyone imagined. "From the nature of his report," Hollins wrote the Navy Department, "it was thought best to proceed at once to Aspinwall."

LIONEL GISBORNE LEFT Caledonia Bay on April 6 aboard *Espiégle,* proceeding to England on a mail steamer on the 11th. Gisborne didn't deny his earlier mistakes. His prior "error in judgement" combined with Cullen's falsity "had completely misrepresented the character of the country." Yet they had accomplished much to be proud of, examining the technical merits of the Darién proposal in a way never before done. A prohibitively expensive tunnel was likely necessary at Caledonia, but he didn't rule out the possibility of a lower pass nearby.

He said he couldn't "sufficiently express my admiration of the perseverance and energy which Lt. Strain has shown, and the almost miraculous manner he has succeeded in reaching the Pacific." Had the British benefited from his cooperation, he added, the survey would have been the better for it.

Despite his keeping the door open (he half hoped to return to Darién next winter), the company dissolved, returning to the shareholders the amounts of their investments, without any deductions. In time Gisborne moved on to other matters, and he never returned— a decision, at least in the short term, that served him well. His reputation was restored, and he spent the rest of his career working on the era's other prepossessing civil engineering challenge, submarine telegraphy. For a time he was a brilliant success. He obtained a concession from the Turkish government for an electric cable from the Dardanelles to Alexandria, and subsequently a concession for a land telegraph through Egypt, from Alexandria to Suez. In 1859 and 1860 he submerged a cable from Suez down the Red Sea to Aden, and another along the northern part of the Indian Ocean to Kurachee—

the two cables, taken together, stretched 3,000 miles, 500 miles longer than the American line across the Atlantic. Several other projects were superintended for the English and the French governments, the latter being a line from France to Algiers. Other projects were pending when the work suddenly dried up.

In practice, none of his cables lasted more than a few weeks, some much less than that. His own government and several others lost millions of dollars. Perhaps the cables failed because they'd been ruptured by harsh currents, or maybe because they were ill-sheathed to begin with, but in point of fact nobody knew. They simply lay at the very bottom of one sea or another, dead and irrecoverable. At the time it seemed like they all short-circuited at once. Gisborne was disgraced. In 1861, at the age of thirty-eight, he died of unknown causes, unemployed. A few years later, British engineers, having seen the flaws in Gisborne's designs and alighting on the necessary improvements, strung together a deep-sea telegraphy line from Brest, France, to Duxbury, Massachusetts, the world's longest.

13 / HOME

They have done nothing further in Congress with re-spect to the Darién Party. . . . The only way to get these things through, however, is by lobbying and pulling the wires, and I don't think any one of the party would condescend to do that.

JACK MAURY, IN AN 1856 LETTER ABOUT AN ANTICIPATED GOVERNMENT COMMENDATION TO THE DARIÉN SURVIVORS

June 25, 1856

41° 30′ N, 71° 20′ W
Newport, Rhode Island

T HE COTTAGE was a lovely white clapboard building with forest-green shutters and a wraparound porch shaded by stately linden and oak trees. The Greek Revival pillars were a common feature in a time when public homage to the antiquities didn't hurt one's gentlemanly standing. Inside, there were framed daguerreotypes, dark Mission-style furniture, and a library study groaning with four walls of old leather-bound books. Pocket journals and great epistolary tomes lay side by side, gobbling every available space in the floor-to-ceiling bookshelves, suggesting they had been pulled and re-pulled. Congressional serials, a compilation of the American world as it stood, took up a yard of shelf space.

True to the era, the intellectual sweep was a bit scattershot, but there was no doubt that a serious traveler lived here: keynote titles abounded, such as Perry's expedition to Japan, James Fenimore's *History of the U.S. Navy*, Humboldt's *Narrative of Travels to the New World*. Many of the books were inscribed, some with feverishly scribbled notes on scraps of paper. A well-worn backgammon board lay at the foot of one of the shelves. Months might pass in this little room. And there, on the wall nearest the sea, was a dashing portrait of the place's owner and architect, Samuel Greene Arnold.

Lazylawn, as Arnold affectionately dubbed his cottage, was a favorite of Isaac Strain's. He and Arnold, a future U.S. senator, had become fast friends after the pair met at Rio de Janeiro in 1847. Arnold was then twenty-six, in the midst of three years of travels that would take him across Europe and South America. He inscribed the journal from those travels "To My Wife—This Gift—The Most Valuable that I Can Bestow—The Result of Three Years Travel With Much Hardship—Is Happily Presented on Her Wedding Day." A shared passion for travel was at the heart of his relationship with Strain too. Upon their first meeting Arnold had remarked how impressive the then-midshipman was—he was a traveler for traveling's sake, he'd cheered. At the time Strain was planning a foray into unexplored Brazil and another "mystical and desperate adventure" that Arnold couldn't wait to be involved with, though he acknowledged he didn't know what it was. Over the years the friendship grew, and in 1856, two years after Darién, Arnold offered him his idyllic seashore retreat to convalesce.

Isaac's days were surely occupied by copious letter writing, long afternoon rambles, and keen social engagements. He often looked from the wraparound porch south by southeast, the vista opening to the ocean breakers and a horizon where the "glass" offered him a view of the ship traffic coming and going from Newport—no doubt quickening his pulse and inspiring him back to the study to plot a new dash somewhere. If his gaze could have extended limitlessly across the ocean, it would have landed along the coast of Spain, near Cape Finisterre.

Unfortunately, Strain's moments of respite were a precious few. He couldn't shake Darién—not the infirmities, not the controversies, and certainly not the feeling that there was still something to prove.

THE *CYANE* HAD ARRIVED in New York on May 17, 1854, only narrowly averting disaster when the ship scraped shoal bottom off Ab-
secon Inlet. Almost immediately, Strain had to address unexpected
rumors that the expedition was ill conceived and ill led. That summer, still two years before Newport, he bunkered himself in Newburgh, New York, a lovely historic village high on the banks of the
Hudson. Here, Strain expected to find a nurturing, leisurely atmosphere where he could pen his official report in peace.

Urged by the secretary of the Navy to complete his account as
soon as possible, Strain soon found himself overwhelmed. It was the
hottest summer in anyone's memory, with one July day after another
topping the 90 degree mark, and several reaching 100. The heat
wave, which began with Strain's arrival and lasted all summer long,
was decimating the local farms and causing a rash of illnesses. Even
the famous mountain view, the staple of Newburgh living that had
drawn society's best and brightest to the little hamlet (including
some of the country's foremost writers), wasn't much of a balm.
One local writer characterized the southward and westward mountains as "nature's arm thrown lovingly around us." For a writer in
the grip of various maladies, and with a view before him that was
strikingly similar to the rising mountains off Caledonia Bay, the embrace probably felt more like a headlock.

Strain asked the department to send him Jack Maury, since Maury
was the expedition secretary and had also been with the main party.
And he pleaded for more time. Both requests were granted, though
Secretary Dobbin reminded Strain that a comprehensive report
wasn't necessary, just something to satisfy Congress. Strain thought
otherwise, believing that the report he produced would need to stand
up against the forthcoming publishings from Gisborne, Cullen, and
others.

In a July 31 dispatch, Strain blamed more delays on his chronic dysentery and the "numerous letters which have been written to me on subjects concerned with the Expedition, especially from friends and relations of those who have died, letters to which, humanity and courtesy requires replies and in some cases, lengthy ones, especially to those written by wives and sisters." In the course of two days, the final ones of July, Strain answered more than twenty letters. He was exhausted.

The final report was not a good deal more complete than what he'd written back on the isthmus for the *Virago* commander Edward Marshall. "For more satisfactory details," he added, "I will be obliged to refer you to the narrative which has been transmitted to the Navy Department for a thorough elucidation of this question." He seemed apologetic. But the several months in the Newburgh highlands wasn't for naught. In the case of one association, it changed his life.

Joel Tyler Headley, who came to know Strain, had only recently moved to Newburgh himself. He was a celebrity author whose best-seller, *Washington and His Generals,* would prove to be one of the most popular books of the time. To a female admirer, he once wrote, "The multitude of requests for my autograph which I receive from gentlemen I dispose of in the briefest possible manner but one from a lady I always regard as a compliment and invariably picture to my-self what sort of a lady she is." (Acknowledging that modesty wasn't his strong suit, Headley went on to inform the woman he saw her as "good looking . . . intellectual," and in possession of a "warm and glowing imagination.")

His prose unabashedly glorified American virtues and pioneer spirit in a way that found wild favor with the public (critics, a good deal less kind, called it pandering). But his interests also genuinely extended to the wilderness: Headley was one of the first to explore and popularly describe the Adirondack region, which he aptly called an "unrecognized paradise." Headley was a romanticist, and didn't let facts obscure the essential truths. It's hardly any wonder he found the Darién story absolutely irresistible—he made a point of calling on the visiting lieutenant.

The two quickly hit it off and agreed to collaborate on a larger story, the one Strain didn't have time to prepare for Congress. Headley was granted access to Strain's journals; he interviewed Maury, Avery, and others. The result was a fifty-thousand-word article for *Harper's New Monthly Magazine,* the first installment appearing in March 1855. *Harper's* was the most important magazine of the day, and the Strain article one of its biggest coups. For weeks, the Panama newspapers excerpted the "thrilling narrative" on the front page. Several American newspapers, including the *Providence Journal,* did the same. The illustrated article made not only Strain but Maury, Truxtun, Avery, and the entire band of Darién survivors heroes all over again.

Yet there continued to be conflicting reports that Strain and Headley had swept aside less favorable features of the expedition. As Strain had expected, both Cullen and Gisborne wrote accounts at variance with Strain's. They portrayed him as amateurishly overeager, having jumped the gun prematurely at Caledonia and misread the situation with the Indians. Had he waited, nobody would have died. British newspapers emphasized the fact that he hadn't rescued the others himself but had done so thanks to the courageous efforts of the *Virago*'s crew.

In early 1856, the criticism came to a head with an article published by Agustín Codazzi, chief of New Granada's survey team. In *Allgemeine Zeitung,* one of the most popular magazines in Europe, he rehashed the Darién expedition story, dredging up the familiar criticisms. The Americans had arrogantly presumed to cross the country without the aid of Kuna guides; they had been ignorant of the forests, unable to identify the appropriate foods to eat or the timber that might have supported their float trip out. But Codazzi went several steps further, employing either outrageous dramatic license or information nobody else had. He said that the Americans had, in their terrible desperation, subsisted on one another, their emaciated bodies serving as "food to the desperate and savage appetites of their companions, in order to prolong an existence constantly bordering on extinction."

On June 17, 1856, Strain made an appearance before the New-York Historical Society, using the forum to make a lengthy rebuttal. The gathering, held in the large chapel of the old University Building in Washington Square, was unusually large, with reporters from several papers sharing booths with gentlemen and statesmen. Reading from his prepared paper, Strain defended himself ably and with passion, drawing rave reviews in the next day's papers. The society itself was charged with indignation, vowing to send correspondence to its affiliates abroad to set the record straight. It was a crowning moment to stand before such an august assemblage, the likes of which included Daniel Webster, William Cullen Bryant, and none other than Don Pedro II, the young emperor of Brazil. Also in attendance, and drawing robust cheers at their introduction, were Strain's cohorts, now Lieutenant William Talbot Truxtun and Frederick Avery. At the conclusion, the party adjourned to one of the upper rooms, where an extravagant strawberry feast had been prepared. A decade earlier Strain had told a friend he hoped to work his way east, finding his way into the right kind of company so he could make a name for himself. On June 17 he was as "east" as one could get.

Days later Strain was back at sea, his first service in two years after a prolonged stay at the large naval hospital in Brooklyn. He'd been appointed executive officer aboard the steamship USS *Arctic* to help execute Matthew Fontaine Maury's pet project: sounding the Atlantic Ocean for a transatlantic telegraph cable. Preliminary soundings over the proposed bed had already determined there was, as Maury put it, a "bottom for it." Having gained a patron in the wealthy New York merchant Cyrus Field, the once derided project in "instantaneous communication" was back on the front burner. Congress appropriated funds for a new survey. By all accounts Strain was overjoyed to be part of the historic undertaking. In 1855 the longest electric cable was a mere 1,000 miles. The lone submarine cable in operation was along the Strait of Dover in the Irish Sea, a comparatively piddling distance of 25 miles. The project—as pragmatic, some said, as a railroad to the moon—almost rivaled a ship canal for visionary flourish.

The expedition, which left St. John in early July, was exceedingly dangerous and difficult. A crew member said the experience of hauling and handling frozen lines in storm-tossed seas was replete with "personal hardship, some imminent dangers, severe unremitting labor and more than ordinary discomforts." The northward seas near Labrador were a harrowing stretch, with icebergs and floes requiring vigilant watches and unerring navigation. The vessel itself, a whaling ship salvaged for the occasion, was barely suitable, with a failing engine and poor technical design. "We flew a pennant and claimed to be a man of war, [but] there was not a gun or other instrument of warfare on board of her," a crew member wrote.

Still, the ship successfully traced the great circle between St. John and Land's End, making some sixty successful casts with its probe of glorified piano wire. At each point on the prescribed route the bottom distance was measured and water temperature recorded. In addition specimens were drawn from the deep, some of the first to be seen at depths averaging 2,000 fathoms. Captain Berryman and Strain placed them—much of the biomass was described as "blue ooze"—in special vials marking the latitude and longitude of each discovery. Field, who had seen the ship off in New York, was there to greet them at Land's End. He was so euphoric at the results of the mission's survey—the line of deep-sea soundings had confirmed the practicability of a submarine telegraph between the two continents—that he provided each of the officers with railway tickets for a holiday in London.

But Strain's involvement was bittersweet. He was a shell of his former self. According to the same crew member, the lieutenant suffered greatly on the forty-day crossing. His Darién-related bronchial problems reemerged under the exertion of duty and exposure to the wind and cold. Before the ship departed for its triumphant homecoming—they were to retrace their route and double-check all readings—Strain was accorded permission to stay behind in England. The *Arctic*'s John Sanford Barnes recalled that Strain had simply never recovered from the Darién exploration: He suffered from several physical disabilities, his missing teeth being the most visceral reminder of what he'd uniquely been through. As Barnes noted, he'd lost them from "eating the beetle nuts."

By the fall, Strain had returned to the United States, settling back in Newport to regroup. His naval career was falling apart. Prodded by Congress, the Navy was aggressively and controversially involved in purging its officer ranks of dead wood. On September 12, 1855, President Pierce backed the findings of the Naval Efficiency Board. Of the service's 712 officers, 49 were dropped and 152 were retired on diminished pay. Somehow Strain survived the "Plucking Board's" first cuts—probably due to his Darién celebrity and his friendship with Secretary of the Navy James Dobbin—but he might not the next. In fact, Strain's ability to stay on the payroll was even more tenuous in light of an incident earlier in the year.

In the spring of 1855 he'd been ordered to the *Cyane*, then under the command of A. B. Fairfax. In the course of a social occasion at the Brooklyn Navy Yard's Mansion House, Strain asked Fairfax the favor of detaching him from duty aboard *Cyane*. Unexpectedly, an agitated Fairfax took the request personally, refusing to hear Strain's "true meaning," and dismissing him in a harsh, preemptive way. Strain returned to the commander's presence a short while later with several letters, one of which was a formal application for detachment. Fairfax boiled over. He confronted Strain as he put on his overcoat and angrily ordered him on board immediately.

"Irritated before," remembered Strain in his letter to Dobbin, "and much excited by his language, this threat as I understood it of personal violence almost maddened me, and the naval officer for the moment was lost in the man—natural instinct arose superior to education—and I replied drawing myself back from him—'If it comes to that Sir I will not go on board.' "

Strain was self-reproachful in his explanation of the "mortifying occurrence," aptly characterizing himself a disciplinarian who "cannot but regret that I should have withheld the obedience which I in turn exact," but Strain also emphasized the emotional reasons at the heart of the disagreement. Though two years removed from the day *Cyane* brought him and other survivors to New York, Strain confessed he was traumatized at the thought of getting back on the ship. "My last cruise in the *Cyane* was the most [onerous] I have ever had in the naval service," he said. In the course of a single five-month cruise he'd gone from a young man to an old one, arriving in port "ill and debilitated." His physical pain had been surpassed, however, by news that greeted him of his seeming betrayal. Theodore Winthrop's private letter home, the last of his updates to William Aspinwall, had appeared anonymously on the front page of the popular *Herald* and had characterized the party as "badly arranged, badly fitted out, badly led, and *mal composé*."

By the spring of '56 the insubordination charges against Strain had been pending for months. The task of assembling witness statements was a cumbersome one, sometimes taking years. Still, a court-martial was in the offing. Yet within days after Strain's unusually emotional letter, Dobbin forgave the incident, detaching him from

Cyane and putting him on standby, awaiting new orders. "I can assure you Sir that you shall have no reason to regret having spared me
the mortification to which an official investigation would have subjected me," wrote an overjoyed Strain. "[It] would have given me a
most unenviable notoriety, when taken in connection with the expedition which has attracted public attention somewhat to my name."
A month later he was aboard the aforementioned *Arctic,* apparently
never to see the *Cyane* again.

DURING HIS APPEARANCE at the New-York Historical Society, a
week before the *Arctic* cruise, several audience members wondered
what had happened to his gallant expeditionary mates. The greater
number, Strain happily told them, remained presently employed in
the service of the country.

In theory the officers were supposed to have received months of
leave time. Their health was quite feeble and totally unable to withstand a sea life, wrote Captain George Hollins; they needed time to
recoup their "original vigor." In practice few got the full measure of
their allotted time. One who got no time was Hollins himself, who
was almost immediately put back aboard the *Cyane* and briefed for a
possible military strike.

He was to redress wrongs done to U.S. citizens at Greytown,
Nicaragua, a flash point in relations between Great Britain and the
United States. Though Hollins bemoaned the "entirely unfit" shape
of the ship and the exhaustion of his crew, the Navy Department ordered the ship out three weeks later. When the *Cyane* arrived off
Greytown in late June, Hollins met with the authorities and among
other things demanded a full apology for the precipitating incident,
an insult suffered by the American minister to Central America. After failing to gain concessions, Hollins issued an ultimatum to the
civilian population that bombardment would commence at 9 A.M.

on the 13th. Within one minute of the time designated Hollins unleashed his controversial—and, many thought, unwarranted—onslaught, blasting away at the town for six consecutive hours. At the conclusion he landed a party that torched any remaining buildings. The action, which seemed to assert in the loudest, most belligerent terms the United States' primacy over the highly strategic Central American isthmus, nearly started a war with England (in fact, the HMS *Espiégle,* under Hancock, steamed to Greytown's defense but arrived only after the *Cyane* had departed).

"There were only about 80 houses in the town, and not to exceed 500 inhabitants," wrote a New York editorialist. It was at once mystifying and shameful that an American vessel should attack and lay to waste such a "miserably defenseless town."

Some would wonder if Hollins's remorseless decision to blow Greytown out of the water had its origins well away from Nicaragua. At Darién, only weeks earlier, he'd been neutralized and then grandly upstaged by his British counterparts, who did far more to help rescue Strain's men than he ever did. Fatigued and antagonized, Captain Hollins was hardly predisposed to hang around and talk.

SAMUEL HOLLAND KETTLEWELL, whose drawings and journal keeping helped breathe life into the expedition for future chroniclers, such as *Harper's* Headley, was one of those who didn't care to go back to active duty. Beginning in 1850 with the Mexican Boundary Commission, he'd served an adventurous five years, traveling through two of the most unexplored and treacherous wildernesses in the hemisphere, the American Southwest and Darién. He was the son of a general in the Royal Artillery, but in the summer of 1854 he returned to civilian life, his wife, Harriet, and their large, growing family. He attempted to set up a civil engineering practice in Baltimore, but Darién-related health problems apparently prevented him from earning much of a living. In 1859, he wrote the new secretary of the Navy pleading for relief:

For six years—almost unremittingly, since my service . . . on the Darien Exploration—I have been a victim to Dysentry— produced by the unparalelled sufferings of that unfortunate expe- dition; in which credit was due to me for the Survey. Mapping. Recording of Journal (so flatteringly mentioned by Headley). The late lamented Secretary of the Navy, in the interview after return of the Surviving Party very handsomely acknowledged my ser- vices—eulogized previously by Lt Strain—and hoped that, should I ever require it the Dept would present some Post worthy of them.

Through all vicissitudes, at one or other occupation as physical strength permitted I have struggled without any application for Office till now, after another severe return of Chronic Dysentry I am compelled there being a dearth of any employment elsewhere to apply for one.

Preparatory to the Congressional Session, Clerks (temporary) are wont to be employed; and I would entreat, not merely on ac- count of the past to which with pain I refer, but of my wife and six children that, whether in the Navy or other Dept., I could find for them means of subsistence.

> *Sir,*
> *Your respectful and obed't*
> *SH Kettlewell*
> *Civil Engineer and Draughtsman*

Apparently Kettlewell was appointed a clerkship, but when the Civil War broke out he sided with the Confederate Army, enlisting as a forty-five-year-old in the Virginia infantry and helping to construct breastworks. Again the durable Kettlewell survived, but two years later his firstborn, Private Edward Randolph, was struck down by yellow fever at Wilmington, North Carolina. For Kettlewell, who had recorded the last wishes of the dying Holmes and Lombard, and who had ministered the ailing from one side of the isthmus to the other, the news of his son's death stirred memories of Darién. Every day they had thought about yellow fever; every seaman did. The yellow tinge came on in only a few hours, then tormenting nausea, violent headaches, and a terrible wakefulness. It was considered the absolute worst way to die.

WILLIAM TALBOT TRUXTUN, Strain's courageous second in command, returned to service almost immediately, moving through the ranks with unusual swiftness. Two years after Darién, in Philadelphia, he married Annie Elizabeth Scott, the daughter of a prominent banker. His forty-year career wouldn't include any more exploring expeditions, nor a single cruise in the tropics. He'd serve throughout the Civil War, commanding several of the ships that formed the North Atlantic Blockading Squadron. Joining the *Chocura*, the first of his ships, was a Darién veteran, John O'Kelly, who had distinguished himself with "self sacrificing attention to the sufferings of the dying." Ironically, the *Chocura* was the mainstay behind the Wilmington blockade, the same blockade that led to increasingly harsh conditions and fever plagues of the kind that took Kettlewell's son.

Yet many of Truxtun's early war experiences had a humanitarian flavor, with his command often providing relief to fleeing slaves. Especially poignant was his account of a plantation burning near Hilton Head. "Soon after leaving the ship a canoe containing three negroes was met who stated that the rebels three hundred strong were at Mrs. March's plantation, killing all the negroes." For weeks afterward Truxtun's ship received dozens of refugees, always in a half-starved condition, "whose appeals for food I have not yet been able to resist, though trespassing rather largely on the ships stores."

In late 1864, Truxtun saw his most significant and important action as part of the force that overwhelmed Fort Fisher, the last major Confederate stronghold. "There has been no other officer in this squadron in whom I have more confidence or for whom I have a higher respect," his commanding officer wrote in the battle's aftermath.

Many years later, in 1885, he was named commander of the Navy yard at Norfolk and promoted to commodore—the same rank as his late grandfathers. When he died two years later, at age sixty-three, his funeral at Christ Church in Norfolk was recorded as the "most imposing and largely attended" since the war.

There is no record of Truxtun ever having written anything about Darién. A report he supposedly prepared for Strain never appeared in the final report of the secretary of the Navy. An indication, however, of the expedition's personal impact might be gleaned from the family papers of his grandfather, Thomas Truxtun, held by the Library of Congress. In them is a copy of the *Harper's* article with a special black leather custom cover inscribed "DARIEN EXPLORING EXPEDITION LIEUT. W. T. TRUXTUN, U.S. NAVY." It was likely presented to Truxtun shortly after the article appeared, perhaps even as a gift from Strain himself. Inside, a note from Truxtun's daughter reads: "This book is one of my most cherished possessions. I am sending it to you with my dearest love, hoping that you will read every word and so realize . . . your grandfather's courage and character during his Darien Expedition experience." His family's pride in what he had accomplished would suggest Truxtun's own. Evidently Strain had long ago unburdened him. He had done the right thing.

BACK HOME IN THE District of Columbia, John Minor Maury's leave from duty only lasted a few weeks. In the summer of 1854 he was ordered to join Strain in Newburgh, New York, where he assisted the ailing lieutenant in compiling his report for Congress.

In the report Strain singled out Maury for special department commendation, remarking that Maury's "physical endurance surpassed that of any member of the party." Strain also related what Truxtun had told him about Maury shortly after they'd reunited at Recovery Camp. The twenty-nine-year-old Virginian, Truxtun said, was the only man he'd ever known who could endure so much and pass through so many trials "without displaying a single instance of selfishness." He had distinguished himself in the one way his lamed guardian Matthew Fontaine Maury never could—as an officer in the field. His family, M.F. included, celebrated Jack as the newest Maury standard-bearer. "He kept the whole party alive by his devoted exertions," wrote his half sister. "For the last two weeks they were out 'Jack' was the only one who had the strength left to carry a shot-gun."

After receiving more praise from a grateful Strain for his help in Newburgh, Maury returned to active duty in the fall of '54, serving aboard the USS *Princeton* in the West Indies. Health ills and troubles with the department began to crop up shortly thereafter. He vigorously protested his next department assignment, a fourth consecutive cruise into the Torrid Zone, again the West Indies. Maury believed the repeated exposure to the tropical climate was jeopardizing his health and rendering him unfit for further service. The department's refusal to reassign him prompted a disgusted Maury to tender his resignation on February 26, 1856.

A month later, Secretary Dobbin, who had refused to accept the resignation, got Maury detached. But Maury's career lasted only a few more months. Continuing to complain of illness and having lost his heart for service, Maury failed to turn up for his scheduled officer's exam and resigned for good on September 17, 1856.

It's unclear what occupied Maury over the next several years, though he likely shuttled between the family home in Fredericksburg and that of his kinsman, Matthew Fontaine Maury, in Washington. In 1861, at the outbreak of the war, Maury partnered with former *Cyane* commander George Hollins aboard the Confederate steamer *St. Nicholas*. Listed as a captain of the Provisional Army of Virginia, Maury and Hollins's force handed the Union one of its most crushing naval defeats, capturing the prizes *Monticello, Mary Pierce,* and *Margaret* in Chesapeake Bay on June 29, 1861.

Like officers on both sides, Maury didn't anticipate either the length or the all-consuming nature of the war. After returning from Darién, he had written passionately about settling down and starting a family—in fact, his decision to quit the Navy was an effort to begin a life where he could have a chance of "trying to get married." In 1860, only months prior to Fort Sumter, he declared his sights set on a lovely Fredericksburg lady, telling an old friend he intended to make a "desperate and most determined assault on Miss Kate" and that he would "dig such a number of pitfalls around her that she must tumble into some of them for I am determined to have her." By 1861 he had his wedding date. But the devastating war, especially in Virginia, threw everything into chaos. After one postponement Maury wrote his best man in October 1862—the month they were originally to marry—to say the engagement was broken: "It is all off . . . I am mighty sorry, but it cannot be helped and there is no use in crying about it or talking about it, suffice it to say that nobody was to blame . . . and that is all I ever expect to tell anybody about it."

In the fall of 1864, the Army of Northern Virginia withstood a major Union assault near Richmond, but the price was costly. Thousands were killed at Chaffin's Bluff, and hundreds more, including

Maury, were captured and brought to Fort Delaware, the same fort he and the rest of the Darién party had marveled over as they wended their way down the Delaware River a decade earlier. Whatever wonder he had once felt at the rising pentagon-shaped structure was replaced by horror: Delaware, a wretched place raked by disease and misery, was one of the most reviled Union-run prisoner-of-war camps. Some thirty thousand Confederate soldiers would spend time behind its 30-foot-high granite walls, thousands of them to die there. Several inmates remembered the "starvation diet" as the worst hardship. In 1865, the U.S. government had reduced the daily ration to Rebel prisoners in retaliation for the mistreatment of Union prisoners at Andersonville. A Georgia private wrote, "Our rations consisted of one-fourth of a half-pound loaf of bread, twice a day. Our meat consisted of a very small, thin slice of salt pork or fresh beef, which made about one good mouthful, with one Irish potato occasionally. . . . I was so nearly starved I was reduced from 140 to 80 pounds."

Near the war's end, Maury and hundreds of other prisoners were loaded onto a transport vessel with the understanding they would be delivered to Richmond and given their freedom. But on the Delaware River, a river he knew well, he watched as the vessel made an abrupt course correction. All around him anxious prisoners appealed to Maury: Where were they going? He knew the channels, had traveled them before, hadn't he? Were they diverting because of a sandbar, some shoals? But the river's course was a mystery, a fuzzy long-forgotten preamble to a much larger story. For a brief time the larger story—the one of his and his comrades' survival at Darién— became a rallying cry, proof of the extraordinary qualities stamped on citizenry from Atlanta to Albany. The story was like Fort Delaware when he first laid eyes on it: a chest-swelling testimony to a nation's better half—to the future.

So in 1865 Jack Maury couldn't tell them that their course, which had in fact reversed, was leading them back to prison. Union and Confederate negotiations had broken down. For the next several months the "Delaware 600" would instead serve as human shields, lined up thicker than the fort's gray granite walls as a flesh-and-bones deterrent to the artillery shelling of their own horrified soldiers. On the other side of the line Union prisoners were lined up just the same.

Maury, whose Virginian ancestor had been an early instructor to Thomas Jefferson, would be one of the last prisoners of war to be released, not gaining his freedom until the late summer of 1865. The reason he'd been detained, one of his kinsmen proudly wrote, was that he had refused to take the oath of allegiance to the federal government, a requirement for clemency. Ultimately the government tired of the battle and released everyone, including those who openly professed support for the Confederacy. Maury, having outlasted another adversary, was welcomed home to Fredericksburg a hero all over again.

IN THE EXPEDITION'S aftermath, Theodore Winthrop was perhaps the lone figure who didn't get any fanfare. Naturally he felt he'd been mistreated in the *Harper's* article—the account of his split with Strain suggested he'd knowingly left the lieutenant and his men in the lurch. He fired off a series of letters to Strain and author Joel Tyler Headley, demanding a retraction. Strain was conciliatory, noting that he now understood the mix-up and saw no reason why they couldn't correct the record. In May 1855, in the *Harper's* issue that included the third and final installment of the Darién story, the editors wrote, "Lieutenant Strain desires us to state that since the completion of the Account of the Darién Expedition he has had an interview with Mr. Winthrop . . . [and] is now fully convinced that there was no intention on the part of Messrs. Winthrop and Holcomb to desert him."

Darién marked the end of Theodore Winthrop's rugged travels. Having temporarily sated the part of him that wanted to ramble, he took a more expected course for an educated society gentleman and began a law practice. Yet over the next five-plus years he also wrote compulsively, sending out manuscripts to Boston and New York publishers with hopes of a literary breakthrough. His attempts at a successful writing life were utterly unrealized. At the outbreak of the Civil War, the family home in Staten Island was awash in rejected manuscripts and articles. He had managed to publish one item, a technical pamphlet. Wrote a friend, "He had seen and felt more than most men of twice his age; and yet he was a nobody. . . . He had essayed the publishing experiment: Grub Street had decided against him."

On April 17, 1861, the thirty-two-year-old Winthrop and his brother William enlisted in the New York Seventh Regiment, an amateur militia represented by many of New York society's leading families. They had been ordered to proceed to Washington, where they would help protect the city until the regular troops arrived. Winthrop, who had also been enlisted as a war correspondent for the *Atlantic Monthly,* dashed off a rousing account of the experience titled "March to Washington." When the Seventh returned to New York a few weeks later—they'd been exuberantly greeted as the first volunteer outfit to arrive in defense of the Capitol—Winthrop stayed behind as a military secretary to General Benjamin Butler. He was informally awarded the rank of major, apparently out of due courtesy to his education and social standing. Other than Darién, he had no previous military experience.

In early June Butler devised a plan—apparently with Winthrop's input—to attack Confederate positions at Little Bethel and Big

Bethel. Near Newport News, on the strategic approach route to Richmond, the Bethels were being used as a base for nightly raids. Fortress Monroe, the Union fort only a few miles away, might be next if they weren't driven back.

By all accounts the surprise night attack was badly bungled. In the dim predawn hours of June 10, a planned rendezvous went awry when one Union regiment inadvertently fired on the other. The engagement killed two, wounded several, and alerted Colonel J. B. Magruder, commander at Big Bethel, of an impending assault. When the Union forces came upon Little Bethel they found it deserted, the Confederates having retreated to their larger and better-fortified position up the road. At 9:30 A.M. the Union officers held a conference at which they inexplicably decided to stick to their plan and move against Big Bethel—this even though they'd long since forfeited any chance of surprise. Upon gaining the ford on Hampton Road they were met by howitzers and a wave of volleys from two companies of North Carolina sharpshooters. Also waiting for them were cavalry and the Third Virginia Infantry. The lopsided skirmish lasted only minutes before a hasty recall, but by the time it was over, eighteen Union soldiers, including Theodore Winthrop, were dead.

Witness accounts greatly differed about Winthrop's death, but all hailed his bravery. He either hadn't heard the recall order or had become separated from the main regiment as he sought to flank the enemy's position through the thick woods. After advancing to within 30 yards of the enemy's lines, and well beyond the protection of his own troops, he was cut down. Some said he'd leaped onto a log to get a better look, others that he was attempting to rally his men and had yelled, "Come on!" when he was shot in the head. General Butler would later console Winthrop's mother, Elizabeth, that he had died instantly, but other eyewitnesses swore he'd risen after his initial wounding and was exhorting his men to follow when another volley put him down for good. According to that report, his men had hesitated to follow.

Those who knew Winthrop and how he'd been haunted by the perception that he abandoned Strain wondered if his actions at Bethel could be traced to the forests of the isthmus. Mindful of Darién, had he rashly leaped to the fore, hoping to prove something to himself or others? Or had he simply lost his way? Whatever the case, news of his dramatic death reached the public almost simultaneously with his "March to Washington" article in the June issue of the *Atlantic*. His courageous behavior and torridly patriotic writing touched a popular nerve. If he wasn't the first Union officer to fall in the field of battle—something he was popularly credited as being—he should have been. With his death, he was famous.

All five of his unpublished novels were rushed into print. By 1863 one of Winthrop's novels had gone through fifteen editions, another twelve, and another seven. In two years he'd gone from obscurity to a beloved, bestselling author.

When he was buried on June 21 at Yale University's Grove Street Cemetery, Winthrop was eulogized as "one of the most brilliant and striking figures who gave to this nation the services of both pen and sword." Brave, brilliant, and unfortunate. His life tracked that of Strain's all too closely. And like Strain's, his star faded just as rapidly as it ascended. By the turn of the century he was virtually forgotten—and so were his books.

THE DARIÉN EXPEDITION'S first death had been George Holmes, a twenty-one-year-old seaman. Seamen were an anonymous lot, their transient, often troubled lives largely unrecorded in department records. Of the four seamen who perished at Darién—Philip Vermil-yea, Edward Lombard, George B. Holmes, and William H. Parks—only Holmes's name has officially survived. He'd been aboard the *Cyane* only a few months when he volunteered to join Strain and the rest of the party on the isthmus crossing. The morning of his death, he told Kettlewell that he wanted to tell him something for the record. His real name was Hooper, George B. Hooper; he had a wife, Catharine, and a three-year-old son, George, living in Washington, D.C.

Apparently he didn't explain the reason for the alias, and in the *Harper's* article Headley elected not to give his true name. The alias stood, denying Seaman Hooper any recognition for his efforts and denying his wife a government pension. Proving the identity of her husband, and that he was killed in the line of duty, would take Catharine Hooper several months of painstaking work. Among those to write the department on her behalf was the minister who'd married them, Truxtun, and Midshipman H. M. Garland, who in 1855 informed the department that Hooper had died because of a badly infected foot and because there were "no means of obtaining proper and sufficient food for him, nor of rendering the attendance which he required." The secretary of the Navy forwarded the letter to the Commissioner of Pensions. Finally, the commission awarded her a $5 a month widow's pension and their son, George, an "Orphan's Navy Pension." In the paperwork the cause of death was listed as "starvation."

IN 1859 FREDERICK AVERY was spending time in Urbana, Ohio, helping his elderly father on the family farm. He'd been living in New York since the time of the expedition; he too had received praise in Strain's official report and the popular articles to follow.

For a time he was satisfied in the business of earning a living, dabbling in various merchant businesses, but in 1859, apparently in Urbana, he was contacted by the department about the most improbable matter of all: another major expedition to the Darién. Reports had surfaced that there was a route between Caledonia and the Gulf of San Miguel that had escaped the notice of Gisborne, Strain, and Prevost. The department, calling on Avery's background, asked him to be "chief pioneer," effectively heading up the expedition to safely guide it across. He'd be supported by the USS *Preble,* a sloop-of-war.

Remarkably, Avery signed up, and by late summer the expedition was taking swift shape. In his prospectus to the department, Avery enumerated three distinct passes through the cordilleras, one of which (the one he had not seen) "I should judge not over 200 feet." It was a few miles northwest of where he and Strain had punched through, directly opposite the Channel of Sasardi. Avery's optimistic assessment was contagious. So many of the *Preble*'s crew rushed to volunteer that several had to be turned away in order to safeguard the ship. Among the trio of civilian volunteers aiding Avery, and steaming for a naval rendezvous at Aspinwall, was a New York naturalist, a surveying expert, and a draftsman. Avery and the others were temporarily sworn into service on September 28, vowing to "bear true allegiance to the United States of America and to serve them honestly, and faithfully against all their enemies, or opposers whomsoever, and to observe and obey the order of the President of the United States of America, and the orders of the officer appointed over me; and in all things to conform myself to the rules and regulations."

But as time drew near for the expedition, the stalwart Avery, perhaps beginning to dredge up what he'd endured only five years earlier, began to fall apart. Beginning in New York and throughout the cruise to Aspinwall, where the *Preble*'s crew eagerly awaited him, he drank heavily. But it wasn't until he arrived in Panama and set foot on the isthmus that he went off the deep end. On one of his first nights on the town, the newly sworn-in Avery drank himself into an uncontrollable, rage-filled fit, hurling invective and the "most gross and abusive epithets toward officers of the Navy." Witnesses to the public display were many, including Captain William Gardner, commander of the U.S. steam frigate *Roanoke*, and officers from the *Preble*. His own colleagues from New York were sufficiently mortified to both report Avery and refuse any future association with him. They withdrew immediately from the proposed expedition. The loss of confidence extended to the *Preble* too, with the once gung-ho volunteers now announcing their reluctance to pursue the special service. On October 12 the disgraced Avery was discharged, only fourteen days after he'd been sworn in. A day later the expedition, never having left Aspinwall, was dissolved.

There's nothing on record to explain Avery's breakdown. Apparently he never attempted to publicly defend himself. Post-traumatic stress disorder, a nightmarish mental ailment first diagnosed in Vietnam veterans, was one intriguing possibility. A mere return to the isthmus could trigger the condition, but there was also a health crisis in Aspinwall when he arrived. Several crewmen aboard the *Preble* were suffering from severe tropical fevers, and a catastrophic outbreak appeared imminent. Or was it something else?

Avery had been a model soldier. In his Navy Department report, Strain richly praised him, saying, "None could have done better than he, with boils on all parts of his person, and five on one knee." Avery would later recover from the Aspinwall debacle to run a successful business in New York and serve on General George McClellan's staff during the Civil War. Aspinwall seemed a gross anomaly. Perhaps Avery's behavior—he'd primarily directed his tirade at the

Navy hierarchy—had a more specific cause, something to do with what had happened to his old commander, Strain. The isthmus was a hotbed of rumors. Some of them concerned the events that had taken place two years earlier in May of 1857. That was the month of the most implausible occurrence of all: Strain's return.

14 / AWAY

> *Besides the body . . . is perishing. It is daily tending to its original form.*
>
> THE REV. ISAAC GRIER, FROM A SERMON
> DELIVERED JUNE 16, 1793

May 5, 1857

40° 45′ N, 74° W
New York City

THE WINTER OF 1857 was unlike any on record. One storm after another blasted the East Coast, first with heavy, gale-driven snows, then with subzero cold. In even temperate coastal areas such as Newport and New York, where Strain spent most of his time, the conditions were brutally arctic. In late January a raging blizzard preceded a succession of days where the temperature never rose above minus 26 degrees Fahrenheit. On the 26th of January the killing cold plummeted to 37 below in Salem, Massachusetts. The situation was no better in the mid-Atlantic. Every river in Virginia and Maryland froze, and solid ice extended a mile and a half from the shore at Chesapeake Bay. Drifts up to 20 feet high were seen in Washington, D.C. Nobody had ever seen anything like the Great Cold Winter. Hundreds died, and shipwrecks littered the seas from Maine to Carolina.

Those fortunate enough not to be in harm's way found themselves holed up and despairing of a suffocating winter that refused to release its grip. Isaac Strain was one of them. Impetuously, he signed onto a Panama cruise. He needed relief, he told his friends. By April, with the storms still lashing the seaports and the subfreezing cold punishing the deep South, anything other than the northern latitudes might have sounded good.

But Strain was by no means the sturdy man he once was, and he hardly seemed to possess the extra physical stamina required for duty in the Torrid Zone, still considered the harshest service in the Navy. He also had emotional reasons not to return, the same ones he'd poignantly expressed to the department in the spring of '56. His past duty had been uncommonly harrowing—ultimately he'd been understood and excused from that part of the world and from the vessel that brought him there. However, on May 5, 1857, Strain went ahead with his new plans and hurriedly boarded a packed New York mail steamer. The *Illinois* was taking him back to Aspinwall, where he would report to none other than the *Cyane*.

Strain's change of heart shocked friends who believed he would stick to the comparatively light duty of the Coast Survey while assembling his papers for a forthcoming book. Moreover, everybody knew the *Cyane* had been stalled off Aspinwall for six months. She was there to stand watch over the railroad transit route, which was thought to be in jeopardy after an anti-American riot at the Panama terminus. Though the violence in Panama City had been intense— the mobs, backed by local police, had killed fourteen Americans and looted foreign-owned properties—nothing had followed in its wake, and the ship's crew was reeling at the thought of staying at the station through the coming rainy season. In fact, the *Cyane*'s crew, which had endured an epidemic scare in the summer of 1855, was already deteriorating. Overcrowding and the coming deluge presaged another wave of fever, the ship's surgeon warned. Hiram Paulding, the Home Squadron's commanding officer, was fairly begging Washington to relieve his entire fleet, but especially *Cyane*, which was faltering in "this climate so pernicious to health."

Strain's decision to steam to Aspinwall anyway—the *Cyane*'s grim conditions had only that month been documented in the *Journal of Medical Sciences*—defied all logic except for one thing: There was breaking news from Darién.

On May 2 Dr. Henry Caldwell, an assistant surgeon attached to the U.S. frigate *Independence,* had returned from a quasi-official exploring expedition into the interior. Caldwell's route, which was roughly between Prevost's and Strain's, took him to within one day's march of the Atlantic. He described a mostly level traverse and said the seaman with him had climbed a tall tree and seen the Atlantic through a distant low pass. The entire party consisted of Caldwell, the seaman, two porters, and the same native guide who had aided Prevost years earlier. He gave credit to Andrew Hossack, the Scotsman who had assisted Strain, as well as Cullen and Gisborne, for informing him of the route and insisting that everyone had missed the true line. Caldwell's effort, though unscientific and filled with problems, appeared to prove the Scotsman correct. "It is not claimed that the practicability of the route is positively decided," wrote Caldwell, "but facts of sufficient importance have been ascertained to justify a careful survey."

Caldwell's cautious language was overlooked. His finding seemed to confirm what some well-placed gentlemen had silently suspected all along: Strain had been mistaken. There was a practicable route. Reported one newspaper, "The long desired route for a ship canal across the isthmus of Darién is found." In London Edward Cullen and others were hawking 600,000 shares, at £10 per share, in a newly formed Darién partnership, the Atlantic and Pacific Ship Canal Company.

The news at Darién also had found a receptive audience in the newly installed secretary of the Navy, Isaac Toucey—he was vigorously investigating several possible ship canal routes. He had already ordered two surveys. One was to examine the Atrato, the southernmost isthmian region championed by the great Humboldt. Another was to instrument the route between Panama and Aspinwall (present-day Colón), which Colonel George Totten, the triumphant engineer of the Panama Railroad, was advocating for. And now Darién was back in the running.

S TRAIN ARRIVED AT THE bustling port of Aspinwall on May 14. The mail steamer *Illinois,* a double-stacked side-wheeler packed well beyond its eight-hundred-person capacity, docked before noon. A severe thunder storm chased them into port, the torrents and fogs forcing most of the sightseers belowdecks. Outside the harbor mouth, a half dozen warships from Great Britain and the United States lay at anchor, each keeping a nervous watch over the others. The isthmus was a flash point, with each government suspicious of the other's motives for being there. Keeping the peace had given everybody a pretext for sticking around, but trouble appeared imminent. William Walker, a highly popular, renegade captain who'd nearly drawn the United States and England into war over his incursion at Nicaragua, was headed for Panama and expected at Aspinwall within days.

Disembarking with Strain was John Bigler, a former prospector, newspaper editor, and California governor. The pair would have had much to talk about on the passage out. They were both natives of Cumberland County, Pennsylvania, and Bigler had even attended Dickinson College, the same school Strain's grandfather graduated from. Now Bigler was en route to Chile as the newly appointed U.S. minister. Of course, Strain knew the region intimately; his *Cordillera and Pampa,* the book he wrote about his South American crossing in 1849, had been published only four years earlier. Bigler was the sort of larger-than-life figure Strain gravitated toward, and given the tendency of travelers to fall into each other, the lieutenant certainly would have shared where he was going and why.

At midday, the quarter-mile-long wharf was a river of people, produce, and products, either coming or going. Slipping into the crowd, Strain immediately saw the new freight rail yard, all housed inside a massive stone structure with three arched entranceways. Further along was the *mingillo,* the native marketplace, where farmers from all over the Atlantic coast, including San Blas, arrived in their loaded dugouts bearing fish, bananas, and ivory nuts. The air was sopping, a sponge to sights and sounds and smells, as thick as the *sancoche* simmering in the large wood-fired kettles along the beach.

Moving along, Strain checked into the Aspinwall House, one of the city's premier hotels. The large American-owned residence wasn't one of the colonial grand dames but newly built and designed to look like a California ranch house. Off the entrance were a bar, card tables, and a billiard room. The lagoon-side quarters offered a perfect view of the booming railroad town, while vistas in the opposite direction offered Aspinwall as it had been only a few years ago: a steamy wall of dense tropical forest. In all likelihood Strain planned to report on the 15th, or perhaps the day after, thus giving him a little time to reacquaint himself with old friends and the news of the day, or walk the *paseo coral,* a beachside track popular with evening promenaders and shell lovers. In Tuesday's copy of the *Panama Star & Herald* he would have found a complete and quite lengthy account of Caldwell's crossing.

But Strain never reported to the *Cyane.* On May 15, the day Strain was expected, Commodore Paulding dispatched a note to Secretary Toucey, announcing it was his painful duty to inform him that "Lieutenant Isaac G. Strain died in Aspinwall last evening at a Hotel having just landed from the Mail Steamer *Illinois.*"

There was no autopsy, no hint of a possible cause of death, and no details whatsoever about the sequence of events that led to Strain's discovery. Paulding didn't even cite the arrangements for his burial.

The *Cyane*'s log recorded little more, except to say he died "suddenly at 11 p.m.," and that the carpenters' morning was occupied making his coffin. The U.S. flagship *Wabash* lowered the colors to half mast. At 3 P.M. some of the ship's officers went ashore to attend the funeral. There was a light rain falling and a sky's worth of gray nimbus clouds overhead. The mourners made the gentle climb to the burial grounds at Mount Hope, or "Monkey Hill," tracing the path of the rail trestles, then veering off on a winding path through the thick undergrowth. The large tropical clearing, chattering with bird life even at midafternoon, came into view. There were thousands of railroad workers buried here, a grim spectacle for isthmus-marooned men half anticipating their own demise. By the time the brief service began, the gathering included officers from the *Wabash*, the British warships *Orion* and *Basilisk*, and some twenty-six sailors from the *Cyane*, fourteen of whom acted as pallbearers and twelve as substitutes for marines. They were joined by a number of citizens of Aspinwall. The chaplain of the *Wabash* read the Episcopal burial service: "Man, that is born of a woman, hath but a short time to live, and is full of misery," he declared, committing the body to the grave with a few handfuls of soil. His funeral was attended by officers who were "strangers to him, and of course, showed but little feeling," lamented George Hamilton Perkins, a young New Hampshire officer aboard the *Cyane*. "Twelve sailors fired a volley over his grave, and three negroes covered him up. Thus ended the days of one of our distinguished naval officers. . . . I wonder what they would do with me!"

For unclear reasons Strain didn't receive full military honors in death. Neither his fellow officers from the *Cyane*, the marines, or the band attended, absences that pained his Aspinwall friends. Commodore Paulding had prevented their attendance for fear of exposing them to sickness, he said. Unclear was whether that sickness was Strain's or the general climate of the isthmus. Also unexplained was why, if a lethal contagion was feared, so many officers from other ships did go.

It's possible Strain was seized with fever, but no official confirmation was ever forthcoming. There were no reports of epidemic sickness aboard the *Illinois*. If he had become severely ill, there was no reason for him to die in his hotel. Even the most sudden and severe bouts of Panama fever would have allowed time for him to get treatment, which in his case was only footsteps away at the large, well-equipped railroad hospital. As the bewildered Perkins wrote in his letter home, "Only twelve hours after his death he was buried, and twenty-four hours before his burial he was laughing and talking." His abrupt decline seemed especially striking because, of course, it was Strain. Even in his diminished, toothless state there was still an aura. He had endured months of disease, hunger, and exposure in a wilderness only a few miles away—and in the end he had walked out with most of his men. If doctors were correct he had earned a lifetime immunity to tropical fevers; more than any who had come before him he was uniquely seasoned.

Amid the murky circumstances surrounding Strain's death one can't help but speculate. Conspiracy-minded types might see amid the high-stakes, big-money ship canal chase some wicked scheme to silence Strain, a man whose experience and influential opinions could easily ruin another's designs. The late hour and tumultuous Wild West backdrop of Aspinwall intrigues others. Had he been out drinking, a vice of numerous seamen but one that had begun to plague Strain since his return from Darién? Had something happened—an insult, a slander—that was settled in the kind of honorable, drawn-pistol fashion the Navy wasn't eager to publicize? Or, darkest of all, had Strain simply had enough and chosen to take his own life? Those who saw him in his last years, how he suffered, might have found such an ending plausible. Perhaps he had come to the conclusion he shouldn't have survived, that the heart and soul of his life had been left on the isthmus. What might have transpired the day of May 14 is a gaping mystery, seemingly as shaded by time and history as Darién itself.

Complicating things is the fact that neither Bigler nor anyone else has ever explained what Strain intended to do on the isthmus. Strain carried with him a government chronometer, a pricey piece of gear that suggested he planned a survey of some sort. He might have intended to help map the Panama-to-Aspinwall line, the present-day ship canal route he personally favored. A note explaining his enthusiasm for the route, evidently written aboard the outgoing *Illinois*, found its way to a naval colleague after his death. Colonel Totten, the railroad engineer who had meticulously surveyed the line, was from Newport and knew Strain. In fact, Totten was one of those private citizens living on the isthmus who had attempted to help rescue Strain at the time of the 1854 expedition.

Of course, Strain might have been rushing to Panama to return to Darién—to prove himself all over again. An obituary in the *Providence Journal*, likely written by Strain's close friend Samuel Greene Arnold, made a reference to the "mental and physical hardships" he'd suffered at Darién and from which he had never entirely recovered. But being unable to "brook inaction," he'd been on his way to join "the same ship from which he had been detached three years before to examine the Darién route."

Years earlier, when some had questioned the practical value of his expedition, Strain had come up with a response. They had safeguarded the public, giving themselves up as virtual guinea pigs in a grisly but necessary experiment of trial and error. By doing so, they had showed the world the deceit of the Darién scheme, thus saving future lives and an incalculable amount of money. Potentially, it wasn't so different from the Scots disaster, where half of the country's circulating currency had been gambled and lost on the failed Darién colony. Strain's men had prevented the impoverishment of a populace ripe to be swindled. They'd done a public service—at a terrific cost, but a public service just the same.

But Caldwell's report suggested otherwise, that the whole matter had simply been mishandled, a waste in and of itself, and that Strain's damning of the route and the route discoverers was less about scientific judgment and more about self-interest and saving face. Though he might have been ill prior to boarding the *Illinois* and known himself unfit for duty, he might not have been able to help himself. It no doubt haunted Strain that he hadn't performed a true scientific survey in 1854. The forces that had reformed and were pulling him south were, like the storm that brought him in the first place, too powerful.

His tragic passing elicited several moving eulogies, one of which remarked on the stunning coincidence of his death in a place where he'd suffered so memorably. It was the stuff of Greek tragedy. A foreign periodical declared his Darién command "a triumph of the soul." Most obituaries recounted his travels to Brazil and Baja and his horseback crossing of the Chilean and Argentine frontier. Alluding to his stamina—and restlessness—a friend said he would have walked to the North Pole on foot alone. To complement pioneering qualities that few could match, he had exquisite conversational and linguistic skills, the eulogies emphasized. His traveling library contained titles in Portuguese, Spanish, and French. "[Strain was] one of the few who, amid the demands of an engrossing profession, found time to cultivate literary tastes to an extent unusual among purely literary men."

Right up until the time he boarded the *Illinois* he was continuing to study the Malaysian language with hopes of realizing his long-delayed exploration of the archipelago. In total he'd served nineteen years in the Navy. Of those, twelve years and three months were sea service and another six years were either shore duty or, more typically, extended unpaid leaves for exploring. It was an exceptionally active record. At one stretch he'd spent some six consecutive years at sea, circumnavigating the globe one and a half times and sailing nearly 50,000 miles.

He never married nor had his own home. A year earlier, in 1856, he had a chance for a different sort of life when he received a 160-acre government land grant for his brief service in the Mexican War. He sold it days later on the secondary market for cash. Presumably he saw little adventure in the settler's life along the Minnesota frontier, or perhaps the money was already spoken for, part of a future trip or the expenses from a past one. He saw his life connected to the sea and the East Coast cities where the most eminent, visionary men gathered. Years earlier he had decided to make a clean break with his home, telling a friend he was starting anew and from that point on would look forward, not back.

Those who knew Strain best—the ones who insisted even as weeks turned to months that he would emerge from Darién alive—were mostly grieved by what he might have done. The bureaucratic Navy shackled young strivers: It was glacially slow with promotions, bedeviled by turf wars, and top-heavy with older, less active, and less progressive-thinking officers. At another time and place, Strain would have realized some of "those great schemes which at all times agitated his restless mind," lamented his obituary writer in the *New York Tribune*, "and proved one of the most remarkable men the Naval service has ever produced."

FOR A TIME STRAIN'S was one of the more prominent headstones at "Monkey Hill," but many years later, in the aftermath of the canal construction, most of the American remains would be disinterred and moved across the isthmus to Corazal, an immaculately groomed 16-acre cemetery a few miles north of Panama City. Probably because they couldn't find them in the overgrown grasses, Strain's remains were left behind.

In the summer of 2001, a long guided search through Mount Hope cemetery revealed nothing either. The asphalt trails were cracked, and the pretty white statuary was stained black with the creeping mildew. There was no Strain tombstone in the oldest part of the cemetery, and even if there were, we might not have seen it. The hilly grounds, lovely and lush, were being reclaimed by the forest. The more modest stones looked as though they'd been cast overboard, their white tips struggling to the surface amid some great sea of high, wild grasses. In the cool mist of an early morning it's still common to see chestnut-mandibled toucans in the highest branches of the highest trees and to hear, as one 1850s visitor put it, the "sweet and sonorous whistle of the turpiale mingle with the harsh cries of the parrot tribe." Off in an eastern direction, away from the canal, the jungle swept away uninterrupted.

For another fifty years the Darién question vexed the U.S. government, never fully going away, never fully answered to everyone's satisfaction. Except for the Civil War years, nearly every administration either sent an expedition or reviewed those previously sent in an effort to resolve the riddle once and for all. The catalyst for many of the efforts was Edward Cullen, who continued to insist to those enlightened enough to listen to him that he'd been wronged and that his route existed. His pleas were irresistible: He wooed each successive administration in such a way that made *not* reexamining Darién somehow irresponsible. He talked of the volunteers who surrounded Strain and their possible allegiances to rival schemes, or his old adversary Gisborne getting a bribe to discourage a Darién canal. Cullen's charges of a fix were fantastic but not impossible.

In 1870, Thomas O. Selfridge Jr., a U.S. naval commander, appeared to put the matter to rest, leading one of the best-prepared, most comprehensive expeditions ever to set foot in the Darién. The extraordinary preparations were a kind of homage to Strain's legendary suffering: the "Darién ration amounted to 53 ounces of solid food per diem, for each man, the meats, breads, etc., being of better quality and of larger quantity than that furnished to any army or navy in the world." There were six hundred pairs of shoes for one hundred men, separate sets of dry, sleeping-only clothes, and a medical kit with enough quinine for daily two-grain prophylactic doses. They strung dozens of miles of telegraph line to ensure they'd never lose contact with the mother ship.

Selfridge said that he himself had been swayed by Cullen, if only because the man was so steadfast in the face of overwhelming criticism. Cullen, by now an old man living in Dublin, had sent him an annotated map from 1854 in which he identified Strain's route and remarked, "The line above marked is that in which Lieutenant Strain crossed. . . . It is the highest point." Several miles further west, or up the isthmus, he temptingly noted, "The Valley for the Canal . . . not approached by Strain or Gisborne."

But after months of running lines, barometrical observations, and paced-off distances—bringing the route to a "strict engineering test"—Selfridge scientifically documented what Strain had tried unsuccessfully to tell everyone: Cullen's pass didn't exist. Along the divide separating Caledonia Bay from the Darién interior, the lowest pass was the one he'd been over, some 700 feet. The headwaters of the Sucubti, the river on the *other* side of the divide, were discovered 553 feet above sea level. "The height of the Sucubti dissipates all idea of a pass," correctly concluded Selfridge, "for were there such, this river would flow to the Atlantic instead of the Pacific, and pricks the bubble of Dr. Cullen's Darién route with its highest elevation of 200 feet." In other words, Strain had been correct.

In 1903, with Teddy Roosevelt's famous "Watch the dirt fly" exhortation, the United States began construction of the present-day ship canal along the line of the old railroad. When it was finally finished, the work was justly proclaimed the eighth wonder of the world. Amid the festive celebrations, soaring speeches, and billowy cigar smoke, there was also a recognition of the horrible cost, and solemn tributes were made to the thousands who sacrificed their lives to make the dream a reality. The seven Darién dead weren't part of any accounting. Unbeknownst to anyone, the graves of the canal's very first casualties anchored the jungle-lined waterway—Isaac Strain at the Atlantic end and his boyhood friend Andrew Boggs on the Pacific.

EPILOGUE

Summer 2001

Isthmus of Darién

THE DAY AFTER my fortieth birthday I flew to Panama. My two Darién guides, Hernán Araúz and Rich Cahill, met me at the airport looking more than a bit hassled. We were to depart for the jungle just after sunrise, and we still had much to do.

The idea had seemed simple enough: to retrace the historic footsteps of the U.S. Darién Exploring Expedition over the infamous Atlantic Divide and then down the contorted run of the 100-plus-mile Chucunaque River. Of course, we weren't likely to uncover any evidence of Strain's march, but we'd get a rough approximation of what they had seen and coped with. The territory remained wild and roadless.

We hit logistical snags almost immediately. Much of eastern Darién lies within the modern political borders of Comarca de Kuna Yala (San Blas province) and Kuna de Wargandi, both autonomous nation-states embedded in Panama. For permission to access the still-sensitive interior lands we'd need to congress with two culturally distinct Kuna villages—Mulatupo on the coast and Morti, a remote hamlet that saw almost no foreign travelers. Lacking any modern communication link with either village, the Panama City–based

Araúz had hired a "runner" several weeks earlier to begin the dialogue and set the stage for our arrival. Our intended route also presented problems: GPS, the American military, and five hundred years of exploring notwithstanding, maps were either unreliable, unavailable, or incomplete. The guides could find no information about anyone taking the "Strain route" in recent times. Like so many trips to set forth across the isthmus, our plans were largely incomplete. As always, you needed to get there.

JUST AFTER DAWN we were flying low over the isthmus in a twin prop. Scanning the countryside, I was thinking of Edward Cullen's famous bird's-eye view of Darién, a sketch so warmly rendered that the U.S. Navy planned to send up an experimental hot-air balloon in 1859 to view what he had. What that gloriously doomed aeronaut would have seen was what we were seeing: the tops of mushrooming trees, all stitched to one another by great masses of vines—in the words of an early naturalist, the "warp and woof" of the canopy.

Being on top of the forest was no more revelatory than being at the bottom. For upward of twenty minutes we didn't glimpse a single break in the canopy. Our future route, if there was a route, was perfectly hidden. Finally, near the San Blas coast, the view abruptly shifted: We saw little pineapple and coconut groves on the mainland, then a series of tiny, densely settled coral islands ringed by breaking surf. At Mulatupo, the small thatch-roofed homes were as thickly bunched as nestled palm fruit. Dugouts skimmed the breezy coastal waters while larger, sail-rigged versions swept toward open ocean and a white-hot horizon. Mulatupo's tiny grass airstrip came upon us in a heartbeat.

We were at the northwestern end of Caledonia Bay, a half dozen miles up the coast from where Strain's party had landed. In a later boat trip from the airstrip to Mulatupo, a distant point of land had been pointed out. "Punta Escoces," announced one of the boatmen. We weren't far. But rather than take the Caledonia River route, or the twenty or so other streambeds that drop to the Atlantic, we were going to tackle the slightly higher Sasardi Pass, a concession to the Kuna men who regularly used the route to trade with the villagers at Morti. Apparently the other route was no longer regularly used—the once-thriving nineteenth-century Kuna villages at Caledonia and along the Sucubti had been abandoned long ago.

The hike to Morti was likely to take us four or five days, we were told. The time estimate seemed suspiciously slow for a destination only twenty or so miles away as the crow flies. We had tropical-weight clothing and ultralight gear and seemed unlikely to be slowed by illness—we had been inoculated against a half dozen jungle diseases, the aggressive regimen suggested for all visitors to this part of the world. Over average backcountry terrain a mile of travel might take forty minutes. Even allowing for the tropical heat and a difficult alpine route that might be twice as long, the numbers didn't compute. Less than 10 trekking miles a day for a modernly equipped, fit, and experienced backcountry party—all of which we were—was hard to imagine. We figured we'd surprise our Kuna guides, who boasted that their toughest comrades traversed the Sasardi-Morti route in a single day.

It took three backbreaking days to ascend the divide alone— practically the same amount of time it took Strain with his rifles, canvas haversack, and a brick-heavy spyglass dangling off his neck. The travel, most of which was in the stony, knee-grinding beds of waist-deep rivers, was fiercely punishing. The 1,200-foot pass, which looked neither high nor terribly daunting from the beach, was moated by rivers, sheer clay-slicked grades, and bands of swarming, spiny vegetation. The trail, when there was a trail, was overgrown and indistinct, often disappearing and leading us across the river to find it again. Even after clawing upward for several hours, it was impossible to see any distance at all, or even to feel like you had achieved a high point. There were no familiar markers to indicate upward progress, as in northern forests. The trees at the top were as broad as those at the base. The steamy heat was barely less oppressive. I marveled anew at those seamen who marched single file behind Strain. After all, I knew the height of the land, could even watch it fall away with a glance at my altimeter wristwatch. They had anticipated a valley.

In coming here, I had expected to add a layer to my archival research and viscerally experience some of what Strain and his men had stoically endured. But atop the divide, after being led on a brief detour to view some old expeditionary debris, it became even more abundantly clear what the Kuna had been through.

The thick plastic battery cases and metal tower bracings they showed us were remnants, I came to understand, from a series of little-known U.S. surveys in the 1960s. In Washington this route was known as "Route 17," and the government scientists who had been here were fact-finding with the idea of excavating a second canal passageway across the isthmus with nuclear explosives. Hernán's mother, a well-known anthropologist in Panama, had been employed by the U.S. Atomic Energy Commission to study the "human impact" of the project. The two dozen underground blasts, each roughly the equivalent of Hiroshima times 100, would have been concentrated on opposite ends of the proposed canal. On the Atlantic side the devices would be detonated on a more or less continuous line from Mulatupo to Morti. Sixty-five hundred square miles of the isthmus was designated as an "exclusion area," meaning the entire indigenous population, an estimated forty-three thousand "highly communal" people, would either need to be moved or suffer radioactive contamination. In the judgment of engineers it would be a minimum of five years before the area was safe to return to. In her report to the Atomic Energy Commission Reina Torres de Araúz had warned that forcibly removing the Upper Chucunaque Kuna from their ancestral homeland was a terrible idea, noting their particular attachment, emotionally as well as economically, to their "small patch of earth."

All the way down the Pacific side of the divide, my mind raced. Mostly I thought about something that happened the previous day. That afternoon the Kuna men had told us they wished to stop early. They said the reason they didn't want to progress any further was their reluctance to overnight in the shadow of Sasardi Pass—a place, they said, that was charged with dark spiritual energy. Initially it was hard to know what to make of the request. Arturo, Edrenio, Joselino, Allen, and Evindion had struck me as a pragmatic group above all else, not overtly superstitious, and in fact they often chose to emphasize their practical relationship with the forest, stopping to show us the medicinal, survival, and construction uses of the flora around us. But that evening all five walked a short distance upstream, curled into the rounded boulders of the riverbank, and lay awake listening late into the night. They swore they heard things.

GETTING TO THE TOP of the divide wasn't the end of our trip. For two more days we followed the broad course of the Morti, one of the Chucunaque's largest and prettiest tributaries. Occasionally there were detours into the forest, but mostly we were in the river, swamping through silty bottoms and water up to our waists. We passed the old village of Morti—it had apparently been abandoned about fifty years ago in favor of the present-day location at the junction with the Chucunaque. There was nothing except memory to indicate anything was here. In its stead were towering cedar trees as wide around as silos and fields of ortiga, their waxy broad leaves waving ominously with acne-like bumps. A painful sting and numbness were the penalty for an inattentive brush. For the first time I dreaded losing sight of or wandering away from the river, where the well-lit views stretched some and where the slow but certain descent toward the Pacific was unmistakable. We were hemmed in by the lushest forest we'd seen yet.

Nobody said much, but the closer we got to Morti, the more anxious we became. By choice, it was one of the most isolated villages in Darién. Unlike the tens of thousands of Kuna that migrated to San Blas, those living at Morti were part of a few thousand that had never left their ancestral homeland of the interior. They were descendants of the Kuna Bravos, the mythic warriors who'd waged war against the Spanish and assorted other intruders for centuries. Morti was where Strain and his men were abandoned and where Prevost's men, mistaken for Spaniards, were murdered. When Hernán and I had originally discussed the Sasardi-Morti route, he'd told me that if we arrived unannounced, we could probably expect the same. The century-and-a-half interim seemed to matter little. The suspicions the Morti Kuna possessed for outsiders were matched by those outsiders held for them. My initial understanding, that the Darién crossing would be a glorified endurance event, couldn't be more off the mark. Even today, maybe especially today, it was something far more personal.

An attempt to shortcut the river's bends seemed like a good idea, but the hilly overland crossing became an epic. When we finally reached the Morti River again, we'd been hiking ten hours. We were just a mile above the village, and though there should have been elation, there wasn't. Our Mulatupo guides took their pay and hurried off through the fields to the village. They were to tell the leaders we were upriver, then send supplies. We'd camp the night and meet with everyone in the morning. Hernán didn't want to presume to spend the night in the village, something the Morti Kuna historically discouraged. When they left, and maybe because of the poor physical and mental state we were in, a bitter read of things took hold. Hernán was sure we'd been ditched.

We were in a bad spot, on a low-lying shelving beach. If the rains returned—we'd been dumped on for much of the day—the rising river would roar right over us. As a half hour turned to an hour Hernán's suspicion turned to certainty. They weren't coming back. "My father always said you can't completely trust the Kuna," said Hernán, repeating a familiar view in Panama, where attitudes about the indigenous population often fluctuate between admiration and disdain. The politically correct part of me found the age-old cynicism sad, even tragic. However, another part of me was so tired, hungry, and scared that I began to wonder if it wasn't true, if maybe we had been left.

Then we spotted two blade-thin dugouts poling upstream: They *were* coming to collect us. They had provisions of a sort—cola drinks and crackers—and the boatmen quickly helped grab the loads lying strewn about the pebbly sandbar. None of our original companions were among them, but no matter. It felt a little like a miracle to be plucked off the shores in this way and escorted onward. The river was wide and shallow and the maneuvering complex, but in a mere twenty minutes we came to the place we'd almost given up on: the legendary confluence of the Morti and Chucunaque Rivers.

Ahead of us were throngs of people gathered on a blufftop. It was near dusk, and the closer we got in the poled skiffs the more we realized they were actually gathered for us. Kids by the dozens came racing down to the waterline, hoping to carry or touch something. But adults, whole families, were also on hand to see us pull up. Flustered, I stumbled headfirst getting out of the boat.

At the riverbank Arturo and the others were there—obviously we'd foolishly misread their rush to dump us. Their rush was to get here; they were hungry and tired too. After climbing nearly vertical footholds notched into the high clay bank, we were led through the village. There were some houses of modern construction, but most were thatched-roof homes with hammocks for sleeping and open fire pits for cooking. A small square outside the gathering house contained a dirt court with *MORTI* lettered across two basketball backboards. Banana and coconut groves formed the outskirts.

Evidently curiosity had been boiling over since Hernán's hand-delivered letter a month ago. Our interest in descending the upper Chucunaque was unusual enough to warrant exactly what we'd walked into: an old-fashioned town meeting. As we were ushered into the cavernous post-and-beam hall, the majority of the village seemed to stream right in behind us.

We sat on a low bench before a trio of town elders, each straddling a centrally hung hammock. One wore a straw boater, another a fedora. They had on white-collared dress shirts, Haggar-like dress slacks cut roughly above the ankle, and no shoes. A wizened man, a shaman, sat across from them, his hatband picketed with exotic avian plumage.

On the near periphery, either sitting on wooden benches or leaning on the unused hammocks, were dozens of teenagers. On the outermost periphery, along the low bamboo-sided walls, mothers nursed babies, toddlers rumbled around, and several older women, adorned with traditional gold nose rings and colorfully beaded limb bindings, threaded *molas*—the reverse-appliqué art the Kuna are world renowned for.

The village chiefs, or caciques, issued long monologues, their rhythmic prose spanning our presence, the issues which impacted the village, and the wilderness that surrounded them. They had known we were coming, but our mission—simply to see the territory without extracting anything; we were ecotourists, Hernán explained—was a concept they wanted to explore. Historically people had not come without wanting something, spoken of or not. The elders were well aware that tourists such as we might, despite the immense difficulty in getting to Morti, beget other tourists. On the San Blas coast the tourist cruise ships were depositing ever greater numbers to see the Kuna, a gawking spectacle that had already caused discord in several communities.

Morti's future was uncertain: The village was afflicted by high infant mortality, TB, desperately bad sanitation problems, and intense outside pressure from mining and timber companies. In the rainy season the river rose dozens of feet and slowly but surely was undercutting their blufftop.

In the near darkness the multilingual back-and-forth continued for several hours, a continuation of a dialogue that had been going on for several centuries. Not surprisingly, there was no historical memory of Strain, nor any of the other expeditions to visit in the nineteenth century. The point seemed clear: Individuals came and went, the conversation was forever. Being even the smallest part of that historic dialogue, of striving to understand and being understood, of listening and being listened to, added a level of meaning to our trip none of us anticipated. "You know what?" said Hernán at one point. "This is really cool. This could be a hundred years ago."

To our surprise, several of our Mulatupo guides spoke up on our behalf, assuring the assembled that we were well intentioned and deeply respectful of the territory we were passing through. And we *were* passing through, they emphasized. Arturo was particularly compelling, cracking everybody up by saying how fussy we were, not allowing anyone to throw even a wrapper or can in the woods. His praise seemed to put us over the top. A happy, accepting mood soon washed over the entire proceeding, and we were invited to stay in the village for the night. Hernán and Rich looked at each other with decided relief: The trip was on. We were hours away from descending one of the tropics' most remote and historic rivers.

This was before we were introduced to the boatman. A downed

bridge lay across the span of the Chucunaque, from bank to bank. The river wasn't navigable and hadn't been for some time. Nobody had been down to Puerto Limón in months. Could we come back another time?

THE RULE OF DARIÉN travel was pretty simple: When in doubt, don't do it. Hernán put it another way: In Darién it's not when you *want* to do something, it's when you *can*. Still, the option of backtracking over the divide wasn't an attractive thought.

Strain's men had been similarly disinclined. Low provisions and armed conflict seemed far less distressing than a return through the torturous canyon they called Devil's Own. Like them, we had none of our own food left. The prospect of going forward, where provisions and our rendezvous boat awaited, seemed far more appealing. The boatman agreed to give it a try.

If we got past the logjam, the boatman would take us as far as Puerto Limón, about 25 miles downriver. We'd overnight there and complete the river trip to Yaviza, or El Real, the following morning.

Our party included the three of us, the boatman, the boat owner, and the cacique, whom we had counseled with last night. He was small but muscular, with skin the soft tan shade of the river and a wide-brimmed sun hat he'd woven from split palm. Our "charter" afforded him an economical opportunity to travel for the first time in years. It was incumbent upon leaders, he'd explained, to be keepers of not only traditional knowledge but also the nontraditional kind too. He clearly relished the opportunity to go away, to explore, and to return with what he'd learned. He'd get out at Puerto Limón, hike several hours to the paved road, then take a bus up the only road in the *provincia,* the not quite Pan-American Highway.

"A traveler for traveling's sake"—that's how many of Strain's friends had memorialized him, and maybe even how he wished to be seen. Had he lived to explore the isthmus again, he undoubtedly would have learned what we did: that the most storied Kuna chiefs of the past were no different, each of them viewed a little more grandly the day they returned than the day they left.

As we descended the river the boatman identified several of the Chucunaque's Pacific-bound tributaries—the Sucubti, the Membrillo, the Chiati. The riverbed was wide and well gouged, but the big rains that fill the Chucunaque and transform it into a menacing presence were weeks away. Lower on the river we'd see an inordinate amount of human traffic—canoes, rafts, and motorized skiffs carting everything from harvest cargos to Panamanian troops—but here the wildlife was the dominant feature.

Black howler monkeys bellowed at us for miles, their commanding leopard-like roars raining down from the highest canopy. Chattering overflights of parrots were their gossipy counterpoint. On the banks, crocodiles abounded—as they had in Strain's time.

He undoubtedly attempted to hunt the behemoths but, like later explorers, watched haplessly as the wounded creatures instinctively drew into the water, eventually expiring at the soft river bottom.

Using old maps and descriptions, and comparing them with modern topographical maps, I hoped we might pinpoint important expedition stopping points. My aspirations to some sort of scientific survey, to find and thus gain insight into the experience of those who'd walked along these banks, seemed laughable once we got under way. Camp Beautiful, Camp Recovery, Hospital Camp, Parting Camp—they were all there somewhere. The true memorial to their being wasn't waypoint coordinates on a GPS but the solid jungle walls flanking either shore. The hothouse greenery simply spilled into the river, obliterating the margins between water and shore, as billowy and knotted and imprecise as 150 years ago.

Back then Darién captured the collective imagination for the evils brewing within it: disease, predatory beasts, savage inhabitants. Of course, twentieth- and twenty-first-century attitudes have flip-flopped. The world's surviving rain forests, such as Darién, are prized as places of almost limitless wonder and creation. Science has made it so; in fact, when scientists first began to investigate how the habitat worked, they went to Panama, both Darién and the Canal Zone—the jungles at America's doorstep. Few forests have received more scrutiny or revealed more biological secrets. In the 1970s British scientists built 300-foot-high aerial walkways a few miles off the Caledonia Bay coast, ushering in the era of serious rainforest canopy study. Much to scientists' amazement, as much as half of all life was found up in the trees. On the ground, foot-soldier scientists, many of them affiliated with the Panama-based Smithsonian Tropical Research Institute, catalogued, combed, and contemplated, uncovering new botanical medicines, species, and theories about the way plants and insects brilliantly conspired in grand co-evolutionary schemes. Underscoring it all was the fact that, far from being a global cesspool, the jungle was our salvation, its preservation directly impacting our own. In a comparative blink of the eye science took a word that for centuries spelled death and made it mean life. In 1981, the United Nations named Darién a World Heritage Site and biosphere reserve, recognizing it as a foremost global priority for conservation.

Yet it is difficult to be optimistic about the survival of Darién. A nuclear-excavated canal might not be built, but the "opening of the Darién" is viewed by many as inevitable. The continuation of the highway from Yaviza to Colombia has been slowed by a lack of funds, not environmental concerns, and new logging roads are pressing deep into the interior, where the best timber remains. Illegal immigrants from Colombia are pouring through the porous border, carving up territory that's not their own. Some are slash-and-burn farmers; others are paramilitary groups or their rebel counterparts, using the thick forest cover for base camps. Hostage taking is a common enough problem that parts of the wilderness have long-standing U.S. State Department advisories against tourist travel. There was one when I went there. Darién's lovely geography—linked but not linked—makes it one of the most attractive and threatened pieces of real estate in the world. Now, as then, it's the ultimate crossroads.

WE MADE IT DOWN the river after all, the water just high enough and our boat narrow enough to slip our way through the logjam. Our rendezvous with Hernán's colleague at Puerto Limón, a nondescript inlet about halfway down the river, worked perfectly. This was roughly the site of Strain's Hospital Camp, and the upper portion of that part of the river is, biologically speaking, uncommonly barren. Rather than camp we decided to try to make it all the way to Yaviza, which we did just before nightfall. From Morti it had taken us about ten hours of boat travel to accomplish what had taken Strain and his men well over a month. The great tidal wash of the Pacific was evident as we approached Yaviza, the muddy shoreline suddenly banded by red mangrove.

We spent a day or two in nearby El Real resting, then extended the journey even deeper into the interior toward the old gold mines at Cana. Strain had remarked on them, but that wasn't why we went. It was simply hard to stop, having come so far. About halfway into the two-day, 25-mile trek, on fairly flat terrain, my feet gave way. I simply couldn't walk anymore, and those with me spent the better part of the morning waiting as I stopped, sat, and repeatedly took my shoes on and off to dress the blisters. Overnight the foot had exploded in some open-sore rash. Each footstep was agonizing, and with the demoralizing pain came the realization that I honestly didn't know what I was going to do. Hernán, the most experienced of us, had already left days earlier, a victim of dysentery.

Only one hundred years ago there had been a bustling trade route where I now stood unable to walk. Roads dozens of feet wide, rail lines, and villages ran from the river to the gold mines. Now there was nothing. As the last of those residents observed shortly before he died, the curse of Darién wasn't a true curse. There was plenty of good that happened; it just didn't happen for long.

I had my shoes off again when a trio came along riding burros. They seemed to materialize out of nowhere. I wasn't sure where they had started from or whether they might help, but apparently my hobbled situation spoke for itself. A self-styled Darién ranger named Alberto took the rope bridle and motioned for me to hop aboard. I might have valorously declined and tried to walk the final few hours—it was the 4th of July, and somewhere in my head I was taken with the idea of finishing this day on my feet—but I would have been foolish.

You come to Darién with the idea that something extraordinary will happen. There are still leopards and harpy eagles and packs of teeth-gnashing peccaries and God knows how many species of plants yet to be discovered. Strain, and those before and after him, shared precisely that expectation: They were bidding on the extraordinary, aware that their trip was as much allegory as epic. Like Dante's journey through the Dark Wood, they were prepared to suffer and face demons because the other side promised so much. Those who couldn't stomach the penance in exchange for the extraordinary had no business in Darién. There was a price to pay. Isaac Strain and almost every man he was with paid the ultimate price. He was brilliant and brave, but never very lucky.

I saw the mule as a gift. I got on and stayed on.

Notes

Not a lot of people are familiar with Isaac Strain and the 1854 U.S. naval expedition to Darién. Though his was the first major government exploration in search of a ship canal route, Strain is a minor historical figure and the story obscure. Even in the small historical societies of western Pennsylvania, where far less adventurous native sons than Strain are generally well accounted for, he is an unknown.

America's ship canal history tends to start in the post–Civil War era with a more conventionally successful venture, the U.S. Darién Exploring Expedition of 1870, an expedition that produced far less human drama but reams of scientific reports, maps, and a fatality-free narrative. Perhaps only a few dozen researchers have found themselves drawn to the enigmatic Strain expedition and then attempted to source the journals and notebooks that the party's men said they produced. Over the last century the Navy Department Library staff has attempted several times to unearth the Darién journals—the most recent occasion being my own two-year search—and in each case their efforts proved fruitless. This, despite the fact that Isaac Strain was a prolific correspondent and is on record as having filed his journals with the Navy depository. They should be there—or in the National Archives or the Library of Congress—but they're not. Darién research mimics Darién reality: Nothing is easy, or for that matter, as you expect it to be.

Most sensible writers would have stopped right there. In explaining why he shifted gears and wrote about only John Adams and not Adams and Thomas Jefferson as he originally intended, the historian David McCullough is fond of saying that you go where the light is. In my case I decided to keep groping along in the dark, stubbornly certain that the same persistence that makes me a tiresome hiking companion would produce that elusive gift, a flaking letter book, bound by dark leather covers and beginning with the words "The U.S. Darien Explor-

ing Expedition of 1854." Never happened. But in waiting for *it* to happen, in re-
searching "around" the journals, I came to believe not only that they had once
existed, as many of the men said they did, but also in the credibility of those portions of the journals that had appeared in print, albeit 150 years ago.

The verbatim journal entries actually appeared in only one place, an account
of the expedition written by the then bestselling historian Joel Tyler Headley.
His story appeared over three successive editions of the 1855 *Harper's New
Monthly,* the most thought-provoking periodical of the day. The diary entries
are pure nineteenth-century expeditionary nuggets, full of odd details and un-
derstated drama. In the decades to come, when Strain's journals couldn't be
found, the question was simple: Were they authentic, or some combination of
the actual journals and Headley's sometimes overheated imagination? In the
countless congressional summaries of the equally countless ship canal exploratories spanning the late nineteenth century, Headley's article was often
cited as an official account of the Strain expedition (though there is an official
government version that Strain himself produced). However, official reports
also undercut it, saying that the author only "claimed" access to the party's
journals. There was no proof since there were no journals to check against. It
probably wasn't beyond Headley to razzle-dazzle a little bit.

There's one obvious reason to think he was, however, faithful to the actual
expedition journal: Strain and most of his men were still alive at the time of the
article's publication and none would have been bashful about correcting him. In
private correspondence from Strain and the others, some of it having to do with
the articles, there's never any hint that what Headley reproduced was anything
but genuine. Strain also trusted Headley as a friend, enough to bequeath a portion of his research and papers to him after he died.

There's other supporting primary material, such as the letter on file at the
Navy Department Library from Samuel Kettlewell, in which the seaman ac-
knowledges his role as the trip's journal keeper (though unfortunately he never
addresses the whereabouts of the darned thing). In order to satisfy myself further about this question and do the unthinkable—that is, treat this secondary
source material as the virtual equal to original manuscript material—I fact-
checked much of the information in the entries, and it stands up. I can't speak
for the rest of his work, but with respect to his journal entries Headley was
faithful. I've used many of them in this account—obviously, I owe Headley a
large debt of gratitude.

The journal entries are a starting point but are by no means the bulk of this
story. I have sought to expand on the blow-by-blow of the Darién survival
drama, to put flesh on the bones of a man (several men actually) and understand
what brought them to do what they did. Whenever possible I've tried to walk

wherever Strain walked. The USS *Constitution,* a ship Strain lived and worked on for three years, is docked only a half hour from my home. Less convenient but just as illuminating were visits to Springfield, Ohio, where he grew up, and of course Darién.

For all the details in the Headley account there are gaping mysteries. There's barely a word of Strain's background, nor that of any of the other principals. Nothing on the British version of events. Nothing on the storm that greeted their launch from Philadelphia or what happened to Darién's "heroes" when their story of survival stopped gripping the nation's readers. Thanks to new original manuscript sources, a variety of untapped historical society collections, countless maritime museums, a few distant relatives, and two trips to the still very wild Darién rain forest, I think a fuller, truer tale is now available.

PROLOGUE

Ignacio Gallup-Diaz, in his *The Door of the Seas and Key to the Universe* (an e-book produced in collaboration with the American Historical Society and Columbia University Press), translates the famous Spanish epigraph slightly differently. His version reads: *Cuando entres al Darién encomiéndate a María; en tu mano está la entrada, en la de Dios la salida.* ("When you enter the Darién/Commend your soul to the Virgin Mary,/Your entrance is in your hands,/But your exit is in God's.") The poem is rumored to have been etched on the walls of an old fort at the entrance of Darién, writes Gallup-Diaz, citing a Spanish historical text.

Panama's Hernán Araúz, the region's most knowledgeable field guide and the son of pioneering Darién scientists Reina and Amado Araúz, provided the more colloquial translation (and oceanic location) I use. Yaviza was a gateway to the Spanish gold mines near the present-day Colombia-Panama border and has been around as a frontier post almost from the start of the conquest. One can still see the fort ruins from the river, and the village itself is newly accessible via the Pan-American Highway. Some of the description in the chapter is informed by my own travels: I visited Yaviza once by the four-wheel-drive road in '91 and again in 2001 along the course of the Chucunaque River. A superb 1988 PBS special, *Tramping the Darién,* also provided a visual background source.

1 / GALES of DECEMBER

Every East Coast newspaper carried accounts of the December-January gales. After the Americans' harrowing expedition to Darién, the storm's significance diminished so much that few of the principals even bothered to remark on it. I could only speculate what they went through, comparing the *Cyane*'s own ship's log and those of others caught up in the Hatteras hurricane, until an account surfaced by the ship's master, William Wilcox. He was a friend of Theodore Winthrop and evidently provided him with an extract of his personal journal. Winthrop, who was planning a book of his own, would have seen very little himself, holding on as he was for dear life in the wardroom cabin, but Wilcox's account provided vivid details and has never been published. I found it among the Winthrop papers at the New York Public Library; it was poorly identified, but I knew it existed thanks to Willard E. Martin's 1945 dissertation on Winthrop, a paper that devotes special emphasis and energy to the novelist's adventurous turn.

One other note: Both the log and Wilcox's account were initially inscrutable to me (a landsman, after all) and required a sailor's interpretation. I was fortunate to get that from Bradley Anderson, a Maine Maritime graduate who served as an officer on several tall ships in the 1980s and '90s, including a cruise aboard the schooner *Ernestina* that took him and a green crew of seventeen students-in-training through October 1991's "Perfect Storm." The *Ernestina* was one of the lucky ones, emerging from the storm (not unlike the *Cyane*) despite losing her engines for several hours and almost all her canvas in the 70-knots-plus gale. Brad's counsel and deep understanding of what it feels like to be under way in a wooden ship beset by hurricane conditions was invaluable.

2 / The SEA and the JUNGLE

Isaac Strain's upbringing is a long-running mystery. The best nineteenth-century references, such as *Harper's Encyclopedia of United States History* and Nathan Crosby's *Annual Obituary Notices of Eminent Persons,* provide little more than his birthplace, parents, and a recitation of his adventurous Navy career. Strain himself, a rather devoted writer and communicator, left no known papers behind to help historians along. If he divulged anything about his childhood it would have been to his magazine biographer, Joel Tyler Headley (who was bequeathed some of Strain's papers), but only the author's twenty-odd books survive, not his papers. Soon thereafter the Civil War absorbed everyone and everything—the present seemed far more crucial than anything that happened in the recent past. Those who didn't play a role in the great conflict, no matter how celebrated they might have once been, were quickly relegated to obscurity. With no direct heirs, Strain's story (and whatever pieces helped construct it) disappeared.

Fortunately the Scotch Presbyterians kept rather exhaustive records, and a small but crucial window into Strain's past is found in the churches that formed the community focal point of frontier living in midcentury Pennsylvania and Ohio. Original documents from Middle Spring Presbyterian Church in Cumberland County, Pennsylvania, record the marriage of his parents, Strain's baptism, and his father Robert's membership in the church. In trying to account for what became of Strain's mother, Martha Grier, I came across countless genealogical treasures, one of them being the *Divorces of Cumberland County* (compiled on CD by Eugene Stroop). The hundreds of cases make for fascinating reading and illuminate the marital hardships that frontier families faced. Finally, I asked genealogical researchers in Franklin, Clark, and Cumberland counties to help find archive materials and hear out my theories on what they might mean. It was reassuring to know that I wasn't the only person who believed the reference encyclopedias had for so long mistakenly given Isaac the wrong mother.

The material on his education at Hopewell Academy comes from several county histories, a popular publishing phenomenon in the latter half of the nineteenth century. Springfield in the 1830s and '40s is documented both at the Heritage Center of Clark County (a building located almost on the very land Robert Strain once owned) and in the stunning book *Heartland,* produced by the Clark County Historical Society.

3 / TORRID ZONE

New Granada, in present-day Colombia, was a busy and virtually unknown place in 1854, a part of the world promisingly situated at the heart of the major trade routes. Under way at the time of the Darién exploration was a massive topographical reconnaissance of the countryside, a project that was awarded to the Italian geographer Agustín Codazzi and seemed to herald a new, commercially auspicious age. At the time of the national survey, it wasn't just their Darién possession that had been inadequately explored but the entire New Granada interior as well. The *Comisión Corográfica* would achieve landmark results, as Efraín Sanchéz argues in his 1995 Ph.D. thesis ("Government and Geography in Nineteenth-Century Colombia"), but the fact that the industrious Codazzi accomplished next to nothing at Darién attests to how complex and difficult an international venture it was. Much of the American perspective about New Granada comes from Theodore Winthrop, who was at the apex of his journal writing with so many free hours, and Isaac Holton's travel narrative, *New Granada: Twenty Months in the Andes* (1857).

William Talbot Truxtun and John Minor Maury left a bit more behind than
their commander Isaac Strain, but not a lot. The bulk of the material comes
from their Civil War days, when Truxtun was helping to run the East Coast
blockade and Maury was trying to bust through it. Maury and his relationship
with his guardian, the famous Matthew Fontaine ("M.F.") Maury, is fascinating
but has never truly been explored in any of the dozen or so books on the
"Pathfinder of the Seas" or in Edward Leon Towle's groundbreaking Ph.D.
thesis. Modern Maury descendants have long thought John Minor and M.F. un-
related and largely unconnected, but the archival material at the Virginia Historical Society, among other places, contradicts their understanding. "Jack"
Maury wasn't only his ward but a confidant and a key advisor on the Matthew
Fontaine Maury project that nearly turned the war for the South, the building of
the first torpedo.

An important point which Towle's Ph.D. and other materials do support is
that the Darién Expedition wasn't as hastily thrown together as some thought.
The senior leaders—Strain, Maury, and Truxtun—were all known to one
another and to M. F. Maury, the driving force behind the Navy's seafaring exploration program. The Navy wasn't simply throwing a ship and some men at
Darién but had instead selected an elite, well-balanced crew. Whatever mistakes happened, their suitability to one another was probably the only reason
they walked out of the jungle. Moreover, their team was small but it wasn't *that*
small by the standards of the day: A few years earlier the secretary of the Navy
detached all of two officers, William Lewis Herndon and Lardner Gibbon, to
conduct a survey of the entire Amazon River watershed. Fifty years before
that, Lewis and Clark had undertaken the first national survey in U.S. history
with twenty-seven men, the same number as the Darién Exploring Expedition.
In applying three officers, three engineers, and more than a dozen ship's crew
to a survey the Navy Department was putting serious emphasis on the Darién
campaign.

One final note about Strain's fateful impatience: He was overeager, says the
naval historian Vincent Ponko Jr. (author of *Ships, Seas, and Scientists*, the foremost reference work on the Navy's antebellum voyages of exploration). Ponko
is correct, but his larger point isn't true, that Strain persuaded an otherwise am-
bivalent Navy Department into the Darién exploration. The evidence is clear
on this: They came to him, not the other way around. Letters from a British
agent trying to arrange the U.S. government's cooperation in a joint survey
back up this crucially different interpretation. A barely legible letter in the Navy
Department files which Strain wrote in August 1853 is cited by Ponko as proof
that Strain was pushing the department for the exploration. However, that mis-

filed letter wasn't about Darién at all, but rather the lieutenant's energetic attempt to lead an East Indies expedition.

4 / DARIÉN GAP

Rough-and-ready modern travelers are well familiar with Darién Gap. It became a hot trekking destination in the '60s, attracting hordes of bandana-clad backpackers who understandably saw something sacrosanct in the blot of roadless rain forest separating South America from North America. To them the "Gap" was defined as the place where the Pan-American Highway—that paved dagger of civilization—stopped, unable to penetrate the natural "obstacles of a continent" nor pick up again until deep in Colombia.

In mid-nineteenth century the Gap, sometimes called Cullen's Gap, was defined altogether differently. For early tropical explorers the Gap was the low spot in the coast-running mountains, the place where they'd lay down that era's more important "road," the one linking the oceans, not the hemispheres. Dr. Edward Cullen, the rogue figure at the center of the Gap excitement, is yet another person whom history has managed to bury. Yet his imprint is everywhere if one looks close enough. He published three books (two editions of *The Isthmus of Darién Ship Canal* and his nasty critique *Over Darién by a Ship Canal: Reports of the Mismanaged Darién Expedition of 1854, with Suggestions for a Survey by Competent Engineers, and an Exploration by Parties with Compasses*) in addition to a lengthy pamphlet about the Darién Indians, an emigrant's guide to New Granada, and an exhausting number of letters to newspaper editors on both sides of the Atlantic. Much of the personal information about him comes from his correspondence with the Royal Geographical Society, the originals of which remain at the London-based society. Dr. Cullen might not have pioneered a route across the isthmus, but he was an early pioneer of a coming art form: media spin.

About the *Virago* expedition: It really hasn't received its critical due in the expeditionary accounts of the Darién exploration. Several important items have never been reported, perhaps because few have accessed the government correspondence at the Public Record Office (PRO) in London or Captain James Prevost's unedited personal account at the Royal Geographical Society. What emerges from those manuscript sources is the startling and wholly unauthorized grab at glory by the Pacific commander Fairfax Moresby and the earnest if flawed effort by Prevost to make good for his father-in-law. Both men paid for their daring plan (according to the Admiralty's *Navy List* for 1854, an annual reference that charted an officer's post and rank changes, each was demoted the same year).

Strain has long been criticized for racing ahead of his British counterparts, but little blame has been put to Prevost and Moresby, who made no attempt whatsoever to negotiate a passage with the Indians and thus were attacked as would-be invaders, an event that had direct bearing on Strain's hardships. The fact that the Prevost expedition was unauthorized and an utter mystery to British parties on the Atlantic side of the isthmus has, to my knowledge, never been pointed out before.

5 / DOOR of the SEAS

The story of the Scots immigration to Darién is perhaps best told in John Prebble's *The Darién Disaster: A Scots Colony in the New World, 1698–1700*. Douglas Galbraith's award-winning fictional treatment of the same historical episode (*The Rising Sun*) is a descriptive tour de force, sharpening the part of the story having to do with the hopes of immigrants and the cruel reality they were unprepared to face. A third impressive voice in the telling of the Scots tale was Strain himself, who perhaps devoted "more time and space" than he should have, he said, in a history-rich paper he read to the New-York Historical Society audience in the summer of 1856 (*A Paper on the History and Prospects of Interoceanic Communication by the American Isthmus*). The story of the Scots at Caledonia resonated with Strain, who was by that time well aware of the speculative mania that both motivated and ruined each of the ventures.

How the journalist Frederick Foster got on board the *Cyane* is a mystery, but his presence isn't terribly surprising. Given the vast amount of print interest and coverage one could make a case that the Darién Exploring Expedition was the first full-blown media expedition. Stories traveling out by both ship and wire gave the proceedings a lively serial feel, and the trio of highly competitive American newspapers in Panama (the *Herald*, *Times*, and *Courier*) were at the heart of it all. The story, involving national survey teams, an engineering feat of historic proportions, and a cast of dashing explorers escorted by the biggest sea powers of the era—well, it was an irresistible tale. Rumors got wide airing and there was much whispering about who was in cahoots with whom. After the fact, in *Over Darién*, Edward Cullen proposed a rather elaborate conspiratorial scheme in which he said many of the freelance men Strain hired had allegiances to rival commercial schemes. On the surface Cullen had a point—Foster, for example, worked for the *Aspinwall Courier*, a newspaper named for the railroad mogul then building the trans-isthmus Panama line—but the truth was probably less dire. The volunteers Strain found in Cartagena and Philadelphia wished to be aligned with whatever project might be successful, and none attempted any bit of sabotage. In fact, Frederick Avery, who Cullen aligned with a rival ship canal group, was later singled out by Strain for his heroic efforts on behalf of the starving party.

Looking for insight on how the crewmen felt about the coming expedition and why they might volunteer (unlike officers they had little to gain professionally), I was assisted immeasurably by Dr. Murray Hamlet, recently retired from the U.S. Army Research Laboratory in Natick, Massachusetts. An avid student of nineteenth- and twentieth-century expeditions and a man who designed and supervised a battery of extreme endurance trials involving foot soldiers, Hamlet is an expert in soldier stamina and psychology. His tests revealed certain timeless universals when it came to seeing why soldiers would take on extraordinary, pain-filled challenges: They volunteered for such duty because they had faith in their leaders and because they were convinced their effort would benefit their foot soldier brethren.

6 / DIVIDE

The tropical climate and a nineteenth-century military man's relationship to it is the subject of Philip Curtin's splendid book *Death by Migration: Europe's Encounter with the Tropical World in the Nineteenth Century*. Curtin establishes the all-too-common seafaring disasters in the Torrid Zone (at Cartagena in 1742 an English siege force lost some 8,000 men to disease in the space of a couple of months), then goes on to explain the scientific world's largely futile attempts to either combat or explain the nature of what was killing them. In the absence of modern disease theory, most medical experts linked human health with human passions and habits of life. "Heat and exercise brought on perspiration, and perspiration affected the humoral balance of the body," Curtin writes. When the humoral balance was adversely affected humans were more predisposed to illness. Some ship's doctors believed the best preventative to the above was to strictly limit a soldier's water consumption in the hot zones; others advised against looser fitting clothing and insisted on insulating materials like flannel (thus isolating the skin from the "miasmic" air). Though Curtin's research focuses on the British colonial experience in the West Indies and India, the American attitude was similar, with most Navy vessels carrying a copy of *Physician for Ships*, a compact, like-minded volume listing fevers, their common symptoms, and a primitive course of treatment (usually bleeding).

In the beginning, scientific-minded researchers believed that white men could readily adapt to the climate if they took certain precautions in the clothing they wore, the places they slept, and the food they ate. However, at mid-century a counter view took hold: The field of medical topography became entwined with the anthropological pseudoscience of phrenology, the attempt to prove intellectual differences among races using physiological measurements. White men died in droves in places like Darién, not because they were weak or unprepared, but because they simply didn't belong there, at least not for long. The higher races in the newly configured hierarchy—something supposedly established by measuring the cranial capacities of skulls—had been designed to inhabit the more climatically advantageous regions of the Earth, the northern latitudes. What this all meant to a typical seaman is debatable, but he was aware of the ongoing misery associated with the tropical climates and more specifically the building of the nearby Panama Railroad. Joseph L. Schott's *Rails Across Panama* is the classic modern account of William H. Aspinwall's enterprise, but another good source, filled with evocative line drawings from the period, is F. N. Otis's *Illustrated History of the Panama Railroad*. I'm also indebted to a fascinating tropical medical journal kept by the *Virago*'s surgeon, Henry Trevan, who was a good deal more sophisticated and insistent than the average American ship physician. He prescribed preventative quinine doses (cut with coffee in the morning and whiskey in the evening) to both the Prevost party and later those that helped rescue Strain's men.

7 / DEVIL'S OWN

U.S. Navy commander Thomas O. Selfridge is widely lauded for his post–Civil War expedition to Darién in 1870, with the historian David McCullough (*The Path Between the Seas*) recognizing his careful and systematic approach as a kind of breakthrough in jungle expeditioning. He succeeded in accurately surveying the Atlantic coast mountains and portions of the Chucunaque valley, and maybe most notably he also emerged unscathed.

However, Selfridge had more than a few shaky moments in the isthmian interior, something largely ignored. In fact, in the earliest days of his exploration, he only narrowly averted disaster, enduring an eerily similar experience to that of Strain and his men. Triumphantly launching himself and his party into the jungle, Selfridge utterly lost his way and was taken for gone when he finally stumbled out three weeks later (he had provisions for twelve days). He and his companions were so ill that the survey was delayed for weeks while Selfridge and others recovered aboard the *Guard*, a warship that was, in one scientist's words, "transformed into a hospital." A few weeks later, in crossing the divide, a flash flood came upon his men "so suddenly that some had barely time to rescue their knapsacks on the bank." Selfridge was well prepared, and for that he deserves ample credit, but he was lucky too. His party could have easily suffered similar (if not more) casualties as Strain's. The biggest difference in the early stage portions of their expeditions is simple: Selfridge turned around and got help, whereas Strain (in a far more anxious political climate) marched on. Self-ridge's unerring expedition has long served to diminish Strain's earlier crossing, making it seem crudely amateurish, but a closer inspection of Selfridge's early troubles is important. It changes the equation and makes Strain's struggles seem far more typical.

8 / CHUCUNAQUE RIVER

The interior narrative comes from a variety of sources: Strain's official accounts to the British and U.S. governments, his collaborative article with Joel Tyler Headley for *Harper's*, and his speech to the New-York Historical Society. Perhaps the best detail comes from Theodore Winthrop's copious notes (in the Laura Winthrop collection at the New York Public Library). Winthrop wrote with particular attention to their separation, a point where Winthrop's attitude about the expedition sours considerably. Whether his famous bad-mouthing of the expedition—"ill led and *mal composé*," he wrote in a private letter to his mentor Aspinwall—was accurate or merely an emotional response to the immense disappointment of a dream denied is up for debate. Knowing Winthrop's wild mood swings (and having reviewed later correspondence in which he shows considerable respect for Strain) makes me think the latter.

My largely positive analysis of Strain's survival strategies was aided by Morgan Smith, who is best known as the founder of the U.S. Air Force's jungle survival school in Panama. Thousands of officers and soldiers have passed through his field training program, as did Apollo astronauts John Glenn, Neil Armstrong, and Edwin "Buzz" Aldrin (NASA wanted them prepared in case their reentry capsules went off course and touched down in remote jungle). Smith's charges made lean-tos from bamboo and palm leaves, learned to identify and drink from the water vine, and skinned and ate iguanas. In the classroom Smith was often assisted by Antonio Zarco, an elder tribesman from the interior of Darién (he also had on-hand a "demystifying" prop, an eight-foot-long boa constrictor named Isabel).

Now in his seventies, Smith has adapted his jungle expertise to business team training, presenting groups with a tropical emergency scenario—specifically, in fact, a plane crash in the Darién—asking them to both strategize in getting to safety and to rank the importance of the items at their disposal. Smith's strategic recommendations in the simulation model ("Jungle Survival Situation"—Human Synergistics) are almost identical to what Strain did, e.g., following "a river course to a larger body of water and possible settlements." Even though Strain ultimately split the group, something Smith cautions against, he did so only after he had done all he could to keep the party together and only upon passing out of the terrain he considered most dangerous (near the hostile Indian settlements). Moreover, Strain was probably justified in halting his raft experiment once it became apparent there was great danger of wetting and ruining their matches. After a machete a disposable cigarette lighter is the most important item to salvage from the plane wreck in Smith's modern simulation. Besides the practical benefits of a fire, he argues that the "psychological comfort . . . is one of the greatest assets for survivors." Among the less helpful items he lists are a pistol ("fairly useless" as a signaling tool "because sound will not travel very far in the forest") and a compass ("may or may not be accurate in the forest since it is possible that it will not maintain magnetic North" in the mountainous, iron ore-rich terrain of Darién).

9 / LIFE and DEATH

Severe swings in morale are well documented in a harsh jungle environment. The unexpected absence of a trusted leader, diminishing food stores, and the accumulated discomforts of "hordes of various kinds of insects" (the words of the physician accompanying the later Selfridge expedition) could easily turn a seemingly healthy party into a barely ambulatory one in a matter of days. According to Murray Hamlet, also an expert in cold weather survival, severe tropical heat is generally more difficult for a soldier to cope with than severe cold for the simple reason that there's little one can do to protect against tropical heat. The body simply can't adequately cool itself. Moreover, at midcentury explorers had far more experience battling Arctic cold, due to the several-centuries' chase for the Northwest Passage, than coping with prolonged exposure to oppressive heat.

Much of the basic narrative information comes from Joel Tyler Headley's *Harper's* 1855 article, which begins by noting his fortunate access to the journals from both the main and advanced party, a book of sketches from the draftsman, and personal interviews with Maury and Avery. He may or may not have seen an account Truxtun penned, which Strain intended to be appended to his lengthy report to the secretary of the Navy but never was. Unfortunately the Truxtun account has never surfaced.

10 / PACIFIC

The Chucunaque River is a complex waterway with a Jekyll and Hyde–like character, especially in the dry season, when it withers to a trickle in spots. The uppermost portions have long supported settlements. Further down, where the Indian presence lessened, the watershed's habitat was still conducive to survival.

Strain was right to believe they could live off the land in this section. James Duke's *Darién Survival Manual,* written in the late 1960s for the swarms of non-native researchers then inspecting the terrain for a nuclear-excavated second canal passage, offers the "big ten" plant species, singling out the palm family as "more important for jungle survival" than any other. In Duke's experience, Strain's high reliance on palms and his comparative lack of success at hunting was perfectly understandable. In spite of the lay perception that the jungle is a lush, animal-rich environment where starvation seems next to impossible, the exact opposite is the case. Big game and even birds are extremely difficult to catch and shouldn't be relied on as major food sources, say jungle survival experts like Duke and Morgan Smith. Reptiles and amphibians are far more accommodating but hardly go a long way in feeding a marching column of two dozen.

In the lower portion of the Chucunaque the pickings get even slimmer. Charles Breder, a New York naturalist attached to the Marsh Darién Expedition, was the first to comprehensively describe the habitat change to "lower arid zone." R. O. Marsh, Breder's leader, immortalized the nonbotanizing parts of the 1924 trip in *White Indians of Darién,* which tells the fascinating tale of another anthropologically driven boondoggle.

Smithsonian Tropical Research Institute in Panama City has conducted further research in the region. Stanley Heckadon-Moreno, STRI's advisor to the director, was extremely patient in answering my questions and updating the current scientific understanding of the Darién ecological life zones. Heckadon-Moreno is also the author of *Naturalistas de Istmo de Panama,* a fascinating book about the history of natural history on the isthmus. Ironically, Darién is still awaiting a soup-to-nuts biological survey. The region is also part of a broader-scale investigation into what STRI scientists call the single most important natural history event since the death of the dinosaurs, the rising of the isthmus three million years ago.

11 / BATTLE ROAD

Given their almost annual flirtation with a new and even bloodier war, a British-U.S. collaborative rescue was a twist to the tale nobody could have foreseen. The fraternity of seamen was a real thing, however, and quite different from the political braying that took place in Washington and London. In fact, a naval ship's crew at midcentury was often comprised of as many foreign-born seamen as those American-born (though regulations required 66 percent of the crew to be U.S. nationals).

In a crew-wide letter delivered to the *Virago* (and written shortly before the

Americans departed Darién for home), the noncommissioned officers and surviving seamen of the U.S. Darién Exploring Expedition wrote: "Words fail us, neither can our tongues express or our pens describe the feelings of our hearts. But, Sir, your kindness and generosity toward us are indeed characteristic of the British gentleman and sailor. To our families in fair and glorious Columbia we shall speak of you, and they shall know you as our deliverer from lingering death; our children shall learn to pronounce your name, and from the altar of our God offer before the throne of the Heavenly Father prayers for your own and family's welfare." In the same letter the men applaud the "almost superhuman exertions of our gallant captain" as well as those of Truxtun and Maury.

Strain lobbied Congress for a reward on the behalf of the Englishmen who helped rescue his party. "Had it not been for their well directed efforts thirteen suffering men must inevitably have perished," he wrote, "notwithstanding every effort that I or the others composing the advanced guard might have made to save them."

The U.S. Congress approved gold medals to the officers and a "liberal grant" of twenty pounds each to his boat's crew, but it's unclear if the men ever saw either the money or the medals. In the summer of 1856 a British naval paper chastised the U.S. government for failing to make good on its promise. The newspaper account in the *Nautical Standard* offers some revisionist details and hints at how the Darién story was evolving in the European press. Among other things, the article says Strain tried to appease the hostile natives with his own stores (thus running out of provisions prematurely). "As the provisions became scarce the natives gradually dropped off, until at length the expedition found themselves in a dense wilderness, without food, and with no one to guide them." The point is untrue but a later detail might be. The rescue party reaching Hospital Camp 2 supposedly found all the edible nuts and berries scoured from the countryside "within seven miles around."

12 / CROSSING LINES

In questioning Lionel Gisborne's widely published claim that he did everything he could to rescue the Strain party I've relied on his original reports, which are found in the Admiralty papers at the Public Record Office in London. His series of "real time" correspondence with the *Espiégle*'s captain, George Hancock (technically, his commander), offers a truer, more in-depth look at his conflicted behavior than his future reports to the Atlantic and Pacific Junction Company stockholders in 1854 and the Royal Geographical Society in 1856.

Gisborne had innumerable reasons *not* to find Strain, who had, after all, raced ahead of him and refused to submit to his authority. He also had a petty streak, a quality that emerges in the privately published version of his book (*The Isthmus of Darién in 1852*). Gisborne seems to have published the latter for the sole purpose of savaging his chief rival at the time, Edward Cullen. In comparing the public and private copies, I found the only significant differences were those portions that concerned Cullen and the liberties he'd taken with the phrase "route discoverer." Of course, the information says something about Cullen's falsity, but perhaps more about Gisborne and his own fervent ambition.

13 / HOME

Knowing the high stakes of the ship canal quest, as well as the partisan nature of route speculators, Strain expected criticism of his findings and his decision to cross independent of the other parties assembling at Caledonia Bay. What he didn't anticipate were the extraordinary charges leveled by Agustín Codazzi, a renowned public figure in Europe and South America, where he had completed topographic surveys in Venezuela and New Granada. Codazzi saw almost nothing of the Darién interior with his own eyes, leaving a few weeks after arriving (a condition that Strain felt should have prevented him from commenting on the trials of others). When Codazzi described the American seamen cannibalizing their dead it meant something. He was an established man of science and to this day, explains Efraín Sánchez in his 1995 Ph.D. thesis, remains a revered figure in Colombia, with villages, rivers, mountain peaks, and a plant species each bearing the Codazzi name.

It's difficult to explain either Codazzi's intent or how he of all people could make such an unsubstantiated charge, but much of his information at Darién was secondhand (something that got nineteenth-century scientific hunter-gatherers like himself and Humboldt in perpetual trouble). Perhaps he had heard the story of seamen Parks and Lombard and their unfulfilled plan of eating the dead and assumed they'd actually done so.

Strain's rebuttal, a paper he read before the New-York Historical Society in June 1856, is both masterful and fairly economical all things considered. It certainly shows his love of research and the fact that his remarkable intellect was undiminished, even as his body wasted away. When U.S. Navy lieutenant John T. Sullivan compiled the *Report of the Historical and Technical Information Relating to the Problem of Interoceanic Communication by Way of the American Isthmus* (1883)—the single best reference on ship canal history the U.S. government ever published—he made special mention of Strain's contribution: "This history . . . should have the merit of brevity," he remarked, "and as it is hardly possible to satisfy these requirements more fully than Lieutenant Strain has in his paper already referred to, his compilation will be quoted. An additional object will be to recognize the merits of this brave officer in a field in which he is but little known."

Sources about Strain's condition in the years after Darién include John Sanford Barnes's *Arctic* trip journal ("My Egotistigraphy," he titled it) archived at the New-York Historical Society. It's also important to note that the material describing Strain's difficulties with Commander A. B. Fairfax comes from a nonindexed Record Group 45 letter in the National Archives. To my knowledge the information in the correspondence between Strain and then Secretary of the Navy Dobbin has never been reported on.

14 / AWAY

The American presence in Panama in the 1850s—something Strain experienced in the last twenty-four hours of his life as he offloaded at Aspinwall—is a remarkable story unto itself. Seemingly overnight the transit had become a crucial oceanic link, drawing multinational warships to oversee it and westward emigrants by the thousands. Between 1850 and 1869 some 600,000 passengers were said to pass through Panama, according to John Kemble's scholarly classic *The Panama Route*.

Tracing a prominent American officer's death might seem to have a reasonably strong chance of success in what was then a prominently Americanized part of the world, but the problems are many. Perhaps one reason why no autopsy was performed and no information was forthcoming was because Strain was still in transit and hadn't yet formally reported to his ship *Cyane*. In essence he was still a private citizen. When U.S. nationals died in foreign ports it was the responsibility of the State Department's consular office to handle the arrangements and report to Washington. In Strain's case the State Department files contain nothing. Why he was buried in Panama and not shipped back home to the United States has a simpler answer: If there was even a hint of fever the remains of a deceased person were not allowed on board a ship, whether it be a naval or a passenger vessel.

Records at the National Archives regional office in New York show Strain's effects loaded aboard the *Illinois* for the return trip to New York. On May 29, 1857, the bill of lading was received at the Brooklyn Navy Yard, and Commandant Thomas Rootes ordered the storekeeper to call for the effects and put them into storage. What became of them, and what precisely they were—the bill of lading has yet to turn up—is a mystery. Some of his journals later found their way into the hands of author Joel Tyler Headley. Perhaps Headley intended to write a book about Strain, and perhaps Strain or his friends left him the material with that understanding, but the project never happened. Instead some of Strain's research—unfortunately without credit—was used in several future Headley articles for *Harper's*.

EPILOGUE

Building a transportation link through Darién remains a hot international issue. Environmentalists (led by the Panama-based Asociación Nacional para la Conservación de la Naturaleza, or ANCON) and indigenous Darién leaders believe extending the Pan-American highway and uniting the continents will destroy the rainforest wilderness and the ancient cultures that inhabit it. They also say the modern *camino real* will open a dangerous hole in the existing natural buffer that prevents passage of diseases from one continent to the other. The governments of Panama and Colombia have agreed not to build the road through Darién National Park, a portion of the greater Darién territory, but opponents are fearful the political climate could rapidly change.

Many are warily watching a major $88 million "environmental development project" in Darién, financed by the Inter-American Development Bank with the support of the U.S. Agency for International Development. Land-use mapping and road-building projects are intended to strengthen the province and create a bigger, better buffer "against the spillover of violence and narco-trafficking activities from neighboring Colombia." The project is touted as a landmark model uniting all Darién interests in a mutually beneficial relationship. Others see it as merely the latest in a long line of nonnative projects impossible to stop.

Selected Bibliography

MANUSCRIPT AND ARCHIVAL MATERIALS

Academy of Natural Sciences of Philadelphia.
British Library, London.
Clark County Historical Society, Ohio.
Cumberland County Historical Society, Pennsylvania.
George N. Hollins, William Henry Winder Papers, Maryland Historical Society.
Henry E. Huntington Library, Berkeley, California.
John Carter Brown Library, Brown University.
John Minor Maury Letters, assorted collections, Virginia Historical Society.
Journal of Samuel Greene Arnold, 1845–48. Private collection; excerpts from Rhode Island Historical Society.
Kittochtinny Historical Society, Pennsylvania.
Library of Congress.
Log Extract, Cyane Master William Wilcox, December 23–27, 1853. Laura Winthrop Papers, Manuscript Division, New York Public Library.
National Archives.
Navy Department.
Naval Historical Foundation.
New-York Historical Society.
New York Public Library.
Public Record Office, London.
Royal Geographical Society, London.
University of New Hampshire.
USS *Constitution* Museum.
Virginia Historical Society.
William Talbot Truxtun, Civil War letter book (1861–64), Hampton Roads Naval Museum, Norfolk, Virginia.

BOOKS

Alden, Carroll Storrs. *George Hamilton Perkins: His Life and Letters.* Houghton Mifflin (1914).

Chapin, Mac, and Bill Thielkeld. *Indigenous Landscapes—A Study in Ethnocartography.* Center for the Support of Native Lands (2001).

Colby, Elbridge. *Theodore Winthrop.* Twayne Publishers (1965).

Corbin, Diane Fontaine Maury. *A Life of Matthew Fontaine Maury.* London (1888).

Curtin, Philip D. *Death by Migration: Europe's Encounter with the Tropical World in the Nineteenth Century.* Cambridge University Press (1989).

Duke, James A. *Darién Survival Manual.* Battelle Memorial Institute, Columbus, Ohio (1967).

Forsyth, Adrian, with Ken Miyata. *Tropical Nature: Life and Death in the Rain Forests of Central and South America.* Touchstone (1984).

Griswold, C. D. *The Isthmus of Panama, and What I Saw There.* D. Appleton and Co. (1915).

Herndon, William Lewis. *Exploration of the Valley of the Amazon, 1851–52.* Edited and with a foreword by Gary Kinder. Grove Press (2000).

Hine, Robert V. *Bartlett's West: Drawing the Mexican Boundary.* Yale University Press (1968).

Holton, Isaac F. *New Granada: Twenty Months in the Andes.* Harper & Brothers (1857).

Howe, James. *A People Who Would Not Kneel: Panama, the United States, and the San Blas Kuna.* Smithsonian Institution Press (1998).

Humboldt, Alexander von, and Aime Bonpland. *Personal Narratives of Travel to the Equinoctial Regions of the New Continent During the Years 1799–1804* (1826). Translated into English by Helen Maria Williams.

Johnson, Laura Winthrop. *Life and Poems of Theodore Winthrop.* Henry Holt (1884).

Kelley, Frederick M. *The Union of the Oceans by Ship-Canal Without Locks.* Harper & Brothers (1859).

Kemble, John Haskell. *The Panama Route, 1848–1869.* Reissued by University of South Carolina (1990).

Lever, Darcy. *The Young Sea Officer's Sheet Anchor, or a Key to the Leading of Rigging and to Practical Seamanship.* Originally published 1819; 2nd edition, Edward W. Sweetman Co. (1963).

Maack, Gerstle. *The Land Divided.* Knopf (1944).

McCullough, David. *The Path Between the Seas: The Creation of the Panama Canal 1870–1914.* Simon & Schuster (1977).

Mitchell, Andrew W. *The Enchanted Canopy.* Macmillan (1986).

Otis, F. N. *Illustrated History of the Panama Railroad*. Harper & Brothers, 2nd edition (1862).

Parsons, Usher. *Physician for Ships*, 4th edition. Damrell and Moore (1851).

Peacock, George. *Notes on the Isthmus of Panama and Darién*. Exeter, England (1879).

Ponko, Vincent Jr. *Ships, Seas, and Scientists: U.S. Naval Exploration and Discovery in the Nineteenth Century*. Naval Institute Press (1974).

Prebble, John. *The Darién Disaster: A Scots Colony in the New World, 1698–1700*. Holt, Rinehart & Winston (1968).

Romoli, Kathleen. *Balboa of Darién: Discoverer of the Pacific*. Doubleday (1953).

Rowett, W. *The Ocean Telegraph Cable: The Construction, the Regulation of Its Specific Gravity, and Submersion Explained*. London: Sampson Low, Son & Marston (1865).

Salvador, Mari Lyn, editor. *The Art of Being Kuna: Layers of Meaning Among the Kuna of Panama*. Fowler Museum of Cultural History, University of California, Los Angeles (1997).

Schott, Joseph L. *Rails Across Panama: The Story of the Building of the Panama Railroad 1849–1855*. Bobbs Merrill (1967).

Selfridge, Thomas Oliver. *Reports of Explorations and Surveys to Ascertain the Practicability of a Ship Canal Between the Atlantic and Pacific Oceans, by way of the Isthmus of Darién*. Washington, D.C.: Government Printing Office (1874).

Stampp, Kenneth M. *America in 1857: A Nation on the Brink*. Oxford University Press (1990).

Strain, Isaac G. *Cordillera and Pampa, Mountain and Plain: Sketches of a Journey in Chili [sic] and the Argentine Provinces, in 1849*. Horace H. Moore (1853).

Thomas, Henry George. *Around the World in Old Ironsides: The Voyage of USS Constitution, 1844–1846* (original log of the ship's carpenter). Edited by Alan B. Flanders. Brandylane Publishers (1993).

Vail, R. *Knickerbocker Birthday: A Sesqui-Centennial History of the New-York Historical Society 1804–1954*. New-York Historical Society (1954).

Valle, James E. *Rocks and Shoals: Naval Discipline in the Age of Fighting Sail*. Naval Institute Press (1980).

Winthrop, Theodore. *The Canoe and the Paddle: Adventures Among the Northern Rivers and Forests and Isthmiana*. Ticknor and Fields (1863).

Wong, Marina, and Jorge Ventocilla. *A Day on Barro Colorado Island*. Smithsonian Tropical Research Institute (1986).

ELECTRONIC RESOURCES

Gallup-Diaz, Ignacio. *The Door of the Seas and Key to the Universe: Indian Politics and Imperial Rivalry in the Darién.* Produced in collaboration with the American Historical Society and Columbia University Press for Gutenberg-e (2003).

Tico Ethnobotanical Dictionary (electronic file updated from the *Isthmian Ethnobotanical Dictionary*): www.ars-grin.gov/duke/dictionary/tico).

CONGRESSIONAL REPORTS

Davis, Rear Admiral Charles H. *Report of Interoceanic Canals and Railroads Between the Atlantic and Pacific Oceans.* Sen. Ex. Doc., 39th Congress, 1st Session, No. 62. Washington, D.C. (1866).

Sullivan, Lieut. John T. *Report of the Historical and Technical Information Relating to the Problem of Interoceanic Communication by Way of the American Isthmus.* House Ex. Doc., 47th Congress, 2nd Session, No. 107. Washington, D.C. (1883).

SHIP CANAL AND DARIÉN ARTICLES

Breder, Charles. "In Darién Jungles," *Natural History,* vol. XXV (July/August 1925).

"Amphibians and Reptiles of the Rio Chucunaque Drainage, Darién, Panama, with Note on Their Life Histories and Habits," *Bulletin of the American Museum of Natural History,* vol. 86 (1946).

Fitzroy, Robert. "Considerations on the Great Isthmus of Central America," *Royal Geographical Society Journal,* vol. XX (1850).

———. "Further Considerations on the Great Isthmus of Central America," *Royal Geographical Society Journal,* vol. XXIII (1853).

Headley, Joel Tyler. *Harper's New Monthly Magazine,* vol. X (March–May 1855).

Kirkpatrick, Ralph Z. *Strain's Panaman [sic] Expedition,* U.S. Naval Institute Proceedings (August 1935).

Maack, Gerstle. "The Secret of the Strait," *Harper's New Monthly Magazine,* vol. XLVII (November 1873).

Trautwine, John C. "Rough Notes of an Exploration for an Inter-Oceanic Canal Route by Way of the Rivers Atrato and San Juan, in New Granada, South America," *Journal of the Franklin Institute,* (March–June 1854).

Watts, George B. "Inter-Oceanic Communications Across the Isthmus of Panama, or Darién," *Bulletin of the American Geographical and Statistical Society* (1854).

DARIÉN ROUTE EXPLORATION

Araúz, Amado. *Cronología Histórica del Darién* (unpublished accounting of major events and exploration in Darién, 1500–1888).

Araúz, Reina Torres. *Human Ecology of Route 17 (Sasardi-Morti Region), Darién, Panama*. Translated and edited by Felix Webster McBryde. Battelle Memorial Institute (1970).

Cullen, Edward. *Isthmus of Darién Ship Canal*. Effingham Wilson: 1st edition (1852); 2nd edition (1853).

————. *Over Darién by a Ship Canal: Reports of the Mismanaged Darién Expedition of 1854, with Suggestions for a Survey by Competent Engineers, and an Exploration by Parties with Compasses*. London: Effingham Wilson (1856).

Gisborne, Lionel. *Journal of the Expedition of Inquiry for the Junction of the Atlantic and Pacific Oceans*. London: Saunders and Stanford (1853). A 2nd edition was privately issued.

————. *Engineer's Report*. Addressed to the Chairman of the Atlantic and Pacific Junction Company, and giving an account of his 1854 expedition to Darién. Printed in London (1854).

Marsh, Richard Oglesby. *White Indians of Darién*. Putnam (1934).

Strain, Isaac G. *History and Prospects of Interoceanic Communication by the American Isthmus*. Paper read before the New-York Historical Society, June 17, 1856. Charles Vinten (1856).

————. October 25, 1854, 33rd Congress, 2nd Session. "Annual Report of the Secretary of the Navy, December 4, 1854, Appendix E, 82-107, House Ex. Doc. 1, part 2, 383–612.

————. *To Commander Edward Marshall, R. N., Commanding Her Britannic Majesty Steamship Virago*, April 8, 1854 (lengthy correspondence describing the expedition, written at La Palma, Darién Harbor).

DOCTORAL DISSERTATIONS

Kazar, John. *United States Navy and Scientific Exploration 1837–1860*. George Washington University (1973).

Martin, Willard E., Jr. *The Life and Works of Theodore Winthrop*. Duke University (1944).

Sánchez, Efraín. *Government and Geography in Nineteenth-Century Colombia: Agustín Codazzi and the Comisión Corográfica*. Oxford University (1994).

Stahl, Gregory John. *The Establishment of America's Stake in an Isthmian Transit Route: 1840–1870*. Georgetown University (1981).

Towle, Edward Leon. *Science, Commerce, and the Navy on the Seafaring Frontier (1842–1861:) The Role of Lieutenant M. F. Maury and the U.S. Naval*

Hydrographic Office in Naval Exploration, Commercial Expansion and Ocean-ography Before the Civil War. University of Rochester (1965).

PERIODICALS

El Tiempo (Bogotá)
Frank Leslie's Illustrated News
Harper's New Monthly Magazine
Illustrated London News
L'Illustration (Paris)
Royal Geographical Society Journal
Natural History (published by American Museum of Natural History, New York)
Transactions of the American Ethnological Society, volumes I–III (1845–1853).
Zeitschrift für Allgemeine Erdkunde (Berlin)

NEWSPAPERS

Aspinwall Courier
The Daily Star (Panama)
New York Herald
New York Times
New York Tribune
Nonpareil (Springfield, Ohio)
Panama Herald
Panama Star & Herald
Philadelphia Gazette
Providence Journal
Springfield Pioneer
Springfield Republic
Times (London)

Acknowledgments

I really couldn't have done this project without these people, all of whom had a role in shaping this book and bringing me through my own little survival exercise. Special thanks to my wife, Patty Adams, a talented editor but an even more remarkable person and partner. Thanks also to my friend Dan Coyle, a gifted story editor who took time from his own writing projects to get me back on track; to Oliver and Nancy Balf for good old-fashioned faith and more; and to Tom Balf for his attempts to shake a sensible outline out of me. I also want to thank longtime friend Bradley Anderson for his energetic eleventh-hour read, a great help to the final version.

On the professional level thanks to my agent, Esmond Harmsworth, who saw his share of ineffectual drafts and didn't panic, and to Kristin Kiser, my editor at Crown, who remained patient and supportive despite many missed deadlines.

A number of folks assisted my research. Thanks to Kathleen Jabs, a U.S. Naval Academy graduate who joined me in sifting through manuscript material at the National Archives and the Library of Congress in D.C.; thanks to Darién guides Hernán Araúz and Richard Drake Cahill for their companionship and trekking expertise; and my thanks to U.S. Army researcher Murray Hamlet and Samuel Greene Arnold descendant Arthur Rogers, who invited me into their homes. Thanks also to Darién authorities Morgan Smith and Stanley Heckadon-Moreno, who agreed to interviews and provided me with fresh perspectives.

I encountered skillful archivists on both sides of the Atlantic. Special thanks to Sarah Strong at the Royal Geographical Society; curator Margherita Desy at the USS Constitution Museum; Jan Herman at the Naval Historical Center; Dan Lewis at Berkeley's Huntington Library; John Stinson at the New York Public Library; Richard Ring at the John Carter Brown Library; and Rebecca Livingston in the early military history division of the National Archives.

Thanks also to genealogical researcher Larry Calimer and curator Virginia Weygant at the Clark County Historical Society in Ohio.

Locally I called on several experts: Special thanks to Dr. Jeff Corbett, Rev. Joel Ives, Vivian Zovala, Lee Grune, and John Young. Finally thanks to the staffs at Salem State College Library, the Phillips Library (at the Peabody-Essex Museum), and Beverly Public Library.

Index

About the Author

TODD BALF, the author of *The Last River* and a former senior editor for *Outside*, is presently a contributing editor to *Men's Journal*. He first traveled to Panama's Darién in 1991—a memorably flawed crossing in which he and his two companions traversed by foot, burro, and dugout canoe yet managed to see neither the Pacific nor the Atlantic.